MASTER
PRESIDENTIAL
HISTORY

FAMILIUS

FAMILIUS

Published by Familius LLC, www.familius.com
Familius books are available at special discounts for bulk purchases, whether for sales
promotions or for family or corporate use. For more information, contact Familius
Sales at 559-876-2170 or email orders@familius.com.

Library of Congress Control Number: 2019953185

Print ISBN 9781641702195
Ebook ISBN 9781641702805

Printed in Hong Kong

Edited by Kaylee Mason and Peg Sandkam
Cover design by Carlos Guerrero and Brooke Jorden
Book design by Brooke Jorden

Images sourced from WikiCommons, Library of Congress,
or licensed from Shutterstock. Editorial credit listed where applicable.

10 9 8 7 6 5 4 3 2 1

First Edition

MASTER
PRESIDENTIAL
HISTORY

DAN ROBERTS
Professor of Liberal Arts and History
Chair, Department of Liberal Arts
School of Professional and Continuing Studies
University of Richmond
Executive Producer and Host, *A Moment in Time*

Dedicated to Mario Mejia Roberts.
He took my name and awakened joy
and inspiration in my heart and mind.

CONTENTS

Acknowledgments. 6

Introduction A: The President
in the United States 9

B: The Electoral College 12

C: Electing the President 14

D: George Washington: Guar-
antor of National Success . . . 17

E: Realignment Elections 20

F: Unitary Executive 22

1   George Washington

2   John Adams

3   Thomas Jefferson

4   James Madison

5   James Monroe

6   John Quincy Adams

7   Andrew Jackson

8   Martin Van Buren

9   William Henry Harrison

10   John Tyler

11   James K. Polk

12   Zachary Taylor

13   Millard Fillmore

14   Franklin Pierce

15   James Buchanan

16   Abraham Lincoln

17   Andrew Johnson

18   Ulysses S. Grant

19   Rutherford B. Hayes

20   James A. Garfield

21   Chester A. Arthur

22   Grover Cleveland

23   Benjamin Harrison

24   Grover Cleveland

25   William McKinley

26   Theodore Roosevelt

27   William Howard Taft

28   Woodrow Wilson

29   Warren G. Harding

30   Calvin Coolidge

31   Herbert Hoover

32   Franklin D. Roosevelt

33   Harry S. Truman

34   Dwight D. Eisenhower

35   John F. Kennedy

36   Lyndon B. Johnson

37   Richard M. Nixon

38   Gerald R. Ford

39   Jimmy Carter

40   Ronald Reagan

41   George Bush

42   Bill Clinton

43   George W. Bush

44   Barack Obama

45   Donald Trump

Endnotes. 462

General Bibliography 477

ACKNOWLEDGMENTS

In 1996 I was asked by the Dean of the then School of Continuing Studies at the University of Richmond to formulate a class based on my public radio program *A Moment in Time*. For the three previous years while I completed my PhD dissertation, I was also doing the basic research and writing the hundreds of program transcripts necessary to broadcast a modular historical program reaching millions of listeners each weekday. It was an exhilarating exercise but was becoming an overwhelming one.

Seeing the Dean's offer as an opportunity for the program, my students, and our *A Moment in Time* production team, I created two courses—one on American history, the other on European and World History. We structured them with a joint faculty and student research component. The students and I would choose the topics from a formula that achieved balance between topics that included North American history, European history, Non-European history, the contributions of women, and the nexus of religion and politics. Then I would add suggestions from my university colleagues, our listeners, and ideas from the students themselves. The students would then produce a topic dossier with a summary essay, topical bibliography, copied sources, and images of the subject in the public domain. I would then take it from there and create the program transcript and broadcast radio script.

Most students are aware that their professors receive and grade their essays, hold them for three years, and then consign them to the bin for recycling or to populate the local landfill.

Not my students.

For a quarter century, I have retained their research work in my archives, where they continue to contribute to the understanding of the topic. In addition to the radio broadcast, their work forms the basic research which is then entered into the topic by volume and program number in our full-service website, www.amomentintime.com.. The students that have taken these courses and my First Years Seminar (FYS) courses have joined with me to do the basic research for future programming on *A Moment in Time*.

When Christopher Robbins, CEO of Familius, suggested a one-minute book on the presidents to be released in time for the 2020 presidential election, I tasked my students in my spring 2019 FYS course, *Taking It to the Streets*, and my Moments in Time American History course to join me in the endeavor. Each of the students produced a dossier on one of the forty-five U.S. presidents. Their work was exemplary and aided me in the research that led to these original essays. Study in my classes has always been a two-way street. I have always learned from my students, even as I have been teaching them. The excellence of their contribution is found all through this volume. For that I am most grateful.

While I am grateful to my students, I am also in deep gratitude to my teachers, who over the years have inspired me with the quality of their intellectual engagement and their encouragement to me to explore the landscape of the mind. To Elizabeth Crutchfield (Music), Mary Ruth Holiday (English), C. Frederick Ulmer (Music and Theater), Hugo Ackerman (American History), Ronald Burnside (American History), Bruce Metzger (New Testament), John Rawson Rilling (English History), and Martin J. Havran (Early Modern English History), my life-long thanks. I am a better analyst, thinker, writer, broadcaster, author, storyteller, dreamer, and a better man because of you.

My thanks also to my fiend and long-time colleague, Dean Emeritus of the School of Professional and Continuing Studies, James Narduzzi. As an accomplished political scientist, Jim very kindly read through my introductory chapters and periodically examined the presidential chapters. His wise counsel and suggestions have made this a better book, and for that, me and my readers are deeply indebted.

I feel profound gratitude to Christopher and the team at Familius who have seen the value of the short form delivery of high-quality information and given this volume and its predecessor a pathway to life. Many thanks also go to my editor, Kaylee Mason, who nursed this project to completion and understood that while hard deadlines are essential, product quality is paramount.

Finally, as some of my readers know, I have struggled for the last two years with the onset of throat cancer and the aftereffects of radiation and chemotherapy. Thankfully at the time of this writing this medical scourge is in remission. I am most grateful for the support and love of my husband, Mario; of my children, Heather, Gerald, Kathleen, Daniel, and Carolyn; of my School and University colleagues; of my dear church friends; and of the many thousands of listeners and broadcast colleagues who noted the change in my delivery and have supported me as I have healed.

Finally, the value of one's life is marked and enhanced by the exquisite architecture of friendship that looks beyond immediate darkness, hungers for the coming light, and remains steadfast.

To
Vaughn Lamar Joseph

Nothing is Better than
The Wind at your Back,
The Sun in Front of you
and
Your Friend beside you.

—After Aaron Douglas Trimble

THE PRESIDENT IN THE UNITED STATES

In summer 1787, delegates from the states met in Philadelphia to update the government of the United States. One of their tasks was to determine if and how the U.S. was to have a chief executive. Under the Articles of Confederation—the national system the delegates were meeting to refurbish—the president was an agent of Congress lacking independence or substantial executive powers.

At first, the delegates were not inclined to disturb the relationship between the president and Congress, but they gradually moved toward creating a government consisting of three independent branches (executive, legislative, and judicial). Each branch would have separate powers, with at least a theoretical ability to check the authority of the others. The intent was to guard against the tyranny against which Americans had brought a Revolution. None of the three branches—especially the executive—would be allowed to grow so powerful as to threaten the liberty of the people.

The Convention eventually structured an executive branch led by the president. In Article II, Section 1, the Constitution provides for the president's election, qualifications, compensation, replacement in case of removal, and oath of office. Article II, Section 2 enumerates the powers of the president to include his command of the armed forces, pardon power, direction of executive officers, making treaties (with the agreement of two-thirds of the Senate), and by implication directing the relationship of the United States with foreign powers. Section 2 also describes the president's appointment power of judges and other officials (with the advice and consent of the Senate).

Article II, Section 3 pronounces the president's obligation to describe the State of the Union to Congress, propose a legislative program to Congress, and provide for the faithful execution of the laws. Article II, Section 4 describes the means by which the president, vice president, and all officers can be removed from office by impeachment and conviction.

Compared to the extensive and detailed description of Congress's duties and responsibilities, the Constitution is relatively restrained in its depiction of the responsibilities and role of the president. In many ways this was intentional. The Founders were divided between those who wished to craft an executive with expansive and robust powers and those who wished to tie down the president to a limited role in national life. The delegates in Philadelphia mapped out a pathway that allowed the occupants of the office to explore the boundaries of their remit.

As we shall see in the pages of this volume, each of the forty-four men* who have led the republic have placed their mark on the office. Some of those marks have been near cavernous—

deep and long-lasting—and others less so, but each has served to further establish the presidency as an equal partner in national governance and, on more than a few occasions, a more than equal collaborator. The office has grown or receded, due in part to the nature and ambitions of the occupant and in part to the circumstances he faced. There have been seasons in which the importance of the presidency has expanded in clear view and others in which the role of the executive has ebbed. It is the hope that our narrative will give clarity to this process and insights into the talents, dreams, motivations, and influence of men who have guided the republic in its political, social, legal, and moral journey.

Shortly after his first election as president, President-elect Franklin Delano Roosevelt affirmed the presidency is "not merely an administrative office. That is the least part of it. It is preeminently a place of moral leadership." In the spirit of Roosevelt's affirmation, at the end of the discussion of each president, I will try to examine the president's moral legacy. The purpose of this exercise is firmly established in the conviction that within the American presidency resides both the potential and challenge to demonstrate and lead the nation in securing our character—our claim to those moral values embodied in Thomas Jefferson's Declaration of Independence, values that have inspired the nation since its inception.

No fair study of American history can deny the national journey has been a flawed one; mistakes have been made, evil institutions have been tolerated, and prejudices have been affirmed. Yet each generation has had a chance to reflect upon Jefferson's words and has in its own way—in sometimes all too slight steps—moved the republic in the direction of the American ideal. Perhaps the genius of this American experiment in freedom is that it has the capacity for renewal and growth, and a potential for consistency. Americans can commit errors and embrace a dark path at times, but they also can spectacularly reverse course and climb in the direction of the light. One important player in this journey of discovery is the American President. Each president has either succumbed to the flaws that encumbered and surrounded him or stuck out for higher moral ground and helped lead the nation to embrace what Abraham Lincoln called, in his First Inaugural Address, the "better angels of our nature."

*In the history of the republic, all who have occupied the office of president have been men. My use of the masculine pronoun in these pages in no way precludes my personal expectation and desire that at some point the American people will choose a woman to lead them in the highest office in the land. In the meantime, the story of the American presidency is the story of forty-four men and the men and women who have surrounded them, challenged them, and helped shape their legacy.

INTRODUCTION: B

THE ELECTORAL COLLEGE

The Electoral College is one of the most confusing aspects of American government—to citizens and foreign observers alike. It is a college that teaches no course. It is an association that has no meeting. Nevertheless, it is an institution that has a powerful effect on national life. It is the means by which the nation selects its president.

At the Constitutional Convention in 1787, the means of selecting the chief executive was a matter of intense debate. The delegates were among the most prominent and prosperous citizens of their respective states. They were part of society's elite. Few of them would have been sympathetic to widespread popular enthusiasm, and they structured the American government to both reflect the will of the people and resist too overt expression of public passions. One of the compelling reasons why George Washington allowed his colleagues to convince him to come to Philadelphia was a fundamental anxiety about looming chaos.

He felt the Articles of Confederation were ineffectual, a "rope of sand" needing serious revision. Shays's Rebellion (1786) had aroused the fears of the American elite class, and Washington was not alone in fearing America was teetering on the edge of "anarchy and confusion." These fears of ill-restrained democracy also loomed over the debate about the president.

Yet, while elitist fears of democracy run amok were shared by most of the delegates, these fears were not the primary reason for developing the Electoral College, for choosing this intricate and often frustrating system of picking a national leader. The real reason was that the Convention was dealing with competing states and regions. Popular direct election of the chief executive would have offended a sizable number of states whose support was required for ratification, states who depended on a favorable national structure to protect their interests—in the House, in the Senate, and in the presidency.

The primary issue compelling the debate over section interests was small states and small states which were also slave states. The Connecticut Compromise offered by Roger Sherman secured for small states equal representation in the Senate—two senators from each state.

When the Convention considered how to determine representation in the House, it stumbled across the issue of slave representation. Northern states insisted that since slaves were property and had no participation in civic life, they should not be counted at all. The South countered that slaves were wards of their owners and should be counted as any other non-voting citizen. States were not similar, but most had some kind of property or tax-paying requirement in order to vote. This limited the franchise to "responsible" citizens who would support the ruling elite in each state or region. Southern slave owners wanted their slaves to be counted as full humans. The solution was the infamous Three-Fifths Compromise in which, for the purpose of determining the size of congressional districts, a slave would be counted as three-fifths of a human.

Having secured voting advantages in both the Senate and the House, the small state–slave state contingent then turned to the election of the president. The Electoral College confirmed their voting advantage because of the number of small state–slave state senators and slave state House members, whose number was enhanced by the Three-Fifths Compromise. In the College, the president and vice president would be elected by a majority of electors, whose number was determined by adding the two senators to the number of House members from each state. If no candidate received a majority of the vote, then the election shifted to the House of Representatives. There, in a so-called Contingent Election, each state would have a single vote for president, whose name would be determined by a majority vote within each delegation. Only three times, 1800, 1824, and 1836 in the Senate for the election of Vice President Richard Mentor Johnson, has this stop-gap procedure been required.

Designed as it was to protect small-state interests, the Electoral College also had a dark side. From Washington through Buchanan—with the exception of John Adams and John Quincy Adams—all elected presidents were either slave-holders or were sympathetic to the slave interest.[1] The College helped preserve that peculiar institution until the election of Abraham Lincoln, who at the time of his election opposed the spread of slavery into the territories.

INTRODUCTION: C

ELECTING THE PRESIDENT

With the ratification of the Constitution, the nation proceeded to begin electing presidents. The first two elections went smoothly, as George Washington was elected unanimously. Warning signs emerged in the hotly contested election of 1800. The rise of the Democratic-Republican Party and its triumph in the November election meant John Adams was eliminated. When the vote was held, Thomas Jefferson and Aaron Burr were tied. This threw the vote into the House of Representatives. There, the intervention of Alexander Hamilton on Jefferson's behalf prevented Burr from being elected. The adoption of the Twelfth Amendment separated the election of the president and vice president in the Electoral College. This made possible the creation of political party tickets in which the candidates for president and vice president run as a team. In the Electoral College, the Electors vote for both along party lines.

Prior to 1800, many states allocated electoral votes by congressional district, thus permitting a possible mixed result between parties statewide. In Virginia, James Madison perceived the election in 1800 was going to be close and hard fought. He arranged for the General Assembly to adopt a winner-take-all election, thus ensuring the Jefferson/Burr ticket would receive all the electoral votes of the Commonwealth since unified voting in the states tends to prevent multi-party splintering of the vote. This arrangement came to be known as the *general ticket system*, and soon most states adopted it. It had the unintended consequence of ensuring the development of a strong two-party system, since unified voting in the states is the only way a party and its candidate can prevent a multi-party splintering of the vote. Only by this unified effort in all the states can a nominee gain enough electoral votes to secure the presidency. The result has been the development of two largely non-ideological, broadly-based parties.

For the most part, the Electoral College has tended to follow the will of the electorate. Only five times has the loser of a popular plurality (under fifty percent but more than the competition) found his way into the White House. John Quincy Adams (1824) prevailed in a vote in the House of Representatives over Andrew Jackson and William H. Crawford, Henry Clay having been excluded from the House vote because he came in fourth in the Electoral College vote. Rutherford B. Hayes (1876) prevailed over Samuel J. Tilden. The latter remains the only losing presidential candidate in American electoral history to have won a popular majority (fifty percent plus one).

Benjamin Harrison (1888) won the Electoral College despite losing the popular vote to Grover Cleveland. George W. Bush (2000) won one of the closest Electoral College tallies in history but lost the popular vote by more than a half-million. In 2016, Donald Trump won the White House over Hillary Rodham Clinton by prevailing in the Electoral College. He lost the popular vote by nearly three million and only succeeded by unexpectedly securing the electoral votes of several key mid-western states. The votes in these states were so close that a change of eighty-thousand votes combined would have thrown the election to Clinton.

The *general ticket system* has two additional effects. First, parties tend to concentrate their political energy on the states with the largest number of electoral votes. This means candidates will select a number of large swing-states and that is where they spend a majority of their money and time. Second, such a system tends to amplify the winning candidate's vote in the Electoral College. For instance, in 1960, John F. Kennedy barely scraped past Richard M. Nixon, winning a popular vote plurality of just over one-hundred-thousand votes. However, in the Electoral College, Kennedy's victory was decisive: 303 to 219.

One of the ironies of the American election system is that on many occasions it has delivered the presidency to the candidate who did not achieve a popular majority (fifty percent plus one). Many have entered the White House having won a plurality of the popular vote but not received a majority of the popular vote, sometimes denied that popular majority by votes for a third candidate. This phenomenon occurred in 1824, 1844, 1848, 1856, 1860, 1876, 1880, 1884, 1888, 1892, 1912, 1916, 1948, 1960, 1968, 1992, 2000, and 2016. In the modern era, the divergence between Electoral College victory and popular vote loss has often provoked calls for serious reforms, including abolishing the College system completely. Should the divergence continue, these calls will only grow louder and more persistent.

INTRODUCTION: D

GEORGE WASHINGTON: GUARANTOR OF NATIONAL SUCCESS

In his examination of the republic's first decade, *Founding Brothers*, Joseph Ellis outlined the prospects for American triumph or failure. On the positive side were:

1. A large and growing, young and fertile white population;
2. A wide continent available for expansion and settlement;
3. Extensive distribution of land owned by the white population; and
4. Nearly a century-and-a-half of experience with Republican governance within the colonial legislatures.
5. Yet, perhaps the most salient factor that gave promise of Republican success was the surety that George Washington would be the nation's first Chief Executive. His presence in the nation's highest office assured a watching world that America was going to be a significant player in the game of nations. This also gave confidence to an often-anxious populace that the republic's future was planted on solid ground.

Shortly before he surrendered his commission in late 1783 and returned to the bucolic slopes of Mount Vernon, Washington dispatched a *Circular to the States* from his standing as the Commander of a triumphant revolutionary army. In it, he revealed the inherent optimism that characterized his public service, first to Virginia and then to the young nation, in pursuit of the "glorious cause."

The Citizens of America, placed in the most enviable condition, as the sole Lords and Proprietors of a vast Tract of Continent, comprehending all the various soils and climates of the World, and abounding with all the necessaries and conveniences of life, are now by the late satisfactory pacification, acknowledged to be possessed of absolute freedom and Independency; They are, from this period, to be considered as the Actors on a most conspicuous Theatre, which seems to be peculiarly designated by Providence for the display of human greatness and felicity; Here, they are not only surrounded with everything which can contribute to the completion of private and domestic enjoyment, but Heaven has crowned all its other blessings, by giving a fairer opportunity for political happiness, than any other Nation has ever been favored with.

George Washington, *Circular to the States*, June 8, 1783

Beyond his enthusiasm for the nation's prospects, in the *Circular* is preserved Washington's Four Pillars that were essential to the "well-being...to the existence of [an independent] United States:

1. An indissoluble union of the States under one federal head;
2. A sacred regard to public justice;
3. The adoption of a proper peace establishment; and
4. The prevalence of that pacific and friendly disposition, among the people of the United States, which will induce them to forget their local prejudices and policies, to make those mutual concessions which are requisite to the general prosperity, and in some instances, to sacrifice their individual advantages to the interest of the Community."

In his *Farewell Address* delivered to the nation in the final days of his presidency, George Washington added an additional Pillar that, if maintained, would help secure the nation's prosperity and success. He asserts that American values could only be sustained by public morality underpinned by religious principles. He is not here advocating dominance of a particular sectarian approach, but rather the general principles undergirding all American religions: loyalty to community; faithfulness to the nation's guiding principles as outlined in Thomas Jefferson's Declaration of Independence; respect for property, reputation and life; equal justice under law; honesty of word and deed; and charity between citizens.

During the Constitutional Convention of 1787, George Washington was the presiding officer. That he was among those calling for a rewrite of the Articles of Confederation and that he would attend the meeting were two of the primary reasons all of the states sent delegates to the Convention. His attendance and his role as president general in Philadelphia were an explicit guarantee. This sent word to the country that, should he occupy any future executive office, power would be executed with judicious restraint, consistent with the modest attitude and reserved behavior he demonstrated in public service and private life.

One southern delegate later explained the Convention was willing to invest the president with significantly greater powers because its members were assured by the prospect of Washington taking office as first Chief Executive. This assurance led the assembly to create the president as an independent player, elected separately and not reliant on Congress.

This was the character, diffident behavior, and convictions of the man who took the oath of office as the first American chief executive on April 30, 1789. He began the process of shaping the president as a co-equal player in those Republican arrangements designed to preserve and protect American liberty.

REALIGNMENT ELECTIONS

In the 233 years since the political system of the United States was formulated, there have been election seasons in which there has been a significant shift in political sentiment on the part of the voting public. Often these moments of change reflect a watershed of surging political alliances associated with what scholars have designated "the party system," but there is not a precise demarcation between systems as identified with a particular election or date.[2]

These specific elections are the time in which an older coalition of voters is replaced by a new, more muscular political construct—sometimes lasting perhaps for decades. These elections are known as *realigning elections*, *critical elections*, or *critical realignment elections*. There is general agreement among historians and political scientists about four such elections:

- 1800: Thomas Jefferson defeated the incumbent President John Adams, thus hastening the demise of the Federalist Party.
- 1828: Andrew Jackson defeated the incumbent President John Quincy Adams, making way for three decades of Democratic Party dominance.
- 1860: Abraham Lincoln emerged triumphant in a field of four candidates to lead the nation through the republic's greatest crisis and the Republicans began seven decades of political ascendency.
- 1932: Franklin Roosevelt defeated incumbent President Herbert Hoover and assembled the New Deal coalition to lead the nation through the Great Depression and World War II. The Democratic Party achieved dominance lasting nearly fifty years in White House elections and sixty years in Congress.

Other observers have identified realignment features in these elections:

- 1876: The corrupt deal between Rutherford B. Hayes and the southern Democrats brought an abrupt end to Reconstruction and sounded the death-knell for African Americans' voting rights. This produced the Solid South for the Democrats and ushered in the reign of Jim Crow apartheid.[3]

- 1896: Changes in fund-raising sources (William McKinley and the Republicans) and campaign tactics (Bryan and the Democrats) secured for the Republicans a long series of blow-out elections.

- 1968: Richard Nixon won a close election through the effective use of the Southern Strategy, with all of its racist undertones, in that he signaled to southern conservatives that he was their champion on states' rights, forced school busing, school prayer, and court appointments. They interpreted this as Nixon intended, as his promise to reign in African American pretention and progress. His Watergate troubles delayed a much more extensive realignment until the Reagan election in 1980; but if this was realignment, it was a slow, decades-long process as the House remained Democratic until 1994—as did the Senate except for a six-year period in the early 1980s.

- 1980: Ronald Reagan's win in 1980 was overwhelming but may have been due as much to the personality of the candidates as it was to an alleged shifting ideological environment. Congress remained solidly in Democratic hands in most years, though Reagan was able to help shift the political orientation of the judiciary.

The study of realigning elections has been an intellectual parlor game for decades, involving sometimes strong contending opinions among political scientists and historians. Some scholars insist the whole idea is unproductive speculation akin to a "Rip

Van Winkle" idea of democracy in which voters come awake every few years and engage in electoral upheaval.

Regardless of the outcome of realignment debates, even a cursory examination of election history can detect occasional, sudden, abrupt changes in voter sentiment, leading to a rearrangement of alliances, coalitions, and political outcomes. Or as the perceptive and concerned New York banker Phillip Hone's scriptural allusion said of the defeat of President Martin Van Buren in 1840, "old things are passed away and, [behold] all things have become new" (I Corinthians 5:7).

INTRODUCTION: F

UNITARY EXECUTIVE

A Unitary Executive (UE) is the idea that the president has full, unencumbered, unchallenged control of the executive branch. It is contrasted to the Plural Executive (PE) configuration in many states in which various executives—lieutenant governor, attorney general, secretary of state, and others—are elected separately and operate independently from the direct control of the governor.

During the George Bush administration and Donald Trump years, a debate has raged over the UE theory. Former Vice President Richard Cheney, several legal scholars in the Bush Justice Department, and President Trump's second attorney general, William Barr, have made extravagant and expansive claims as to the magnitude of presidential power, particularly in the realm of national security. Barr has gone so far as to claim the complete absence of restrains on the president's ability to work his will within the executive branch on other matters as well. The outcome of this debate has real-world consequences, because it governs the extent of presidential power in a Republican democracy.

There is no doubt that the Constitutional Convention in Article Two established a UE. The Founders expressly intended to invest a single official with full control and responsibility under the law—along with full accountability. They wanted a president who would act with vigor and rectitude. He could not hide behind any other person, engage in unexamined criminality, or blame other people for his appointments, policies, actions, character, or behavior. In the words of one of Harry Truman's favorite dictums about presidential authority, "The Buck Stops Here," meaning he could not pass the blame or responsibility to anyone else.

Congress, in Article One, has a long enumeration of its powers to make laws, which the president must execute. If constitutional, laws must be executed that are "necessary and proper" to carry out its legislative function or perform its vested constitutional powers or in controlling the government, any department, or officer. This enumeration includes regulation of the armed forces.

The president, in Article Two, has relatively few enumerated powers. Absent constitutional restraint or congressional mandate, from the beginning the president has been able to vigorously explore the boundaries or limits of the presidential remit. This is certainly true within the executive branch and in circumstances requiring him to fully execute the role of Commander in Chief of the armed forces.

Since the Constitution created a UE, the debate among scholars and reflected in the actions of various presidents is between a weak UE and a strong UE.

A strong UE is described as having almost unfettered power within the executive branch. He can hire and fire officials with no restrictions, set policy within the legal limits as imposed by Congress, and fully marshal the resources of the government during times of war or national emergency. Under this definition the president himself determines the extent of his willingness to exercise power. Presidents such as George Washington, Thomas

Jefferson in his appointments and the Louisiana Purchase, Andrew Jackson, James K. Polk and Abraham Lincoln during wartime, Theodore and Franklin D. Roosevelt, Woodrow Wilson, Lyndon Johnson, Ronald Reagan until Iran-Contra, George Bush after the attacks on the World Trade Center, Barack Obama in some domestic issues, and Donald Trump have either expanded or tried to expand presidential power under the strong UE paradigm. John Dean writes of the more extreme interpretation of UE, "Neither Congress nor the federal courts can tell the president what to do or how to do it," particularly on national security.

A weak UE is described as exercising power within the executive branch, but either through philosophical deference,[4] personal weakness, or indecision finds their exercise of power attenuated by Congressional action, judicial fiat, or contemporary national or international circumstances.

The behavior and approach of individual presidents has ranged across the spectrum between weak and strong unitary executives. Wherever the president stands on the continuum of UE, there is still a struggle between the three branches. In his exercise of power, he is constantly rubbing against the limits of the power of the other two co-equal branches, Congress and the Judiciary.

Both the courts, Congress, and the president have cross-branch powers—all have either primary or secondary legislative, judicial, and executive functions and can check the prerogatives of the other branches. Presidents appoint judges with the Senate's advice and consent and can influence legislation by vetoes or threats of vetoes. Congress can pass laws that the president has a constitutional obligation to enforce, even laws regulating the armed forces. Through judicial review, courts can void even lawfully passed congressional legislation and can alter, impede, encourage, or protect executive action within the executive branch or in the execution of constitutionally lawful measures.

Congress can investigate the actions and functions of the

executive branch through its oversight role, exposing illegal acts, unethical behavior, or fraud, often bringing such malfeasance to an end or securing the resignation of corrupt officials. Through its appropriation utility, it can reign in the president and his appointees, alter their policies, or either encourage cooperation or cut off the fiscal means of defying Congressional mandates. Congress can also enlist the judiciary as an ally in tempering presidential conduct or prerogatives. Finally, Congress can apply the ultimate sanction on the president and his minions through impeachment, though that is a blunt instrument rarely attempted and constitutionally difficult to accomplish. In 2019, articulating a strong UE paradigm, under the leadership of Attorney General William Barr, the Trump administration attempted to interdict congressional oversight and block all Congressional subpoenas and appearances of executive branch officials. Barr refused to appear under congressional subpoena and was sanctioned with criminal contempt by the House of Representatives. How this clash is resolved will likely depend on court intervention—and will have influence on the future of the UE debate.

Congress has, on occasion, attempted to limit the president's ability to conduct his constitutional duties. In 1867, Congress passed the Tenure of Office Act, essentially limiting the president's power to remove certain federal officials from office without the approval of the Senate. President Andrew Johnson defied the act and attempted to fire Secretary of War Edwin McMaster Stanton because the two had clashed over enforcement of Reconstruction legislation. Congress then impeached and tried Johnson, but failed to remove him by a single vote margin in the Senate. The law was significantly modified in 1869 and repealed in 1887. In 1926, the Supreme Court in *Myers v. United States* declared the Tenure of Office Act was likely unconstitutional.

1

GEORGE WASHINGTON

GEORGE WASHINGTON: LIFE PAGE

Born: February 22, 1732, Popes Creek, British Colony of Virginia

Parents: Augustine Washington and Mary Ball

Married: Martha Dandridge, 1759

Delegate from Virginia to First Continental Congress: September–October 1774

Delegate from Virginia to Second Continental Congress: May–June 1775

Commander in Chief, Continental Army: June 14, 1775–December 23, 1783

President General, Constitutional Convention; State House, Philadelphia, Pennsylvania: May 25–September 17, 1787

First President of the United States: April 30, 1789–March 4, 1797

Senior Officer of the United States Army: July 13, 1798–December 14, 1799

Slaveholder who manumitted his slaves at his death

Died: December 14, 1799, Mount Vernon

Additional resources available for this president at www.amomentintime.com.

GEORGE WASHINGTON: DEVELOPING LEADERSHIP-I

George Washington was born in 1732 into one of Virginia's older families. His father Augustine Washington was of middling gentry but did not possess the large land-holdings or social standing that would have insured the family be included among the colony's major planting families. Augustine never sat in the House of Burgesses, but at his death he bequeathed a respectable ten-thousand acres to his heirs. Young George had little formal education, but he could turn a decent English phrase and was drawn to mathematics, and thus he became a competent surveyor by the age of sixteen. He soon demonstrated strong communication skills—his letters to the Continental Congress during the war were powerful, succinct, poignant, and at times moving.

With his fortune building, he found himself drawn into military service, and by his early twenties he had attained the rank of major in the Virginia militia. In 1753, the Ohio Company, a group of land speculators, in whose number his brother Lawrence was counted, desired to build a fort near present-day Pittsburgh. Unfortunately, the French were attempting to claim the same area. Washington's military experience and familiarity with the west made him a natural choice to deliver a letter from Virginia's governor demanding the French leave the Ohio Valley. The French respectfully declined the demand and Washington returned to Virginia, where he wrote a report of this expedition. Impressed, Governor Robert Dinwiddie had the report printed and it significantly enhanced Washington's reputation.

GEORGE WASHINGTON:
DEVELOPING LEADERSHIP-II

In the years prior to his emergence on the national and international stage, in many ways the personal and professional destiny of George Washington was forged in Ohio Valley. In 1754, Virginia Colonial Governor Dinwiddie sent him back to the Forks of the Ohio (the confluence of the Allegheny and Monongahela Rivers) at the head of an expedition to remove the French from the area and capture Fort Duquesne, the stronghold France was building at the Forks.

Leading 150 men, Washington discovered French troops were ranging far southeast of the Forks near present-day Uniontown. He threw up a fortified camp he called Fort Necessity and, with his Indian allies, attacked an enemy column that had strayed too close to the colonials, capturing or killing most of the French—including their commander Joseph Coulon de Jumonville. The French from Fort Duquesne counter-attacked, surrounded Washington's band, and—after a bloody clash—forced him to surrender.

Though he was taken prisoner, Washington conducted himself well and emerged with standing intact. This encounter was the initial skirmish in a giant geopolitical confrontation known in Europe as the Seven Years War or in America as the French and Indian War. Despite the loss, he wrote his brother Lawrence, expressing his emotional state while under fire, "I heard the bullets whistle, and, believe me there is something charming in the sound." His expressed sentiment quickly spread, reinforcing Washington's reputation and notoriety.

GEORGE WASHINGTON:
DEVELOPING LEADERSHIP-III

In 1755, London determined to drive the French from the Ohio Valley. They sent a large expedition of British regulars under General Edward Braddock to capture Fort Duquesne at the Forks of the Ohio. George Washington joined Braddock's staff as a lieutenant colonel, but on the trail, Washington became severely ill. Fortunately, he re-joined the Braddock column in time to participate in the Battle of the Monongahela. Braddock was a brave but incompetent leader, unused to wilderness fighting, and when his forces stumbled into an ambush by the French and their Native American allies, he suffered a catastrophic defeat. It is counted among the worst the British suffered in the war. Braddock was killed and Washington rallied the remaining troops, took command of the rear guard, and organized an orderly and strategic retreat—even though he was still wracked with fever and a severe headache. His performance in battle and in the retreat won him admiration from his men and the authorities in both Virginia and London.

By 1758, the skirmishes on the North American western frontier between France and England had spilled over into a wider European, even world-wide, conflict. That year, Washington led a Virginia detachment as part of a large British attempt under General John Forbes to finally take Fort Duquesne. When they arrived, they found the fort burned and abandoned. They rebuilt it on a different, more defensible site and named it Fort Pitt for William Pitt, the British first minister who ordered the expedition to capture this strategic site. The British now had undisputed control of the Ohio Valley, and the scene of the war gradually shifted elsewhere.

GEORGE WASHINGTON: COMMANDER IN CHIEF

At the end of 1758, Washington resigned his commission and retired to Mount Vernon. He married well, secured his fortune as a wealthy tobacco planter, and embarked on a political career that would eventually return him to military service. He served as Justice of the Peace and then a member of the Virginia House of Burgesses. While he was not an orator in the likes of Patrick Henry or a constitutional theorist such as James Madison or a brilliant legislator, his experience, character, and mature judgement won him the respect of his peers.

Washington served in the First Continental Congress, where he left a lasting positive impression when—upon hearing of the closing of the Port of Boston—he offered to raise, equip, and lead a large force to defend American liberty. He returned to the Second Continental Congress and was selected to command the American army. Supplemented with regiments from Virginia and the middle colonies, he left to join and lead the New England forces surrounding Boston after Lexington.

In early July 1775, the new commander arrived at the mustering grounds in Cambridge. Washington was unsure of the ability of the men he would lead against the greatest military enterprise in Europe—perhaps the world—but his gravity, intelligence, and personal integrity served him well as he led his troops to ultimate victory. He was sustained by a sense of almost divinely inspired destiny and an uncompromising devotion to what he called the "glorious cause," the achievement and preservation of American liberty.

GEORGE WASHINGTON:
THE AMERICAN CINCINNATUS

In 458 BCE, a Roman consular army was surrounded on Mouth Algidus, a segment of the Alban Hills southeast of Rome. The Romans were trapped by the army of the Aequi, one of Rome's traditional enemies. Desperate for leadership, they turned to Lucius Quinctius Cincinnatus (born c. 519 BCE), who at the time was working his farm not far from the city. Cincinnatus gathered a rescue force and defeated the enemy, it is said, in a single day. He was then honored with a triumph in the city, retained his power only for the time it took to bring Rome through the crisis, resigned, and returned to his farm.

George Washington served the new United States as Commander of the Continental Army from mid-1775 through the end of 1783. He was no tactical genius in the likes of Stonewall Jackson or Douglas McArthur, but he stubbornly adhered to his strategy of defensive war. With some surprisingly effective initiatives by him and his subordinates when the advantage was clearly on the American side, he wore down the enemy's resources and resolve. The Continental Army suffered many setbacks in the course of the war, but also successes. By 1781, it was clear the British were ready to deal, and with the signing of the Treaty of Paris (1783), Washington saw that his mission was complete. He surrendered his commission and, like Cincinnatus, returned to his farm.

At the end of his military service and presidency, Washington gave up the reins of power—thus bearing witness to the requirement of modest leadership and self-denial that is essential for the success of Republican governance.

GEORGE WASHINGTON:
CONSTITUTIONAL CONVENTION (1787)

By the middle of the 1780s, Washington, James Madison, and many of their friends and confidants were deeply concerned about the state of the nation they had labored so hard to free. Washington especially believed that the current constitution, the Articles of Confederation, was a "rope of sand" that was leading America into anarchy. When Shay's Rebellion lit up western Massachusetts, Washington was convinced substantial change was necessary to preserve America's Republican experiment.

After much hesitation, he accepted the logic of Madison and others and reluctantly agreed to attend the Convention, set for Philadelphia in May 1787. His presence assured an anxious nation that the way forward would be of salutary effect. Washington's lack of offspring and expressed hostility to monarchy and clear lack of ambitions guaranteed his leadership would be transparent and positive.

At the Convention, over which Washington presided, he demonstrated restraint, allowing others to do the theoretical debate and the "horse-trading" necessary to create the new government. When the new Constitution was complete, he signed it with much satisfaction and returned to Mount Vernon to await the decision of the states. When, in late June 1788, ten states—including his own Virginia—had ratified the Constitution, Washington was confident—though the document was not perfect—it laid the foundation for a brighter future for the United States.

GEORGE WASHINGTON: UNANIMOUS ELECTION AND PARTY POLITICS

There were few doubts as to who would be the first president under the new Constitution. In fact, Washington ran unopposed and garnered all the votes in the Electoral College. The same situation applied leading to his second term. The lack of electoral opposition did not mean Washington's administration was free of controversy. The requirements of his position was that nearly everything he did set some kind of precedent. He was aware the nation—indeed the world—was watching, so the first president acted with appropriately Republican discretion.

One of the first imbroglios was over the presidential title. Washington finally established "Mr. President" as the title, but not before some rather grandiose and silly titles were floated in Congress. "His Highness the President of the United States of America, and the Protector of their Liberties" was certainly ear catching, but thankfully fell by the wayside.

In his first inaugural address, Washington warned against "local prejudices" and "party animosities" that would distract the new government from the impartial execution of its burden to provide equality of governance. Washington and the other Founders were certain that political parties were disruptive and had no place in the bright Republican future. It is clear they would be disappointed, so much so that Washington would agree to stand for a second term in order to tamp down divisions in the country and the Cabinet. These divisions only grew with the passage of time, and during the presidency of John Adams calcified into competing political parties. This set the stage for a lively American political future.

GEORGE WASHINGTON:
FOREIGN AFFAIRS

In addition to the continued evolution of partisan politics and the so-called Whiskey Rebellion, the second Washington administration was consumed with foreign policy concerns. As a result of the French Revolution, by 1793 France and Britain were at war. The U.S. was expected to enter the war on France's side. This, of course, would alienate the British. Defying the partisans on either side, Washington issued the controversial Neutrality Proclamation of 1793.

In 1794, Britain began seizing American ships in the Caribbean. The Republicans pounced, thinking this was an obvious affront from the secret malevolent hand of Alexander Hamilton. To cool the growing hostility to Britain, Washington sent Chief Justice John Jay to Britain to negotiate a settlement. While Jay was in London, farmers in Western Pennsylvania rebelled against the federal excise tax on whiskey. Because time and distance prevented them from shipping grain to eastern markets, they distilled their grain into whiskey—which was taxed, while cereal grain was not. Washington declared them in rebellion and sent twelve-thousand militia to put down the uprising. The mere threat of this enforcement tamped down the agitation.

When Jay returned, he brought a treaty that, on the face of it, conceded most of the issues to Britain, but Washington was relieved issues between the two nations were resolved and war was avoided. Trade was resumed, Britain stopped seizing American ships, the U.S.–Canadian border dispute was rationalized, and pre–Revolutionary American debts were wiped away.

GEORGE WASHINGTON: LEGACY

In many ways, Washington defined the presidency. Historian James Thomas Flexner calls him the "indispensable man," whose service guaranteed the survival of the United States and set the stage for the republic's rising greatness. Given the scantiness of description in the Constitution, Washington found himself making up his job as he went along. The people admired and trusted this Virginia farmer and placed in his capable hands the first stages of the national journey.

Political necessity required the Founders to leave two issues for resolution in future decades: (1) the relationship between federal and state governments and (2) slavery. Washington's stewardship of the revolutionary victory and his service as the first president forms the core of his legacy. With increasing intensity he grew skeptical of slavery, and at his death he set into motion the eventual manumission of most of his slaves. Though Washington found partisan groupings to be personally repellant, the first two great American political parties emerged from a long running personal and political dispute between two great personalities in Washington's own Cabinet. Yet as it emerged, the political parity system formed a salutary and necessary part of Republican maturity.

On December 14, 1799, after a short illness, George Washington died at Mount Vernon. News spread and the national mourning was genuine and deep. He is routinely ranked by the people and historians at or near the top of the list of American presidents.

2

JOHN ADAMS

JOHN ADAMS: LIFE PAGE

Born: October 30, 1735, Braintree, Massachusetts

Education: Harvard College, BA and MA

Married: Abigail Smith, 1764

Vocation: Attorney

Delegate, First Continental Congress: 1774

Delegate, Second Continental Congress: 1775–1778

Commissioner to France: 1777–1780

Commissioner to United Kingdom: 1782–1783

Minister to the Netherlands: 1782–1788

Minister to the United Kingdom: 1785–1788

First Vice President of the United States: 1789–1797

Second President of the United States: 1787–1801

Defeated in the election of 1800

Retired to Quincy, Massachusetts

Died: July 4, 1826

Additional resources available for this president at www.amomentintime.com.

JOHN ADAMS: FOUNDING BROTHER

John Adams was born into one of Massachusetts's oldest families.
Though his training at Harvard was a classical one, Adams was
inclined to seek a vocation that would lead him into a life of high
reputation; he wanted to be a great man and believed that training and
service as an attorney would lead him in that direction. He was admitted to the bar soon after he received his MA from Harvard in 1758.

From the beginning, few could deny Adams was a man of great
honesty and profound integrity, but he demonstrated early-on a raw,
irascibility that was off-putting and constantly hampering his public
career. Many people just did not like John Adams; though they were
impressed by his intellect and dedication to the cause of liberty, they
often found it difficult to hold him in affection. One clear example
of this contrast was his legal defense of the British soldiers involved in
the so-called "Boston Massacre." He was the best lawyer in Boston and
managed a successful defense, but his hatred of the mob action that led
to the conflict (conduct that he excoriated in the trial) diminished his
popularity for several years.

Elected as a delegate to both the First and Second Continental
Congresses, he soon established a national reputation as perhaps "the"
champion of independence in Philadelphia. He served on the committee
that helped draft Thomas Jefferson's Declaration of Independence and
was the foremost defender of the document in the congressional debates.
In *Founding Brothers*, Joseph Ellis counts Adams (along with Washington,
Jefferson, Franklin, and others) as one of America's founding brothers. A
good case can be made that Adams was first among equals.

JOHN ADAMS:
DIPLOMAT AND VICE PRESIDENT

After helping to organize and manage the Continental Army, John Adams was appointed Commissioner to help Benjamin Franklin and Arthur Lee negotiate relations with France. On his way to Paris, Adams heard France and the U.S. had signed an alliance. Yet, from the time of his arrival in Paris, there was tension in the delegation. Adams felt that Franklin's obsequy[1] toward the French had few limits. Consequently, Adams's relations with French Foreign Minister Charles Gravier, comte de Vergennes, were particularly frosty. Vergennes would only deal with Franklin, and so Adams left France.

John Adams was appointed Ambassador to the United Kingdom in 1785 and, with his wife, Abigail, at his side, negotiated the early stages of that unusually touchy and complicated relationship. He resigned in 1788 and returned to Massachusetts, and an exultant welcome, and awaited political developments. Adams, as a New Englander, was chosen as vice president to George Washington to balance out the ticket.

His service as vice president was frustrating to Adams. George Washington and the rest of the political class largely ignored him, but his votes in the Senate were consistently supportive of the administration's policy. In the second Washington/Adams term, the rift between Thomas Jefferson and Alexander Hamilton burst into view. Because he was essentially a conservative Republican revolutionary, distrustful of broad-based popular democracy, Adams gradually migrated toward the Federalists.

JOHN ADAMS: ELECTION OF 1796

The election of John Adams in 1796 was a strange affair. There was little active campaigning by the candidates (Aaron Burr being the exception), and the voters in only a minority of states selected the electors. In most of the states, the legislatures chose the electors. Thomas Jefferson and Burr were the candidates of the Republicans. Thomas Pinckney and Adams were supported by the Federalists. It was a bitter campaign of newspaper and flyer assaults and rallies—and the results were very close.

Alexander Hamilton, however, was fully engaged in the election. He was convinced that though Adams was a Federalist, the vice president would be haughtily resistant to the Hamiltonian counsel. Therefore, the former treasury secretary contrived to throw the election to Pinckney. When the conspiracy became public, it backfired and probably shattered Hamilton's political career. It did secure the election for Adams, who won by a margin of three votes in the Electoral College. The turmoil ensured Jefferson was elected vice president. It was the only election in U.S. history where candidates from differing tickets were elected.

JOHN ADAMS: XYZ AFFAIR

Foreign policy dominated Adams's term of office. Specifically, the president was determined to keep the United States out of the war embroiling Europe between France and Britain. Jay's Treaty had settled Anglo-American issues, but it angered the French and they began detaining U.S. commercial shipping. This heightened the tension within an already divided citizenry.

To deflect the growing war fever, Adams sent a peace commission to Paris, but at the same time he announced increased spending on military preparations. The latter enraged the pro-French Republicans, who saw the military build-up as hostility to the French Revolution and support for the monarchist British. When the commissioners—John Marshall, Charles Cotesworth Pinckney, and Elbridge Gerry[2]—arrived in Paris, they were greeted with demands that the U.S. pay huge bribes both to French Foreign Minister Talleyrand and the French government in order to secure an amicable peace. The Americans abruptly rejected this corruption. When the collapse of the mission became public, it was a source of embarrassment to Thomas Jefferson, who had colluded in private with the French to secure a pro-French outcome. The country was incensed, and popular sentiment became to turn against France. Remarkably, because of his firm rejection of French corruption, Adams, for the first time in his life, was a popular politician.

JOHN ADAMS:
ALIEN AND SEDITION ACTS

As war fever ramped up after the XYZ Affair and as engagements increased between ships of the new U.S. Navy and the French, disputes between Federalist and Republican newspaper and partisans rose to white-hot intensity. Republicans accused Adams and the Federalists of having monarchist inclinations. Federalists spat back that Republicans were Francophiles seeking to undermine American independence.

The Federalists took their antagonism to the floor of Congress. In June 1798, Congress passed and Adams signed the Alien and Sedition Acts, a series of laws designed to stifle Republican obstruction and suppress the influence of émigrés and to restrict immigration. This legislation aroused profound public disapproval, especially the Sedition Act.

Under the Sedition Act, the administration indicted at least fourteen individuals, including one congressman, and sued a number of Republican newspapers. The Republicans made these laws a campaign issue in 1800, using arguments mustered in the Kentucky Resolution and the Virginia Resolution (secretly authored by Thomas Jefferson and James Madison). In language that would haunt the national memory in the 1830s' Nullification Crisis, and then in justifying southern secession in the 1850s and 1860s, the two Republicans wrote that states had the "natural right" to nullify (invalidate) federal laws they considered to be unconstitutional.

JOHN ADAMS: QUASI-WAR

The all-consuming issue that dominated the single Adams term was the frayed relationship between the U.S. and France. French leaders were anxious to get America to honor its treaty obligations and enter the Anglo-French conflict on the side of France. George Washington refused to take the bait, and John Adams continued this policy. He tried to drive a path between pro-British partisans and the pro-French Republicans.

In May 1798, French privateers[3] began seizing American ships. This was the beginning of an undeclared naval war known as the Quasi-War. In response to France's aggression, Adams and Congress established the Department of the Navy and began building a group of swift, potent frigates, including USS *Constitution*. This young navy demonstrated resourcefulness and bellicosity and was soon beating back the French challenge on the sea.

In the meantime, Congress had to pay for its new ships and Army and so passed an extraordinarily unpopular direct tax—a land tax. Protests against the tax, among them the largely nonviolent "Fries Rebellion," ended when Alexander Hamilton and the Army suppressed the uprising. Negotiations with France were so promising that by the middle of 1800, Adams and Congress disbanded the Army. The final peace treaty was passed and signed by Adams on February 3, 1801.

JOHN ADAMS: ELECTION OF 1800

A s the election of 1800 approached, it was clear that re-election would be a challenge for John Adams. His Federalist allies were deeply divided over the war and negotiations with France. The opposition Republicans were incensed about the political repression of the Alien and Sedition Acts and nervous about a large standing Army led by Alexander Hamilton.

Amidst an effusion of bitter rhetoric—printed and shouted—and partisan electioneering, the election of 1800 sullied the political landscape. Both sides were guilty of insults and rumors designed to smear the reputations of Republican candidate Thomas Jefferson and the incumbent president seeking re-election.

In the end, Adams fell victim to widespread but largely inaccurate supposed "monarchist" inclinations. He was also hurt by a divided Federalist party. This division was amplified by an increasingly irrational Hamilton, who attacked Adams's character, values, and behavior in a vicious pamphlet. It was supposedly intended to influence "internal" deliberations within Federalist ranks, but it was leaked to the public and undermined Adams's support.

The election was very close, with Adams carrying New England and Jefferson carrying the South, and the deciding votes came from the state of New York.

JOHN ADAMS: LEGACY

Of the Founders, perhaps none were more responsible for American independence than John Adams. With great tenacity, he hammered away at loyalist hesitation within the Second Continental Congress and then shepherded Thomas Jefferson's Declaration of Independence to adoption. He organized support for the Continental Army and the early stages of the war effort in Congress. Adams assisted in diplomatic discussions with France and Holland, and he represented the U.S. in negotiations that led to independence, and he then served as ambassador to the United Kingdom.

After two frustrating terms as vice president, he served a single term as president during the tumultuous first decade as the American republic sorted out its political arrangements. He secured a peace treaty with France and kept the young nation out of what could have been a disastrous war for which America was ill-prepared. He is considered the father of the U.S. Navy and established the Library of Congress. He and Mrs. Adams were the first presidential family to live in the executive mansion in the rough new national capital of Washington.

For all his accomplishments during his life of ambition, Adams struggled against the near-universal conclusion that he had an off-putting irascible personality. He tended to lecture his enemies and friends, expecting that high office was his to command rather than something to be earned. Page Smith asserts Adams was his "own worst enemy." Adams made a friend of history, but few friends and numerous enemies in the political world he inhabited.

3

THOMAS JEFFERSON

THOMAS JEFFERSON: LIFE PAGE

Born: April 13, 1743, Shadwell, Virginia

Education: College of William and Mary

Married: Martha Wayles, 1772

Had children with Sally Hemings

Vocation: Attorney

Delegate to Second Continental Congress: 1775–1776

Primary Author of the Declaration of Independence: 1776

Governor of Virginia: 1779–1781

Author of *Virginia Statute for Religious Freedom*: Drafted 1777, Enacted 1786

Delegate to Confederation Congress: 1783–1784

Minister to France: 1785–1789

Secretary of State: 1790–1793

Vice President of the United States: 1797–1801

Third President of the United States: 1801–1809

Founder, University of Virginia: 1819

Died: July 4, 1826

3-A

Additional resources available for this president at www.amomentintime.com.

THOMAS JEFFERSON: A GROWING AFFINITY FOR FREEDOM AND INDEPENDENCE

Thomas Jefferson was born in the Virginia heartland in Shadwell near Charlottesville. Peter Jefferson, his father, was a prosperous planter and slave-holder who provided a rich education and financial legacy for his children. Jefferson attended the College of William and Mary. After a first year of frivolous partying, Jefferson buckled down and came under the tutelage of several professors, including George Wythe, who all saw Jefferson as a man of sterling intellect and talent.

Young Jefferson clerked for Professor Wythe and was admitted to the Virginia bar in 1767. His legal advocacy on behalf of several slaves seeking freedom revealed a growing commitment to personal liberty. Jefferson's rhetorical skill laid to paper attracted the attention of Congress's leading proponent of independence, John Adams. Their rich friendship lasted during the remaining fifty years of their lives, though was unfortunately interrupted by bitter political animosity in the early years. Adams secured Jefferson's membership on the committee to draft the Declaration of Independence (1776). In a whirlwind of graceful prose, Jefferson hammered into eternity the dreams of a people desiring self-determination. Each generation of Americans have seized Jefferson's idiomatic vision and struggled to make it their own.

THOMAS JEFFERSON: WARTIME GOVERNOR, RELIGIOUS FREEDOM, AND DIPLOMAT

After the vote on independence, Jefferson returned to Virginia to prepare for war. He served with the Virginia militia and in the House of Delegates, where for three years he led in the drafting of the Commonwealth constitution and the state legal infrastructure.

While in Williamsburg, one of his most cherished projects dealt with freedom of religion. Jefferson was particularly interested in breaking the fiscal grip the Anglican Church had on Virginia's citizens. In 1779, he introduced the "Bill for Establishing Religious Freedom," but it failed to pass. In 1786, James Madison resuscitated Jefferson's creation and secured its passage in two bills, the first disestablished[1] the Anglican Church and the second secured passage of the *Virginia Statute of Religious Freedom*.

From 1779 to 1781, Jefferson served two one-year terms as governor. He moved the state capital from Williamsburg to the more defensible city of Richmond and led the state militia in its defense against General Benedict Arnold's invasion in 1781. From 1784 to 1789, Jefferson served in various diplomatic posts, succeeding Benjamin Franklin as Minister to France. In Paris, he witnessed the dramatic early months of the French Revolution and drew close to many of the Republican leaders, particularly the Marquis de Lafayette. Jefferson retained pro-French inclinations for the rest of his political life.

THOMAS JEFFERSON: *JEFFERSON AGONISTES*—CONFLICT OVER SLAVERY AND SALLY HEMINGS

Of all the Founders, Thomas Jefferson was most conflicted over the issue of slavery. At times, he worked hard to restrict the institution. As a Virginia Burgess, he attempted—but failed to take from the colonial government—control over slave owners who might desire to emancipate their slaves. Though it failed to make the final draft, he attempted to insert an anti-slave trade clause in the Declaration of Independence. On the other hand, his intellectual struggle was soon compounded by affectional reasons. While serving as Minister to France, Jefferson brought his daughter Polly to Paris. Her traveling companion and Jefferson's slave was a teenager, his deceased wife's half-sister, Sally Hemings. According to Hemings's family testimony, Jefferson began a sexual liaison with Sally while in Paris, and Sally was soon pregnant. This relationship continued and produced several children.

Inter-sexual relations between master and slave were a fairly common phenomenon in slave society, but they represent a particularly poignant aspect of Jefferson's life. He was so clearly uncomfortable with the institution and his participation in it, and yet was so completely incapable of extracting himself from it for personal, social, and political reasons.

THOMAS JEFFERSON: VICE PRESIDENT AND A NEW POLITICAL PARTY

Jefferson returned to America from his sojourn as Minister to France in 1789 with the full expectation of going back. He was an enthusiastic supporter of the French Revolution, though uncomfortable with its more extreme and violent aspects. However, President George Washington interrupted his plans by appointing him secretary of state. In the Cabinet, Jefferson frequently clashed with Treasury Secretary Alexander Hamilton over national finance. Jefferson was opposed to the idea of a national debt and a national bank to manage that debt. Washington mostly sided with Hamilton on fiscal matters, but Washington and Jefferson prevailed in the Compromise of 1790—which placed the nation's new capital on the Potomac River.

He and his partner, James Madison, were strong supporters of states' rights and opposed the preference for centralized concentration of power they saw in Washington, John Adams, and Hamilton. Jefferson and Madison formed a new political grouping known as the Democratic-Republicans, often known simply as Republicans. They supported Jefferson's bid for the presidency in 1796. In that election, he lost narrowly to Adams (seventy-one to sixty-eight in the Electoral College) and spent four frustrating years presiding over a Federalist Senate.

THOMAS JEFFERSON:
ELECTION OF 1800

If the first American Revolution began with the Declaration of Independence and the second was hammered out in the Constitution (1787), the election of 1800 may be called the third American Revolution—a political one. It was the first election that occasioned the peaceful transition of power between opposing political parties, but it was a rancorous process.

Republican's painted Adams and his party as having monarchial tendencies. Federalists described Thomas Jefferson in lurid terms as an immoral wretch heavily influenced by the French. Even the latter's relationship with Sally Hemings was trotted out to demonstrate his lascivious inclinations.

Adams was eliminated in the Electoral College, but due to an anomaly in the Constitution, Jefferson and his running mate Aaron Burr were tied in the Electoral vote with sixty-three votes. This threw the election into the House of Representatives, where each state had a single vote. In this contingent election, Jefferson prevailed (nine states to four), oddly as a result of lobbying on his behalf by arch-rival Alexander Hamilton. He felt Jefferson less a threat to national harmony than Burr, expressing he would rather have as president a man with wrong principles than one "devoid of any."

THOMAS JEFFERSON:
ELECTIONS HAVE CONSEQUENCES

Some historians consider Thomas Jefferson to be one of—if not the most—influential presidents of his century. This resulted from his two terms, followed by two terms each served by two of his closest associates, James Madison and James Monroe. These three were able to place their stamp upon the Federal enterprise in ways that had a lasting if not permanent effect. Jefferson believed in the "improvability of the human mind, in science, in ethics, in government"—and no limits could be placed on that progress.

Jefferson began rooting out Federalist influence by replacing office holders, military officers, and judges—particularly John Adams's late term "midnight judges." He eliminated various taxes that the Federalists had used to finance their economic system, cut the U.S. Navy fleet in favor of cheaper gunboats, and began to pair back on the national debt. In his inaugural address he made a standard plea for unity: "We are all Republicans, we are all Federalists," but then organized his presidency along partisan lines.

At his first inauguration he arrived unaccompanied, on horseback, in plain clothing and personally secured his horse in a nearby stable. Each step of his program was designed to move beyond what he considered to be the backward-looking program of his predecessors and to clear the way for a new, different, better Republican future.

THOMAS JEFFERSON: BARBARY INCURSION AND LOUISIANA

During the colonial period, the British Navy protected American vessels on the shipping lanes. But beginning with American independence, that security went away. The U.S. was on its own. One particularly vexing hotspot for conflict was the North African coast. Congress declared war on Tripoli in the First Barbary War (1801). Jefferson's aggressive efforts during the war were one of the main diplomatic and military accomplishments of his presidency.

In 1800, Spain gave France the Louisiana Territory. Aware that to have a major European country holding the Mississippi and Missouri watershed was a threat, Jefferson sent James Monroe and Robert R. Livingston to Paris to negotiate. Napoleon Bonaparte made them a counter-offer: all of Louisiana for $15,000,000. This would virtually double the size of the United States. Jefferson's constitutional scruples led him to believe the government could not make such a purchase, but the purchase was politically popular so he swallowed his principles and made the deal.

To explore this new acquisition, Jefferson commissioned his secretary Meriwether Lewis and William Clark to explore the new region as far as the Pacific Coast. The Louisiana Purchase probably guaranteed Jefferson's election in 1804.

THOMAS JEFFERSON:
POST-PRESIDENCY AND LEGACY

For nearly two decades, the sage of Monticello sat on his mountain, engaging multiple correspondents and visitors on the political and cultural issues of the day. From before his first term he had been interested in establishing an educational institution, free of religious influence, whose professors and students might explore topics that other schools did not. In 1819, Jefferson founded the University of Virginia. He designed the buildings and grounds, helped plan the courses, and guided the institution as rector in its early years. This, along with his founding of the U.S. Military Academy, placed Jefferson in the front rank of educational innovators in early America.

Beginning in 1812, Jefferson and John Adams re-established their relationship in a remarkable run of correspondence, 158 letters, fleshing out events from their own perspective and discussing the significance of the Revolution they helped mid-wife. In an amazing coincidence, the two adversaries, now re-united, died on the same day, July 4, 1826, the fiftieth anniversary of the signing of the Declaration of Independence. Jefferson was swamped with debt at his death and was not able to leave a monetary legacy to his heirs. In his will, he freed the children of Sally Hemings, but his goods and slaves were sold at public auction.

4

JAMES MADISON

JAMES MADISON: LIFE PAGE

Born: March 16, 1751, Port Conway, Virginia

Education: College of New Jersey (Princeton), AB

Married: Dolley Payne Todd, 1794

Delegate, Congress of the Confederation: 1786–1787

Delegate, U.S. Constitutional Convention: 1787

Member, U.S. House of Representatives: 1789–1797

U.S. Secretary of State: 1801–1809

Fourth President of the United States: 1809–1817

Died: June 28, 1836

Additional resources available for this president at www.amomentintime.com.

JAMES MADISON: PREPARATION AND THE CONSTITUTION

James Madison was born into a wealthy planter family in the Virginia Piedmont. He was educated by Presbyterian clergymen and excelled as a student at the College of New Jersey. Madison was diminutive in stature and often suffered from health-related maladies, but he was intellectually gifted, having a mind bent on acquiring knowledge and an understanding of the Enlightenment philosophy of eighteenth-century liberalism.

Returning from Princeton he became involved in the independence movement. After helping draft the Virginia constitution, he served in the Virginia House of Delegates as an ally of Governor Thomas Jefferson. Later, while in Congress, he saw the weakness of the central government and disunity between the states. He began to advocate for a reform of the Articles. Together with Alexander Hamilton, he secured support for the Philadelphia Convention (1787), which would consider amendments to the Articles.

The Philadelphia Convention began on May 25, 1787, and the influence of Madison was felt in all deliberations from the beginning. He and other home-state delegation members presented the Virginia Plan, which formed the basis for debate: three branches of government (legislative, executive, and judicial) and a bi-cameral legislature with House and Senate. Madison spoke over two hundred times on a variety of topics. He kept a meticulous journal on the proceedings and, while he did not get all he wished, he believed the new Constitution was a vast upgrade to the Articles.

JAMES MADISON: WAR OF 1812-I

Arguably the greatest mistake of Thomas Jefferson's presidency was his imposition of the Embargo Act (1807), which cut off all foreign trade and was designed to punish the warring powers, Britain and France, to get them to stop attacking American ships and impressing[1] American sailors. The embargo was incompetently enforced, ineffective, and wildly unpopular because it did serious damage to the American economy—much of which was based on overseas trade. This was like shooting himself in the foot. Congress repealed the worst aspects of this draconian measure just as James Madison came into office.

To stop the attacks on American shipping, the new president in 1809 tried a diplomatic sanctions maneuver. He promised to trade exclusively with whichever of the belligerents would cease its commercial warfare with America. Both powers played Madison as a diplomatic incompetent and neither would cease attacks on American shipping. Public opinion was growing restive over the continued attacks, especially becoming irritated with Britain, and in the mid-terms of 1810 elected a Congress dominated by "war hawks" such as John C. Calhoun and Henry Clay. This was symptomatic of a general outburst of war fever. Riding this wave of belligerence, Madison asked Congress for a declaration of war in early June 1812.

JAMES MADISON: WAR OF 1812-II

The problem with prosecuting the war just declared was that there was no real army or navy—due to severe cutbacks directed by former President Thomas Jefferson and aided by Madison. Madison and Congress had to create new fighting forces almost from scratch. The president and many Americans thought they could easily capture Canada, but American invasion attempts were repeatedly defeated throughout the war.

Though peace talks were continuing, the British (finally victorious over Napoleon Bonaparte) brought in troops and landed them in the Chesapeake Bay. They scored a major victory over the Yanks at the Battle of Bladensburg in August 1814, during which they almost captured the American president. They then proceeded to Washington and burned the Capital, the president's home, and much of the city. After the Americans fended off the Brits at the Battle of Baltimore,[2] the British withdrew from the region.

Public opinion in Britain was turning against the war, and both sides began looking for a means of extracting themselves from this unfortunate little war. After weeks of discussion, it became clear that a treaty simply affirming the pre-war status quo would be the only satisfactory result. The treaty was signed on December 24, 1814, then affirmed by the British and ratified by the U.S. Senate on February 16, 1815.

JAMES MADISON: LEGACY

James Madison left office a popular president who had ushered in the Era of Good Feelings, but over the years his presidency has not received universal acclaim from historians or political scientists. During his second term, he was the beneficiary of two things: (1) relief that the war had ended and (2) that his opponents, the Federalists, had earned public disdain because of opposition to the war and were collapsing politically. He was one of the key Founders of the Democratic-Republican Party and was on the winning side of most of the issues that faced the infant republic.

His inability to keep the U.S. out of the War of 1812 is considered by historians to be one of the greatest mistakes made by any American president. Nearly all observers, however, rate his brilliant work in creating and preserving the Constitution to be his most lasting legacy. Historian Noah Feldman believes Madison's idea of "liberty-protecting constitutional government" to be one of the most influential American political ideas.

Madison was one of the authors of America's unfinished business, the two great constitutional failures of the Founders: slavery and ambiguity on federal/state sovereignty. Madison did little to correct this unfinished constitutional business. He remained a slave-holder throughout his life and did little to modify the moral stain on America. His approach to federal/state relations was so inconsistent (or, to be kind, so multifaceted) as to have been pretty much devoid of help in resolving this issue.

5

JAMES MONROE

JAMES MONROE: LIFE PAGE

Born: April 28, 1758, Westmoreland County, Virginia

Education: College of William and Mary

Married: Elizabeth Kortright, 1786

Military Service: 1776–1780

Delegate Confederation Congress: 1783–1786

Member, United States Senate: 1790–1794

Minister to France: 1794–1796

Minister to Britain: 1803–1807

Secretary of State: 1811–1817

Fifth President of the United States: 1817–1825

Died: July 4, 1831, New York City, New York

Additional resources available for this president at www.amomentintime.com.

JAMES MONROE:
MILITARY AND EARLY SERVICE

James Monroe was the last of the Revolutionary-era presidents. By the time he took office in 1817, the U.S. was moving into a new period of economic and social transformation.

He interrupted his education at William and Mary to serve in the Revolutionary Army and was wounded at the Battle of Trenton. He endured the frigid Valley Forge encampment with General Washington during the winter of 1777. There he shared a log hut with his life-long friend John Marshall and forged a friendship with the Marquis de Lafayette.

Monroe's long political career began in 1782 with election to the Virginia House of Delegates. Service in the Confederation Congress was followed by a term as U.S. Senator, various diplomatic posts, and a term as Virginia governor. President Thomas Jefferson sent Monroe and Robert R. Livingston to Paris where they negotiated the Louisiana Purchase. After serving a term as Ambassador to Britain, he returned to his plantations and law practice until his appointment as Madison's secretary of state. During the War of 1812, Madison relied heavily on Monroe's advice and made him Secretary of War. His vigorous leadership helped bring an end to the conflict with the signing of the Treaty of Ghent (1814) and General Andrew Jackson's surprising victory over the British at New Orleans.

Monroe ran for president in 1816 and, in the wake of the Federalist Party collapse, faced no real opposition and won overwhelmingly.

JAMES MONROE: MISSOURI COMPROMISE—FIRE-BELL IN THE NIGHT

The Panic of 1819 created substantial resentment toward banks, in general, and The Bank of the United States, specifically. Also causing offense in the South and West was the Supreme Court's decision in *McCulloch v. Maryland* (1819), which affirmed Congress's right to charter The Bank of the United States and protect it from state taxation. Further, the unanimous Court declared the supremacy of federal over state law if federal law was constitutionally approved as "the supreme law of the land."

Yet the issue generating the most passion was the attempt to prevent Missouri from entering the Union as a slave state. Congressman James Tallmadge offered amendments to the bill, which would prevent more slaves from coming into Missouri and make future children of slave parents free at the age of twenty-five. Three days of rancorous debate followed.[1] Eventually a compromise was achieved— the Missouri Compromise. Missouri could come into the Union as a slave state. Maine would come in as a free state. Slavery would be excluded from all states (except Missouri) north of the southern border of Missouri.

There was no more acute observer of this crisis than former President Thomas Jefferson. He considered the outcome to be chilling, describing it as a "fire-bell in the night" and predicting the Missouri Compromise to be a threat to the survival of the Union.

JAMES MONROE: MONROE DOCTRINE

If the Monroe administration's domestic accomplishments were meager, its achievements in foreign policy were exceptional, due in large part to the partnership between the president and his secretary of state, John Quincy Adams.

General Andrew Jackson invaded Florida in 1818, supposedly to attack the Seminole nation, which was harboring escaped slaves and stirring trouble for white settlers. Spain then realized its position in the region was tenuous at best. Negotiations led to the Adams-Otis Treaty (1819), in which Spain ceded Florida to the U.S. and the northern border of New Spain was defined—thus freeing the Louisiana Purchase of any threat of Spanish interference in U.S. western settlement. Once the treaty was ratified by both sides, the U. S. was free to recognize the new Latin American republics (Argentina, Peru, Columbia, Chile, and Mexico) that had recently declared their independence from Spain. After recognizing these republics in 1822, Spain's only remaining American colonies were Cuba, Puerto Rico, and Santo Domingo.

In his 1823 message to Congress, President Monroe issued what came to be known as the Monroe Doctrine, but which probably should be called the Monroe/Adams Doctrine. The U.S. promised to stay out of European conflicts, but said America would not tolerate further colonization of North, Central, or South America. The Monroe Doctrine is considered by many to be one of the cornerstones of American foreign policy.

1750   1775   1800   1825   1850   1875

JAMES MONROE: LEGACY

James Monroe's presidency has often been characterized as the "sleeping presidency," and as far as domestic policy is concerned, he pushed no great initiatives. His greatest legacy lay in diplomatic efforts to secure American interests. He and Secretary of State John Quincy Adams won Florida from Spain and fixed the southern border of the Louisiana Purchase to protect U.S. western expansion. During his terms, the Supreme Court moved aggressively in two landmark decisions to affirm Federal law as the supreme law of the land.

His most singular achievement was the so-called Monroe Doctrine, a cornerstone of American foreign policy. While it had no immediate effect, the Doctrine firmly established the U.S. as the preeminent power in the region and successfully prevented future challenges to this guardianship of Republican governance within its sphere of influence.

As a slave-holder, Monroe worked to protect the slave interest before and during his time in the White House. Quietly, in the background, he aggressively supported the southern/slave position in the negotiations that led to the Missouri Compromise. At the Virginia Constitutional Convention in 1829, he characterized slavery as a blight imposed upon Virginia by the British Crown. Like many southerners, he held the illogical and perverse position that slave-holders were free of any personal responsibility for the horrors of slavery, but rather were innocent victims in an institution forced upon America by outside forces. His solution to the perineal problem: not emancipation but deportation.

6

JOHN QUINCY ADAMS

JOHN QUINCY ADAMS: LIFE PAGE

Born: July 11, 1767, Braintree (Quincy), Massachusetts

Education: Various European universities; Harvard College, BA

Vocation: Attorney

Married: Louisa Johnson, 1797

Minister to the Netherlands: 1794–1797

Minister to Prussia: 1797–1801

U.S. Senator: 1803–1808

Minister to Russia: 1809–1814

Minister to United Kingdom: 1815–1811

Secretary of State: 1817–1825

Sixth President of the United States: 1825–1829

Member U.S. House of Representatives: 1831–1848

Died: February 23, 1848, Washington, D.C.

Additional resources available for this president at www.amomentintime.com.

JOHN QUINCY ADAMS: EARLY SERVICE AND CONTESTED ELECTION

Educated by private tutors, young Quincy accompanied his father, John Adams, on diplomatic missions to Europe even while continuing his education. He returned to Harvard, where he excelled academically and began a legal practice in Boston. Appointed by President Washington as Minister to the Netherlands, he began a series of diplomatic posts: Portugal, Prussia, Russia, and Great Britain.

As President James Monroe's secretary of state, Adams helped President Monroe articulate the so-called Monroe Doctrine, which became one of the great cornerstones of American foreign policy.

In the 1824 election, no candidate won a majority of electoral votes, requiring a contingent election in the House of Representatives—only the second of three such elections in U.S. history.[1] Andrew Jackson had won the popular vote, but that was largely irrelevant in the House. Adams worked the state delegations and won Henry Clay's support. Adams won and appointed Clay as secretary of state. This—the so-called "corrupt bargain"—election left a sour taste in the mouth of Jackson supporters, who made life miserable for President Adams and almost immediately began to plan for the election of 1828.

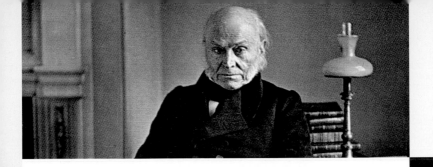

JOHN QUINCY ADAMS: POLITICAL DIVISION AND 1828 DEFEAT

Adams and his secretary of state, Henry Clay, shared an approach to public action that has come to be called the "American System." To this system, Adams added recommendations for an Interior Department, a naval academy, a national university, and a national bankruptcy law. They and the Supreme Court found support for this activity in the "commerce clause" and the "necessary and proper clause" (Article 1, Section 8) of the U.S. Constitution.

Political opposition was another matter entirely. It formed early and hard, was able to almost completely eviscerate the Adams/Clay program, and laid the groundwork for the election of 1828. Adams supporters soon came to be known as National Republicans, and Democrats supported Andrew Jackson.

The election was one of the bitterest in American history. Partisans on both sides attacked the personal life of the two major candidates. Adams was criticized as an elitist, Jackson as being too impetuous and violent for high office. Even the fragile Rachel Jackson was dragged into the fray, accused of bigamy in terms so extreme that Jackson was convinced it caused her early death.

In the end, Adams was swept away in an Electoral College stampede and in a huge popular landslide that was not equaled until that of Theodore Roosevelt in 1904. Adams was so horrified by the tenor of the election that, like his father before him in 1801, he refused to attend the inauguration of his successor.

JOHN QUINCY ADAMS: POST-PRESIDENTIAL TRIUMPH

Adams intended to retire from public service, but gradually became disgusted with Andrew Jackson's policies—particularly the introduction of the "spoils system," as the new president cleaned out the ranks of federal employees not allied with the Democrats. As a result, Adams decided to disregard the custom that former presidents not offer themselves for public service subsequent to their term. This was a course of action only taken by himself and future President Andrew Jackson. He was elected to the U.S House of Representatives and remained there for eighteen years.

Adams was not idle as a member of the House. He worked hard for a high tariff regime to protect native industries. Southern opposition to tariffs was predicated on the desire to make it easier to sell agricultural products overseas. Tactics sharpened during the so-called "nullification crisis," which threated disunion if the South did not get its way and helped force the U.S. to adopt lower tariff rates. Adams came to detest the single-minded intensity and power of the Southern slave-based interest in Congress and he worked to oppose that force with all his rhetorical and political skills.

Adams opposed the annexation of Texas and cast one of the few votes against the Mexican War, believing both were intended to increase slave-based representation in Congress.

JOHN QUINCY ADAMS: LEGACY

The second President Adams saw his presidency as a flawed one, something most historians are agreed upon. He was one of the most effective diplomats in the nation's history and was certainly qualified to be president. Given the circumstances of his election—a contingent election in the U.S. House—to achieve re-election Adams would have had to recognize his peril early on and taken steps to counter-act the revolutionary partisan forces that were closing in on him and the nation he led.

On the nation's unfinished business, one can only say "he tried." He shunned the mantra of states' rights and advocated a steady growth in federal power and participation in the economy and life of the U.S. He was only marginally successful in implementing his program of federally funded infrastructure projects, high protective tariffs, and a steady economy managed by a national bank.

His principled, vigorous stand against slavery (along with his father) marked him as the only president in the years between 1800 and 1860 to have been neither a slave-holder nor allied to the slave interest. Historian Daniel Walker Howe deems Adams's intellect "and courage [to be] above reproach." His political skills were circumscribed by the changes that were whip-sawing the American electoral system, but his personal rectitude and moral leadership mark him as an average president with above-average—even superior—instincts and profound wisdom as he sought to advance the national interest.

7

ANDREW JACKSON

ANDREW JACKSON: LIFE PAGE

Born: March 15, 1757, Waxhaw Country on the Carolina border (Jackson claimed South Carolina)

Vocation: Attorney

Married: Rachel Donelson Robards, 1794

Military Service:

- American Revolution, Volunteer Military Courier: 1780–1781
- War of 1812, Creek Campaign and Battle of New Orleans: 1812–1815
- First Seminole War, Florida Invasion: 1816–1821

Member, U.S. House of Representatives: 1796–1797

Military Governor of Florida: 1821

U.S. Senate: 1823–1825

Seventh President of the United States: 1829–1837

Died: June 8, 1845, Nashville, Tennessee

Additional resources available for this president at www.amomentintime.com.

ANDREW JACKSON: PUGILIST

After admission to the North Carolina bar in 1787, Jackson moved to the frontier community of Nashville, Tennessee, where he met and married Rachel Donelson Robards, the daughter of his landlord. After Tennessee achieved statehood, Jackson was elected to the U.S. House of Representatives in 1796 and the following year to the U.S. Senate. He did not find legislative service to be fulfilling, and he resigned in part because of this, but also in disgust with the John Adams administration.

Jackson purchased the Hermitage, a large plantation near Nashville, and prospered as a slave-holding cotton planter and merchant with large land holdings in Tennessee and Mississippi.

As he built his fortune, Jackson advanced his statue as Commander of the Tennessee militia. In that capacity, he gained great repute as a fierce Indian fighter, leading troops against the Creek Confederation during the War of 1812. For his service, Jackson was promoted to Brigadier, then Major General in the U.S. Army. In the decisive Battle of New Orleans on January 8, 1815, British General Pakenham attacked Jackson's lines and was completely defeated, losing his own life in the process. British writer Alexis de Tocqueville, who was no fan of Jackson's, pilloried "Old Hickory," saying Jackson's elevation to the White House was due solely to the recollection, twenty years old, of this victory under the walls of New Orleans.

ANDREW JACKSON:
ELECTION OF 1828

Almost immediately after the election of 1824, Jackson and his allies began preparing to take on President John Quincy Adams in 1828. The Adams's forces took the name National Republicans to distinguish themselves from the Democratic-Republican coalition that was galloping toward Jackson. As befit the custom, the General did no active campaigning, leaving the heavy lifting to a growing network of pro-Jackson newspapers and clubs.

The rhetoric on both sides was intensely personal. Adams was accused of aristocratic pretensions, corruption, of being a closet Federalist, of placing a billiard table in the White House at government expense, and even of obtaining a prostitute for Czar Alexander I while serving as minister to Russia. Jackson was portrayed as a cruel slave-holder and slave trader, and as a violent pugilist, whose father was a mulatto and mother a "common prostitute."

Jackson won overwhelmingly, both in the popular vote (56 to 43.6 percent), where that was allowed, and in the Electoral College (178 votes to 83 votes). In the bittersweet aftermath of this sweeping victory, Rachel Jackson died, probably of a heart attack. Her grieving widower was convinced his enemies had murdered his beloved wife with their unrelenting slanderous attacks.

ANDREW JACKSON:
THE EATON AFFAIR

The early months of the Jackson administration were consumed with one of those classic Washington cat fights that have so fascinated political insiders since the beginning of the republic. One of Jackson's closest political allies was Secretary of War John Eaton. Rumors accused Eaton's wife, Peggy, of questionable morals, dating from her days as a barmaid in her father's tavern and her behavior in the months before their marriage.[1] The wives of the Cabinet—led by Floride Calhoun, wife of the vice president—ostracized the Eatons, asserting that allowing a "prostitute" so close to the president was unacceptable. Jackson, already tender over the loss of his wife, considered this dust-up all too reminiscent of the treatment his wife received prior to her death. He vigorously defended Peggy Eaton, taking umbrage with her persecutors.

By early 1831, Jackson had had enough and, at the suggestion of close ally Secretary of State Martin Van Buren, demanded the resignation of all his Cabinet members. He sent Van Buren in a recess appointment as Ambassador to London, and when Vice President John C. Calhoun blocked Van Buren's confirmation, the latter returned to Washington. There he took his place as leading member of a group of informal advisors, Jackson's so-called "kitchen cabinet," on whose counsel the President came to rely in the years ahead.

ANDREW JACKSON: SPOILS SYSTEM

Jackson entered office determined to root out what he considered to be corruption and lax management. He encouraged Congress to restructure federal accounting practices so as to eliminate waste, fraud, and abuse and then began to eliminate office holders from previous administrations, putting in place loyalists from the Democratic Party. He began to use the Tenure of Office Act (1820) as a cudgel to enforce his belief that only rotation in office would make hiring conform to the will of the people. He intended this to preclude a corrupt and hereditary civil service, but in reality his solution only served to embed a corrupt and partisan-based civil service. Jackson only rotated out about 20 percent of federal office holders, but his choice for replacement was governed by political kinship, friendship, or geographical origin—hardly criteria designed to secure talented, unbiased public servants. The President simply duplicated the hiring practices of his predecessors; now there were Democrats in the place of Federalists or National Republicans, hardly a prescription for improved, more efficient, governance.

Jackson's changes had a lasting effect. Those presidents who followed him developed this system in an elegant and efficient way. Jackson's idea of partisan rotation in office came to be known as the "spoils system"—as in "to the victor go the spoils." Later in the century—when the voters and politicians alike had grown disgusted with this unethical, shady arrangement—serious reform came under President Chester A. Arthur with the passage of the Pendleton Civil Service Reform Act (1883).

ANDREW JACKSON:
NULLIFICATION CRISIS-I

Acquaintances of Andrew Jackson knew of his legendary temper, which could burn with white-hot intensity and sometimes manifest itself in verbal and physical ways. Only the most foolish or intrepid dared to intentionally arouse Jackson. Poking the bear did not often end well.

Nowhere was this instrument more on display than during the so-called Nullification Crisis of the early 1830s. And, oddly enough, it was over the most tedious of topics: tariffs. Beginning in 1816, a tariff was laid to protect American producers of military goods and other manufactured products. These tariffs were raised significantly in 1824 and 1828 and slightly in 1832.

The problem arose when foreign countries retaliated with tariffs of their own, making it difficult for Americans—particularly from the South—to profitably sell their cotton and other agricultural goods overseas at a profit. The Tariff of 1828 was particularly egregious and was called by Southerners, the "Tariff of Abominations."

Following the precedent outlined in the Kentucky and Virginia Resolutions (1800), Vice President John C. Calhoun articulated a theory of resistance known as nullification and expounded on it anonymously in "The South Carolina Exposition and Protest" (1828). In it, he declared any state had the right to "nullify"—declare illegal or void—this tariff (or any federal law within their state they deemed to be unconstitutional). By this, he was definitely poking the bear.

ANDREW JACKSON:
NULLIFICATION CRISIS-II

After the passage of a series of tariffs (taxes on imported goods) to raise federal revenue—but more importantly to protect American manufactures from foreign competition—European countries retaliated by slapping tariffs on American exports—particularly southern cotton. South Carolina responded by nullifying this tariff (and by extension any other federal law), because it deemed the law to be unconstitutional. President Jackson correctly concluded that if allowed, such a practice would doom the Union. He suspected the author of this theory was Vice President John C. Calhoun of South Carolina, who presented it anonymously.

Jackson was sympathetic with the South's position on tariffs and supported a partial, but lawful, reduction in the tariffs. He would not, however, tolerate seditious behavior. When, in 1832, South Carolina nullified the tariffs of 1828 and 1832, Jackson sent U.S Navy ships to Charleston harbor and promised to hang anyone for treason who supported either nullification or secession. He also ordered the tariff be collected off Charleston before ships could land.

In December, he issued a proclamation in which he thundered that nullification contradicted both the letter and spirit of the Constitution. He asserted South Carolina was on the brink of insurrection and treason, and he appealed to the people of the state to reaffirm their loyalty to the Union. Fortunately, both sides began to back down and found a solution that gradually reduced tensions and the tariff—but it was a closely held thing.

ANDREW JACKSON: INDIAN REMOVAL

Andrew and Rachel Jackson were unable to have children of their own. They adopted three sons: Theodore, an Indian; the son of Rachel's brother, whom they named Andrew Jackson, Jr.; and Lyncoya, a Creek Indian boy orphaned after the Battle of Tallushatchee. The irony of the Jacksons' apparent personal affection and generosity toward his Indian children is in marked contrast to his treatment of the eastern Indian tribes.

As late as the 1820s, many Indian nations lived in nearby proximity to the growing white population. Recognizing the inevitability of white settlement, these clans (especially the Cherokee) had begun to shape their lifestyles to accommodate white desires—all to no avail.

On close votes, Congress passed the Indian Removal Act (1830) and many of the tribes began to move west. The Cherokee successfully argued their treaty rights before the U.S. Supreme Court, but Jackson refused to enforce the Court order. Neither Federal nor state authorities were sympathetic to the Cherokee cause. The largest group in the Cherokee Confederation rejected peaceful removal and, later under President Martin Van Buren, were forced west to Oklahoma on the "Trail of Tears"—on which thousands of Cherokee suffered cold, starvation, and death. Almost a fourth of their number died on the way.

ANDREW JACKSON:
CRUSHING THE BANK-I

Andrew Jackson loathed banks. To him, they represented a corrupt concentration of wealth and power he felt undermined democracy and Republican values. His opposition was part historical, part political, and profoundly emotional. He was particularly distrustful of the Bank of the United States (BUS). Chartered by Congress in 1816, it was up for renewal in 1836. This confrontation was a long time in the making.

The American Revolution dramatically changed the economic landscape. Banks were an essential part of this transformation. This market revolution, which had opportunities for both success and failure, created hope and, at the same time, anxiety—which was then conveyed to elected officials. Andrew Jackson was one of those suspicious of this market revolution—many parts of which threatened his understanding of the Jeffersonian ideal.

Jackson's opposition to the BUS, and banks in general, was rooted in his suspicion of debt and paper credit. His ideas were questionable from an economic viewpoint but politically quite popular. The government kept its gold and silver on deposit in the BUS. The bank took this capital and issued loans in the form of paper money to investors who built factories, roads, canals, and other profit-making enterprises. Its currency was the most reliable in the country. All this was good, but Jackson hated it.

ANDREW JACKSON:
CRUSHING THE BANK-II

A ndrew Jackson had a primitive understanding of economics. This ineptitude brought him into conflict with the Bank of the United States (BUS) and its president, Nicolas Biddle. Banks were wrong in general because, the President believed, they created a social and political hierarchy built on paper money. Unfortunately, Biddle allied himself with Jackson's enemies, particularly Henry Clay, who wanted to use the Bank as an issue in his 1832 campaign against Jackson.

BUS allies did not wait for the 1836 renewal date, but rather put forward an early re-charter bill in 1832, which Jackson thunderously vetoed. In the election, despite the thousands of dollars Biddle threw into the campaign to defeat him, Jackson won in a landslide. He won 54 percent of the popular vote and 216 electoral votes.

Jackson withdrew federal funds from BUS and deposited them in so-called "pet banks" at the state level. The closing years of Jackson's second term witnessed a soaring economic boom, a spectacular rise in cotton prices, and inflationary lending by the pet banks. Without the restraining influence of the BUS, land speculation spun upward and there was no restraint on the economy. When the cotton market collapsed just after President Martin Van Buren took office, the U.S. entered several years of painful economic contraction known as the Panic of 1837.

ANDREW JACKSON: LEGACY

Andrew Jackson left a lasting imprint on the presidency—in part because of his commanding personal and political temperament, and also because, with modifications, he extended the influence of Jeffersonian Republicanism through the middle of the nineteenth century. His understanding of the changing economic circumstances of America was primitive at best, but his sterling political instincts were rock solid. His attacks on banks as agents of un-democratic corruption secured victory for his party in three successive elections (until the long economic contraction known as the Panic of 1837, for which his policies had to shoulder a significant part of the blame). This downturn gave opportunity to his political enemies and ushered in the Whig coalition, confirming the launch of the Second Party System (1828–1854).

His attempts to bring true reform to political hiring were largely ineffectual. Basically, Jackson solidified the old way of hiring into what his foes called the spoils system. His appointments were generally of sub-standard quality, though his rotation of political office-holders was comparatively small compared to his successors. The problem only grew worse until the advent of serious civil service reform in the 1880s.

Perhaps the darkest part of Jackson's legacy was his policy of Indian removal. Long before he caused the removal of more than forty-five thousand Native Americans to Indian Territory, he had earned the Creek name for Jackson: *Jacsa Chula Harjo*—"Jackson, old and fierce."

MARTIN VAN BUREN

MARTIN VAN BUREN: LIFE PAGE

Born: December 5, 1782, as Maarten Van Buren

Vocation: Attorney

Married: Hannah Hoes, 1807

Surrogate (Probate Judge) of Columbia County, New York: 1808–1813

Member, New York State Senate: 1813–1820

Attorney General of New York: 1815–1819

U.S. Senator: 1821–1828

Governor of New York: 1829

U.S. Secretary of State: 1829–1831

Minister to the United Kingdom: 1831–1832

Vice President of the United States: 1833–1837

Eighth President of the United States: 1837–1841

Died: July 24, 1862

Additional resources available for this president at www.amomentintime.com.

MARTIN VAN BUREN:
LITTLE MAGICIAN

Born Maarten Van Buren to a lower-class New York provincial family, he was the only president to speak English as a second language, Dutch being his first. He was a political genius, often called the "Little Magician," and made his way to the highest office in the land—not through aristocratic preferment, but rather by intelligence and hard work. Yet, he hungered after the symbols of gentility—elegant homes, clothing, and entertainment—even while creating the political machine that lifted ordinary working people into power, thereby changing the nature of American political life.

Van Buren served in various state positions, eventually moving to the national stage as a U.S. senator. There he fostered his goal of re-animating a two-party system based on ideological differences. During the Adams administration, he actively opposed the Adams/Clay American system of extensive public works, and he moved quickly behind the 1828 candidacy of Andrew Jackson as the best way to bring his new creation—the Democratic Party—to life. His primary vehicle of creation was the so-called "spoils system," the principles of which he had perfected as a Bucktail[1] leader in New York state.

Van Buren used his iron-fisted control of New York politics to gain re-election to the Senate (1827), a brief term as Governor of New York (1829), and, through Jackson's election, elevation to secretary of state.

MARTIN VAN BUREN: VICE
PRESIDENT AND ELECTION OF 1836

As secretary of state, Van Buren scored a series of spectacular successes. France settled U.S. claims from the Napoleonic era. The Ottoman Empire at last permitted U.S. vessels access through the Bosporus Strait into the Black Sea. Finally, he was able to gain trade entree to the British West Indies, something that had eluded Presidents James Monroe and John Quincy Adams.

Significant political energy was expended in the early years of the Jackson administration over the so-called Petticoat Affair. Peggy Eaton, wife of Secretary of War and close Jackson-ally John Eaton, was shunned by the wives of official Washington because of alleged improprieties surrounding her marriage,[2] as well as her outspoken, brash, assertive personality. Only Van Buren and Postmaster General William Barry sided with the Eatons, thereby winning Jackson's gratitude. The President refused to meet with the Cabinet for years, but instead gathered Van Buren and a group of informal advisors derisively known as the "Kitchen Cabinet."

Van Buren enjoyed the strong support of Jackson in the election of 1836 and so received the Democratic nomination. He faced three candidates, members of a loose coalition of anti-Jackson sentiment that gradually was coalescing into the Whig Party. The combination of Jackson's support, strong Democratic organization, and a weak, fragmented Whig campaign gave Van Buren the White House.

MARTIN VAN BUREN:
PANIC OF 1837

In a manner of months, Van Buren's dream of a lifetime was almost completely swept away. Literally days after his inauguration, the nation's economy was assaulted by a major economic contraction: the Panic of 1837. This led to a grinding five-year, double-dip depression. At the same time, Mexico began making financial demands and threatening war over Texas. The abolitionist movement enjoyed a growth spurt and flooded the nation with anti-slavery propaganda, leading to sectional tensions. And then a rebellion in Canada and a Maine border dispute threatened war with Britain.

Van Buren, committed to laissez-faire economics, was philosophically opposed to government intervention in the economy to right the ship. He advocated a plan to withdraw all government gold and silver from state banks and institute an independent treasury, but, once finally passed in 1840, it failed to deliver the promised stability. The slavish devotion of Van Buren and Jackson to Jeffersonian rejection of high tariffs and federally funded public works projects meant the U.S. became dependent upon foreign investment and imports for the construction of the Erie Canal and other public works projects.

Ironically, the funds used to finance the "Trail of Tears"—$50 million—gave a powerful boost to the economy in 1838, and economic activity revived temporarily. By the end of 1839, however, the simulative effects of this government spending were exhausted. In the end, economic bad times swept Van Buren from office. In the face of unprecedented crises, the Little Magician had run out of tricks.

MARTIN VAN BUREN: ELECTION OF 1840 AND POST-PRESIDENTIAL LIFE

In 1839, President Van Buren was looking forward to his re-election. The Panic of 1837 had subsided, and it seemed as though his Jeffersonian/Adam Smith non-interventionist approach to righting the economy was working. Southerners had been anxious to follow-up Andrew Jackson's diplomatic recognition of the Independent Republic of Texas. Van Buren dodged the Texas bullet by refusing to consider annexation.

Then, at the end of the year, catastrophe struck when Britain raised interest rates and the country was plunged back into depression. Van Buren had to face the voters during this double-dipped catastrophe and defend his miserable economic record. The Democrats were divided over Texas and the Whigs carried the day. The voters denied Van Buren a second term and elected William Henry Harrison of Indiana, though the election was breathlessly close.

President Van Buren had a productive political life after he left the White House. He came close to winning the Democratic nomination for president in 1844, but his opposition to the annexation of Texas turned away most Southern delegates, and his supporters withdrew his nomination at the last minute.

During retirement, Van Buren became increasingly vocal in his opposition to slavery—which was an almost complete reversal of his position when he needed Southern votes to sustain his climb to power.

MARTIN VAN BUREN: LEGACY

Martin Van Buren is the father of the modern political party. He funded and built it using the "spoils system" approach to the appointment of state and federal officials. He believed it was necessary to preserve the Republican ideals he held dear—free market economics, states' rights, and no federal funding of public works. In the end, his creation struck him down and he was denied the second term for which he hungered.

On America's unfinished constitutional business, he came down hard on the side of the states in the competition for supremacy among the nation's centers of power. He emphatically rejected Henry Clay's American System, precluded federal involvement in the economy and support for infrastructure projects. He helped Andrew Jackson crush the Bank of the United States and generally opposed high tariffs (with the possible exception of the Tariff of 1828, which observers suspect was a political maneuver to embarrass President John Quincy Adams).

On the issue of slavery, Van Buren, who owned a single slave early in life, allied himself with the slave interest in the Democratic Party in order to win nomination and election as president. But in retirement, a growing personal opposition to slavery began to emerge. In public statements such as the so-called "Barnburner[3] Manifesto," he argued the Founders looked forward to slavery's abolition. Prior to his death in 1862, Van Buren supported President Abraham Lincoln's efforts to restore the Union by military force.

9

WILLIAM HENRY HARRISON

WILLIAM HENRY HARRISON:
LIFE PAGE

Born: February 9, 1773, Charles City County, Virginia

Education: Hampden-Sydney College and University of Pennsylvania

Vocation: Military service and politician

Married: Anna Symmes, 1795

Secretary of Northwest Territory: 1798–1799

Delegate from Northwest Territory to U.S. House of Representatives: 1799–1800

Governor, Indiana Territory: 1801–1812

Member, U.S House of Representatives from 1st District of Ohio: 1816–1819

U.S. Senator: 1825–1828

Minister to Columbia: 1828–1829

Ninth President of the United States: 1841

Died: April 4, 1841, Washington, D.C.

Additional resources available for this president at www.amomentintime.com.

WILLIAM HENRY HARRISON:
TIPPECANOE AND TECUMSEH TOO!

The ninth president of the United States was the well-educated younger son of one of Virginia's first families. He chose a career in the military and eventually public service. Harrison served with the Army in the 1790s before resigning his commission to take the position of secretary to the Northwest Territory. He represented the region in Congress until President Adams appointed him governor of the Indiana Territory. During his time as governor, he attempted to open the territory to slavery, but a large number of anti-slavery settlers secretly conspired with President Thomas Jefferson to thwart Harrison's efforts.

Harrison served terms in the U.S. House and Senate before spending a year as Minister to Columbia. He was one of three Whig candidates for president in 1836 in a scheme to deny Vice President Martin Van Buren a majority in the Electoral College. The plan failed and Harrison retired to his farm in North Bend, Ohio, where he continued to serve as clerk of the Court of Common Pleas for Hamilton County. Nevertheless, the siren call of presidential politics continued to tempt him; as the Panic of 1837 ground down the Van Buren presidency, William Henry Harrison and his Whig Party allies began to sense an opportunity.

WILLIAM HENRY HARRISON: SHORTEST PRESIDENCY

If Martin Van Buren created the modern political party, William Henry Harrison taught the nation how to use Van Buren's creation. Though the Whigs made slight gains in the 1838 mid-term elections, the Democrats held control of Congress—and it seemed as though the economy was righting itself. Unfortunately for Van Buren, at the end of 1839, the economy again collapsed. With tens of thousands of men out of work, the fields were ripe for a Whig Party harvest.

Harrison easily won the party nomination for president and then unleashed the famous "Log Cabin Campaign" against the incumbent, whom the Whigs settled with the epithet "Van Ruin." When the Democrats attempted to deride Harrison as a country bumpkin sitting on the porch of his log cabin sipping hard cider, the Whigs seized the images and turned them to their advantage in seeking the votes of common people.

Harrison was inaugurated on a cold, rainy day and gave the longest inaugural speech in presidential history. In late March, he gave evidence of a severe cold which developed into pneumonia. Within a month of his inauguration, William Henry Harrison died, having served the shortest period of time of any U.S. president.

JOHN TYLER

JOHN TYLER: LIFE PAGE

Born: March 29, 1790, Charles City County, Virginia

Education: The College of William and Mary

Vocation: Attorney

Married: Leitia Christian, 1813 (died 1842); Julia Gardner, 1844

Member, U.S. House of Representatives: 1816–1821

Governor of Virginia: 1825–1827

U.S. Senator: 1827–1836

Vice President of the United States: 1841

Tenth President of the United States: 1841–1845

Member, Confederate Congress: 1861–1862

Died: January 18, 1862, in Richmond, Virginia

10-A

Additional resources available for this president at www.amomentintime.com.

JOHN TYLER: HIS ACCIDENCY

John Tyler fully expected to spend four leisurely years as vice president. When the death of President William Henry Harrison in April 1841 shocked the country, Tyler seized the moment, rejected any attempt by his political opponents to relegate him to care-taker status as some kind of acting president, and took the oath of office. His opponents may have derisively assigned to him the epithet "His Accidency," but fortunately for the country, Tyler knew the nation needed a constitutionally affirmed president. His decisive action established an important precedent until the passage of the Twenty-Fifth Amendment in 1967 resolved most questions of succession.

Harrison had called a special session of Congress to deal with appointments and pressing legislation, and Tyler worked with the Whigs in the early days to accomplish their goals. He signed national bankruptcy legislation, a law ending the Independent Treasury,[1] and legislation permitting sale of national lands to settlers, but on the infamous bank issue he choked. By early September 1841, as a life-long opponent of a national bank, he had vetoed two bills re-establishing the Bank of the United States. Henry Clay stubbornly refused to accept any of Tyler's reservations on the bank charter, imprudently assuming the Whigs could override Tyler's veto.

JOHN TYLER: LEGACY

Tyler's legacy can best be described in two words: succession and annexation. To the nation's benefit, Tyler immediately took the oath of office upon the death of William Henry Harrison. This established a precedent for succession that carried through the assassinations of Abraham Lincoln, James A. Garfield, William McKinley, and John F. Kennedy. Their vice presidents—Andrew Johnson, Chester Arthur, Theodore Roosevelt, and Lyndon Johnson—immediately took the oath of office and assumed the responsibilities of a regularly elected president.

Tyler's most important goal was the annexation of Texas. He believed it would strengthen the slave interest in Congress and expand and protect the institution in the foreseeable future. He made it an issue in the campaign of 1844 and succeeded in procuring statehood for Texas in 1845.

As to the nation's unfinished constitutional business, Tyler worked strongly to maintain the status quo on both unresolved issues. In the struggle over sovereignty between state and federal governments, he was a strong advocate of states' rights. As a life-long slaveholder, he may have possibly believed the institution to be evil, but he never freed his slaves. Politically he was a strong advocate of the slave interest and worked tirelessly to protect, extend, and strengthen it during his state and federal service.[2]

11

JAMES K. POLK

JAMES K. POLK: LIFE PAGE

Born: November 2, 1795, Pineville, North Carolina
Education: University of North Carolina, Chapel Hill, BA
Vocation: Attorney, Slave-Trading Planter
Married: Sarah Childress, 1824
Member, U.S. House of Representatives: 1825–1839
Speaker, U.S. House of Representatives: 1835–1839
Eleventh President of the United States: 1845–1849
Died: June 15, 1849

Additional resources available for this president at www.amomentintime.com.

JAMES K. POLK:
DARK HORSE CANDIDATE

Born and educated in North Carolina and raised in Tennessee, James Polk was an acolyte of Andrew Jackson and rode the Jackson wave to political advancement. The young attorney's family was close to Jackson's, and while Polk served in the Tennessee legislature, he gave support to General Jackson's rise to power. After 1825, he was a member of the U.S. House for several terms, serving in the prestigious post of Speaker for the last few years of his tenure. In the House, he worked for Jackson's agenda (and later that of President Martin Van Buren), opposing federal support for infrastructure projects and supporting the President's battle over the Bank.

Polk was a slave owner and surreptitious slave trader even during his years in the White House—and worked tirelessly to advance the slave interest throughout his political career. By the late 1830s, he was nursing presidential ambitions and left Congress to run for Governor of Tennessee. He won once (1839) and then lost twice more (1842, 1843). This series of defeats would have crushed most men's political motivation, but Polk hammered on.

When Van Buren faltered at the Baltimore Democratic National Convention and his preferred alternate candidate, New York Senator Silas Wright, revealed that he too opposed Texas annexation, Van Buren dropped out and the convention turned to Polk—who became America's first so-called "dark horse" candidate for president.[1]

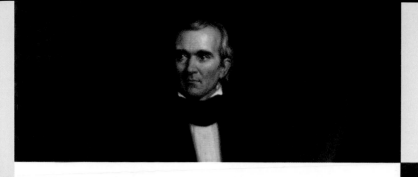

JAMES K. POLK: POLK'S GOALS— TARIFF AND INDEPENDENT TREASURY

James K. Polk had a well-earned reputation among all parts of the electorate for political duplicity. He would hide his true intentions to secure support from one group or another and then, in the White House, proceeded to do what he had intended to do all along. For instance, to protectionist-tariff advocates in Pennsylvania, he issued a letter which seemed to promise continued support for some type of protection. Supporters of Martin Van Buren were the key to his victory in New York, but once in office, Polk angered the Van Burenites by appointing officials who had helped derail Van Buren's nomination. Some might call this the clever actions of a savvy campaigner. Others just called him a liar.

During his term, Polk had four major goals: (1) elimination of protective tariffs, (2) restoring the Independent Treasury [see discussion in John Tyler: His Accidency], (3) settling the Oregon boundary dispute with Britain, and (4) acquisition of Upper California, then a possession of the Republic of Mexico.

Shortly after taking office, Polk instructed Secretary of the Treasury Robert J. Walker to prepare a new and lower, non-protective, tariff bill. The measure passed Congress and Polk signed it in summer 1846. The lower tariff helped fuel a thriving trade with overseas partners, particularly Britain.

JAMES K. POLK: POLK'S GOALS— EXPANSION TO OREGON

From the beginning of his single term in the White House, Polk demonstrated a passion for U.S. expansion. There is no evidence he articulated the term "manifest destiny,"[2] but it certainly fit with the major passion of his presidency.

Oregon emerged as a point of contention only after the election of 1844. Early on, Polk identified U.S. interest in acquiring the territory through negotiations, but with hawkish rhetoric, he threatened military action if America and Britain could not reach an accommodation. Polk called on Congress to pass a resolution, giving Britain a one-year notice of U.S. intentions to end joint occupation of the territory. The Brits sent word that it would settle for a division along the forty-ninth parallel. The Treaty was signed, submitted to the Senate, and approved in mid-1846.

Unfortunately for Polk, the result of his oh-so-clever backroom maneuvering may have resolved the international conflict with Britain, but it left a bad taste in the mouth of Northern Democrats. Many of them had loyally helped secure statehood for slave-holding Texas, but then were denied the prospect of more free states when Polk gave away Oregon north of the forty-ninth parallel. The President seemed to be unaware that his policy of unrestrained expansion was creating widespread sectional animosity with disastrous results in the next decade.

JAMES K. POLK: POLK'S GOALS— EXPANSION AND THE MEXICAN WAR

When Mexico frustrated his schemes for grabbing the territory west of Texas, Polk moved to declare war. He sent General Zachary Taylor into disputed Texas territory west of the Nueces River and just north of the Rio Grande. Polk was clearly taunting Mexico into an attack. Mexican leaders swallowed the bait and sent forces into disputed territory north of the Rio Grande. They ambushed U.S. troops and overwhelmed them in the so-called Thornton Affair.[3] Polk pounced.

Instead of asking Congress for a declaration, he simply asserted that Mexico's aggressive action had "shed American blood on American soil" and that a state of war already existed between the two countries. Asserting his presidential prerogative as Commander in Chief, he took full control of the machinery of government and micromanaged the war from beginning to end. In battle after battle, Yank troops overwhelmed the out-led and out-gunned Mexican forces, in the end capturing Mexico City.

The Mexican government held out until February 1848, repeatedly refusing to accept President Polk's humiliating and insulting demands. The Mexicans finally gave in. The two parties signed the Treaty of Guadalupe Hidalgo (1848), thoroughly dismembering the Republic of Mexico.

JAMES K. POLK: POLK'S GOALS— EXPANSION AND THE MEXICAN CESSION

The Treaty of Guadalupe Hidalgo was signed in early February 1848. By it, the U.S. paid Mexico $15 million, the border of Texas was fixed on the Rio Grande River, and Mexico paid a huge territorial indemnity that encompassed the future states of New Mexico, Arizona, California, Utah, Nevada, and part of Colorado.

There was a bitter debate in Congress over the Mexican Cession. Some senators wanted the U.S. to receive no Mexican territory from the war. Others were determined to block the introduction of slavery into the Cession. In response, freshman Pennsylvania Democratic congressman David Wilmot introduced an amendment to an appropriations bill banning slavery in any state carved from the Mexican Cession.

James K. Polk was a slave owner and slave trader and supported the institution, yet, for him, slavery was tangential to the main focus of his energy—expansion to the Pacific. In a supreme irony, other than Missouri and Texas, no state sculpted from territory acquired in the wake of the Mexican War or from the Louisiana Purchase came into the Union as a slave state.

Everett Historical / Shutterstock.com

JAMES K. POLK: LEGACY

Considering the bizarre way he had secured the Democratic nomination and his reputation for political duplicity, James K. Polk was a remarkably successful president. Some historians consider him to be one of the most effective pre–Civil War presidents—certainly in comparison to most of the others of that era. His high rankings are largely attributable to his ability to accomplish those things he set out to do.

Along the way—either through political naiveté, frustration over Mexican stubbornness, or an unarticulated desire to expand slavery—Polk barreled through the bloody humiliation of a weaker neighbor to secure Upper California and, in the Mexican Cession, what became the entire American Southwest. Polk's accomplishment was real and extraordinary. Though of questionable morality, it did contribute to the future grandeur and prosperity of the United States.

While his primary focus was on expansion of the nation's physical boundaries, he was also a slave owner, a slave trader, and was sympathetic to the unencumbered spread of the institution. He did not go to war—as some of his contemporary critics alleged—to make room for more slave states, but as someone fully engaged in that dissolute institution, he did nothing to help resolve that pressing moral issue save to perpetuate it. Ironically, his expansion did not expand the reach of slavery but may have pushed the nation closer to Civil War because it intensified the raw, emotional debate over slavery and the slave interest; a debate about slavery's expansion.

12

ZACHARY TAYLOR

ZACHARY TAYLOR: LIFE PAGE

Born: November 25, 1784, Barboursville, Orange Country, Virginia

Vocation: Military Service—U.S. Army, 1808–1849

- War of 1812
- Second Seminole War
- Black Hawk War
- Mexican War

Married: Margaret Smith, 1810

Twelfth President of the United States: 1849–1850

Died: July 9, 1850

Additional resources available for this president at www.amomentintime.com.

ZACHARY TAYLOR:
SECTIONAL TENSIONS

When Zachary Taylor took the oath of office, the major issue facing the republic was the disposition of the territory taken from Mexico after the war. It was becoming increasingly clear that California, whose population was bursting after the discovery of gold east of Sacramento in 1848, wanted to come into the Union as a free state.

Taylor, though a slave-holding southerner, saw his first responsibility was to preserve the Union. He began to work for compromise with Daniel Webster and other Northerners opposed to slavery and even worked with Henry Clay. Webster and Clay began to stitch together the vaunted Compromise of 1850. The plan included free statehood for California, the balance of the Mexican Cession under federal control, a ban on slave trading in Washington, D.C., and a strict new fugitive slave law.

The compromise was not realized during Taylor's brief term, but he was heavily engaged in the negotiations that laid the foundation for its future passage during the term of his successor. To his fellow Southerners—whose white-hot pro-slavery passions were stirring talk of secession and treachery—he thundered, "[anyone] taken in rebellion against the Union, he would hang . . . with less reluctance than he had hanged deserters and spies in Mexico."

ZACHARY TAYLOR: LEGACY

Historians have not generally ranked Zachary Taylor among the best presidents, though some count him the most effective among the four Whig presidents (Harrison, Tyler, and Fillmore).

President Taylor died in summer 1850 of an indistinct intestinal disease (possibly gastroenteritis, though termed cholera at the time of death), which was unrelated to the Asiatic cholera epidemic gripping the U.S. that season. His death was so sudden and mysterious that rumors abounded he was the victim of poisoning by pro-slavery agents. In 1991, his body was exhumed and tested. The study demonstrated very low levels of arsenic in analyzed body parts and speculated the President may have succumbed to contaminated food followed by incompetent medical treatment. Subsequent examination of the evidence has done little to resolve the controversy.

On slavery itself, he was an unashamed slaver, owning by his own words upwards of three hundred slaves. Only Thomas Jefferson, George Washington, and possibly Andrew Jackson owned more slaves than Taylor. He was the last president to maintain slaves while in the White House, but he expressed general opposition to the spread of slavery into new federal territory. Taylor was the last Southerner elected to the White House until Woodrow Wilson was chosen in 1912.

13

MILLARD FILLMORE

MILLARD FILLMORE: LIFE PAGE

Born: January 7, 1800, Moravia, New York

Vocation: Attorney

Married: Abigail Powers, 1826 (died 1853); Caroline McIntosh, 1858

Member, U.S. House of Representatives: 1833–1835 and 1837–1843

Comptroller of New York: 1848–1849

Twelfth Vice President of the United States: 1849–1850

Thirteenth President of the United States: 1850–1853

Died: March 8, 1874, Buffalo, New York

13-A

Additional resources available for this president at www.amomentintime.com.

MILLARD FILLMORE:
COMPROMISE OF 1850

As vice president and president of the Senate, Fillmore had presided over some of the most impassioned and articulate debates in the history of the republic. The issue was the spread of slavery into the territories. In order to soothe the tensions between North and South, early in 1850 Henry Clay of Kentucky began putting together a compromise "Omnibus" bill that would give each side something. President Zachary Taylor had advanced competing proposals that did not contain provisions advocated by Clay and was opposed to the Omnibus bill. The debate was intensified as Clay and Taylor publicly mocked and ridiculed each other and their respective positions.

When Fillmore became president, he made it his objective to get something like the Compromise through Congress. The making of congressional sausage[1] assumed legendary proportions, as both sides swapped and traded their way to resolution. Instead of Clay's Omnibus Bill, Fillmore worked to break its parts into separate pieces of legislation and soon the Senate, then the House, had passed the Compromise of 1850. In it, California was admitted as a free state, the boundary of New Mexico was set, and Texas was compensated for land it claimed but would not get in the settlement. The slave trade, but not slavery, was banned from the District of Columbia.

| 1750 | 1775 | 1800 | 1825 | 1850 | 1875 |

MILLARD FILLMORE: LEGACY

In November 1850, a member of the Whig party—recalling the treachery of the hated John Tyler and the current apostasy of President Millard Fillmore—wailed, "God save us from Whig vice presidents." To earn this level of contempt, Fillmore presided over the construct of the Compromise of 1850, particularly the Fugitive Slave Act. He declined to join the migration of the Whigs' and Know-Nothings into the new Republican Party, as he was opposed to abolition.

He did not seek but accepted the nomination of the American Party (Know-Nothing) in 1856. His association with the xenophobic, anti-Catholic, religion and race-baiting party has damaged his historical reputation—though there is no evidence he harbored the nativist sentiments of that party. By 1856, the Know-Nothing starburst was dying, and Fillmore was only able to carry a single state and 10 percent of the popular vote.

President Fillmore's support of the Compromise of 1850 did little to resolve the tense relationship between the federal government and state governments, though some of the parts of the Compromise laid the groundwork for enhanced federal control of territories. Fillmore personally opposed slavery, but for constitutional reasons believed the federal government could not interfere with the institution in the states and territories.

Milliard Fillmore suffered two devastating strokes in 1874 and died shortly thereafter.

14

FRANKLIN PIERCE

FRANKLIN PIERCE: LIFE PAGE

Born: November 23, 1804, Hillsborough, New Hampshire

Vocation: Attorney

Married: Jane Appleton, 1834

Education: Bowdoin College

Member, U.S. House of Representatives: 1833–1837

U.S. Senator: 1837–1842

Military Service, New Hampshire Militia and U.S. Army: 1831–1848

Fourteenth President of the United States: 1853–1857

Died: October 8, 1869, Concord, New Hampshire

Additional resources available for this president at www.amomentintime.com.

FRANKLIN PIERCE: POLITICIAN, SOLIDER, ELECTION OF 1852

Pierce inherited his interest in politics from his father, Benjamin Pierce, a Revolutionary War veteran who was a prominent New Hampshire state legislator. Benjamin believed in education and sent Franklin to Philips Exeter Academy and Bowdoin College—where the boy developed into an amiable, if not brilliant, student. A rising Democratic star in New Hampshire, the younger Pierce served in the legislature, the state militia, U.S. House, and U.S. Senate. In the House and Senate, he adhered to the Democratic program of opposition to banks and support for the Southern slave interest.

Pierce's support for Henry Clay's Compromise of 1850 demonstrated his commitment to those features of the legislation that benefited the South—most specifically the Fugitive Slave Act. Pierce gained the Democratic nomination in 1852 as a classic come-from-behind dark horse candidate on the forty-ninth ballot and ran on a North–South unity ticket with Alabama Senator William R. King. The platform opposed abolitionist "agitation" and offered strong support for the Compromise of 1850. They were elected in a popular and electoral vote landslide with strong Democratic majorities in both houses of Congress.

Shortly after his election, tragedy struck the Pierce household. On a train trip from Boston, their railroad car derailed, and their youngest and sole-surviving son, "Benny," died in the crash. Both Franklin and Mrs. Pierce suffered from depression from this event, which likely contributed to her withdrawal from public life for most of his administration and to his poor performance as president.

FRANKLIN PIERCE:
KANSAS-NEBRASKA ACT

Perhaps nothing contributed to the general failure of the Pierce presidency as the Kansas–Nebraska Act, a creation furthering the political ambitions of Democratic Senator Stephen Douglas of Illinois. Douglas wanted the transcontinental railroad to connect the west coast with Chicago. To secure needed Southern support for the project, as well as for his years-long quest for the presidency, he offered to repeal the prohibition in the Missouri Compromise (1820), which prohibits slavery north of the 36°30' line along the southern border of Missouri stretching out to the Pacific. In place of this, Douglas offered the idea of "popular sovereignty," or more derisively "squatter sovereignty." When territories applied for statehood, local settlers would determine whether the new state would be slave or free. President Pierce was reluctant to support this initiative, but he signed the bill anyway. The aftermath ruined his term and prevented his re-election.

The Kansas–Nebraska Act unleashed powerful sectional hostility. Suddenly Kansas became the cockpit of racial and political antagonism, a paradigm of a nation losing control of itself. Pro-slave settlers from Missouri flooded into Kansas, and soon migration was over-matched by those opposed to slavery. Bloody battles between the two sides prolif-erated and soon the territory took on a terrible autograph: "Bleeding Kansas." Pierce reacted to the turmoil by siding with the clearly out-num-bered pro-slavery side. His intercession on behalf of the pro-slavery minority and inability to suppress the violence in the territory made him seem weak and feeble, and this damaged his reputation.

FRANKLIN PIERCE:
OPENING TO JAPAN

Japan was ruled by the Emperor, but actual power was held by his chief military officer, the Shogun, Tokugawa Ieyoshi. The Shogun's chief advisor was Masahiro Abe, a realistic politician with a keen intellect. He led a faction that was opposed to expanded contact with the West, but recognized that European and American power was so overwhelming that Japan needed to make the best deal it could with the foreigners, lest it be abused and carved up as had been China.

In late November 1852, before Franklin Pierce took office, President Millard Fillmore dispatched Commodore Matthew C. Perry to Japan to encourage Japan to open itself to international trade. As Perry's flotilla approached in July 1853, Japan's government was rendered impotent by divisions in the shogunate and Ieyoshi's incapacity due to illness. While the Japanese government temporized, Perry ignored repeated demands that he leave and began sending surveying ships further up Edo Wan (the ancient name for Tokyo Bay). Finally, after extended negotiations, he came ashore at Kurihama to deliver a letter from the president of the United States. The Japanese still wanted him to leave. Unfazed, Perry promised to return the following year.

In February 1854, Perry and a stronger American fleet appeared, and Abe forced through the government a decision to open Japan to the Americans. Gifts were exchanged on March 13, 1854. By receiving the dour American shogun—Matthew Perry—Japan had reluctantly turned from isolation and begun its journey into the modern world.

1750 1775 1800 1825 1850 1875

FRANKLIN PIERCE: LEGACY

Franklin Pierce is generally ranked among the least effective of U.S. presidents. It is certain that few leaders could have navigated the turmoil that gripped the American political landscape of the 1850s. It is also certain that Pierce lacked the talent to overcome the challenges he faced as president.

He largely failed to address the nation's unfinished constitutional business. As a Northern Democrat beholden to the South for the votes that put him in the White House, he was seen as a Southern ally in the sectional conflict of the decade. He hated slavery as an evil institution but supported the pro-slave position to get ahead politically and was incapable of finding a resolution of the issue that was dragging the nation in the direction of a bloody schism. On issue after issue he sided with the slave interest, thus staining his reputation and rendering as impotent as his administration of justice.

When Pierce left office, he and Mrs. Pierce began a long European odyssey, returning to New Hampshire in 1860. During the run-up to and during the Civil War, Pierce was a critic of President Abraham Lincoln's policy of restoring the Union through force of arms. He was particularly agitated by Lincoln's increasingly vigorous approach to emancipation. Often accused of being a pro-Confederate with traitorous tendencies, his denials of these allegations fell on deaf ears. Pierce was a heavy drinker, particularly in his later years, and died in 1869 of cirrhosis of the liver.

15

JAMES BUCHANAN

JAMES BUCHANAN: LIFE PAGE

Born: April 23, 1791, Cove Gap, Pennsylvania

Education: Dickinson College, BA

Member, Pennsylvania House of Representatives: 1814–1816

Member, U.S. House of Representatives: 1821–1831

U.S. Minister to Russia: 1832–1833

United States Senator: 1834–1845

U.S. Secretary of State: 1845–1849

U.S. Minister to the United Kingdom: 1853–1856

Fifteenth President of the United States: 1857–1861

Died: June 1, 1868, Lancaster, Pennsylvania

Additional resources available for this president at www.amomentintime.com.

JAMES BUCHANAN:
DRED SCOTT DECISION

Few presidents have achieved the White House with more seasoning and capability than James Buchanan. He was known as a political "trimmer," a politician who publically held no firm position on various issues, often supporting both sides so as to avoid criticism. On one issue, however, he was adamant. While Buchanan may have nursed deep inside some inchoate moral opposition to slavery, on public policy he was a strong supporter of the South and the institution of slavery. He soon earned the unflattering epithet "doughface," a Northerner sympathetic to the South.

Two days after Buchanan's inauguration, Chief Justice Roger B. Taney delivered his infamous decision in *Dred Scott v. Sandford*, denying Dred Scott his freedom and even his right of appeal as a black slave—asserting no African American had any rights. It was a broad-based decision that declared the slavery restrictions of the Compromise of 1820 to be unconstitutional, and by a seven to two vote, it banned any federal interference with the institution of slavery in the territories or the states. Only states could ban slavery in their precincts. Buchanan publicly supported the decision and, in fact, knew the outcome in advance. He had inappropriately interfered with the decision and encouraged Tawney to make the decision a comprehensive one. Buchanan believed a decision so emphatic would end the slavery controversy. He could not have been more wrong. *Dread Scott* only served to enflame sectional animosity.

Perhaps the most pressing issue facing the new Buchanan administration—and one that yielded a disastrous result—was the disposition of the territory of Kansas. First pro-slavery settlers, then anti-slavery settlers, descended on the territory, determined to secure Kansas for their side. To become a state, the settlers had to develop a constitution for submission to Congress. Pro-slavery emigrants chose Lecompton, Kansas, as their capital and developed a constitution that allowed slavery. Free-Soil emigrants made Topeka their seat of government and developed a constitution which banned slavery. As each month passed, the number of Free-Soil Kansans increased as anti-slavery settlers poured in to claim the territory for their cause. Soon they outnumbered pro-slavery settlers.

A pro-slavery Lecompton Constitution was sent off to Washington for congressional approval. Buchanan's representative in Kansas, Robert Walker, denounced it as a fraud, and Buchanan pulled every available lever to have the pro-slavery constitution accepted. The President offered federal jobs, contracts, and even direct bribery (some say as much as forty thousand dollars). The Senate accepted the Lecompton Constitution, but in the end the House rejected it.

It was then sent back to Kansas for a new vote. Voters overwhelmingly rejected the pro-slavery constitution. This signaled that eventually Kansas, after so much blood and bitterness, would enter the Union as a free state. The Republican Party took control of the House and was able to block all Buchanan's initiatives in the remaining two years of his term.

JAMES BUCHANAN: THE ANGUISH OF JAMES BUCHANAN

After the mid-term elections of 1858, President Buchanan faced a hostile Congress that blocked pretty much all of his legislative priorities. He had become obsessed with the idea of annexing Cuba as a new territory that might eventually become one or more states (potentially boosting pro-slavery forces in the country). The Republican House repeatedly blocked his attempts. He exacted his revenge when he vetoed important parts of the Republican agenda—including the Homestead Act and the Morrill Act.

To compound his problems, in his first year as president, the country experienced a brief but severe economic contraction: The Panic of 1857. The Buchanan administration did practically nothing to curb the suffering, and the public blamed Buchanan and the Democrats for their inaction in the face of wide-spread distress.

In the House, the dominant Republicans began to look into government corruption. They found treasury money had been given to Democratic legislators and direct bribes had gone to congressmen in exchange for voting in favor of the Lecompton Constitution. Evidence was insufficient to impeach Buchanan, but the Republicans used the Covode Committee Report as a weapon extensively in the 1860 election campaign.

JAMES BUCHANAN: LEGACY

It is difficult to find a historian or observer of the Antebellum period who fulfills James Buchanan's prediction on the day before his death: "History will vindicate my memory." In the parlor game of presidential rankings, he is almost always placed among the least effective presidents. Some place him at the bottom as the worst of the lot.

In another more serene era, his experience, moderate disposition, and talents might have made for a more salutary result, but Buchanan was too fixed in his convictions to help a nation cracking at the seams and hungry for firm, consistent, and balanced leadership. It was not, as some critics have opined, that indecision made execrable his presidency. It was his steady, strong support for the South and the institution of slavery which made him incapable of leading the nation on a better path. He was reviled in the North because he let the South slip into secession and reviled in the South because he denied that region the right to secede.

Aas a committed Jacksonian, he acted vigorously in behalf of states' rights. He may have had some indeterminate opposition to slavery "in the abstract," but he defended the slave interest at every point. He defended those who trafficked in slavery claiming that slaves were "treated with kindness and humanity."

It seemed, as the hours ticked down on his term of office, that all he desired was to throw his presidential remit into the lap of his successor and flee in terror. Nevertheless, Buchanan spent the rest of his life defending his record—to little avail. By 1861, James Buchanan's moral, legal, personal, and professional failure was nearly absolute, and most players in the national divide were glad to see the back of him.

16

ABRAHAM LINCOLN

ABRAHAM LINCOLN: LIFE PAGE

Born: February 12, 1809, Sinking Spring Farm, Kentucky

Education: Self-educated, enthusiastic reader, read for law

Vocation: Attorney

Married: Mary Todd, 1842

Member, Illinois House of Representatives: 1834–1842

Member, United States House of Representatives: 1847–1849

Sixteenth President of the United States: 1861–1865

Died: Assassination on April 14, 1865; died April 15, 1865

Additional resources available for this president at www.amomentintime.com.

ABRAHAM LINCOLN:
PRAIRIE LAWYER

Lincoln was born near Hodgenville, Kentucky. His father, Thomas Lincoln, was a farmer who moved his family first to Indiana, then Illinois. His mother, Nancy Hanks Lincoln, died in 1818 and his father re-married in 1819. Lincoln was quite close to his stepmother, Sarah "Sally" Lincoln, but grew increasingly estranged from his father and, in 1831, left home and settled in New Salem, Illinois.

Lincoln was drawn early to the world of the mind. He became an avid reader, though he did not avoid his chores, and developed skill at wielding an axe. He said of his self-taught education, "I studied with nobody." He was physically strong and athletic, and he had little trouble intimidating those who might try to take him on. In New Salem, he and some friends were hired by a local merchant to take a flatboat of goods to New Orleans. There he had his first exposure to slavery, the institution that would come to define his life and presidency.

He established a lucrative traveling law practice and soon became well-known throughout Illinois as an excellent and witty advocate for his clients. In 1842, he married Mary Todd, the daughter of a family of slaveholders from Lexington, Kentucky, and became a dutiful and loving husband and father. He and Mary had four sons, only one of which lived beyond childhood. They bought a home in Springfield, Illinois, where Lincoln parlayed his growing law practice into a political career.

1750   1775   1800   1825   1850   1875

ABRAHAM LINCOLN: THE ADVENT OF A POLITICAL MODERATE

As the U.S. population grew and pushed west into the continental heartland, the controversy over slavery trailed not far behind. The Missouri Compromise (1820) had excluded slavery from states above the southern border of Missouri on a line that stretched to the Pacific. Southerners saw this as imperiling their ability to protect slavery's expansion, which would significantly transform the balance of power in Congress—to the South's disadvantage.

Abraham Lincoln's advent as a national leader emerged from the dispute over slavery's expansion into the western territories.

After a single term in the U.S. House in the mid-1840s, Lincoln returned to Springfield and further built his lucrative law practice. His principled condemnation of the Kansas–Nebraska Act signaled his re-emergence to active political engagement. As a Whig Party member, he was faced with a dilemma. The Party had begun its steady decline, eventually becoming enfolded into the newly evolving Republican coalition. That is where Lincoln found his home as an anti-slavery advocate, though not an abolitionist at this point. His opposition was rooted in his conviction that the institution violated the principles of the Founders: freedom, equality, and democratic self rule.

ABRAHAM LINCOLN: SENATE DEBATES AND COOPER UNION

During the presidential election of 1856, Lincoln joined the new Republican Party. In 1858, he received the Party nod to run for U.S. Senate against Stephen Douglas.

The two candidates met in seven of the most famous debates in American history. The tall, lean, athletic Lincoln stood in marked contrast to his short, rotund opponent. Their arguments perfectly tracked the national debate, with Lincoln accusing his adversary of subservience to the "slave power" in his distortion of the values of the Founders about the equality of all men. Douglas, he said, wished to spread slavery nationwide. Douglas countered that Lincoln had sold out to the abolitionists and western settlers should be able to determine whether their new state was slave or free. The Republican's argument was essentially a moral one, whereas Douglas tended to focus his argument on the legal issues surrounding the *Dred Scott* decision.

Douglas was re-elected, but in defeat Lincoln was able to expand his national exposure. His speech at New York City's Cooper-Union Hall in early 1860 emphasized the moral imperative in opposing slavery—no middle ground between right and wrong. His precise intellectual formulation of the issues facing America scored points with this key constituency and pushed Lincoln into the front ranks of national Republican contenders.

ABRAHAM LINCOLN:
ELECTION OF 1860

The election of 1860 was one of the most fractured in American history. There were two candidates in the North and two in the South. Lincoln and Stephen Douglas competed for Northern votes. Vice President John C. Breckenridge and John Bell of Tennessee focused their campaign in the South.

Despite this splintering, Lincoln won a plurality of the popular vote and decisively in the Electoral College (180 to 123 combined). The Republican triumph was engineered by clever manipulation of Lincoln's image: "Honest Abe the Rail-Splitter." They developed a youth outreach effort and an intensive media strategy, blanketing the North with newspaper stories, posters, and pamphlets. At thousands of Republican rallies, speakers promoted Lincoln and the Party's program.

The Republican Party was a coalition of old-line Whigs with their interest in internal improvements and business progress, Know-Nothings who opposed immigration (particularly Catholic immigration), and anti-slavery abolitionists. While this alliance had no appeal in the South, victory did not require Southern votes—particularly since Southern popular and electoral votes would be split between Breckenridge and Bell. In the end, Lincoln shut out Douglas in the North, Breckinridge took the South, and Bell grabbed his home state of Tennessee, the border state of Kentucky, and Virginia.

ABRAHAM LINCOLN: SECESSION-I

The election of Republican Abraham Lincoln as president brought an end to the long struggle of the South to use its virtual control of the federal government to protect the institution of slavery. Since the ratification of the Constitution, effective leadership, unified support of the Democratic Party and its antecedents, and the all-too-effective counting of the slave population as three-fifths human beings had secured the "Slave Power's" dominance of the central government. The last thing in the world the South desired was states' rights, because increasingly individual states were taking actions hostile to slavery.

As Southerners saw it, the Compromises of 1820 and 1850 conceded minor gains to the South in exchange for significant incremental advances for the anti-slavery side. Any hopes Southerners might have had that Kansas–Nebraska's doctrine of "popular sovereignty" would increase the number of new slave states crumbled in the experience of "Bleeding Kansas." Anti-slavery forces were becoming too strong, and the Northern population was becoming too large and increasingly impatient with the spread of slavery. It was clear that despite all the violence on both sides, political maneuvering, and illegal efforts of pro-slavery settlers, Kansas would come into the Union as a free state. If Kansas could not be forced in the pro-slavery direction, there was little hope that any future state could be. South-erners began to listen to their most radical advocates and conclude that their region's economic well-being was imperiled if they remained in the Union.

Despite the Constitution's infamous Three-Fifths rule—which for the purposes of representation in the U.S. House of Representatives and the Electoral College declared that black slaves would be counted as three-fifths of a human being—by 1860 all the avenues of Southern control of the federal government were closed off. The South had lost control of the House, then the Senate, and then the Electoral College, and they no longer had influence in the White House with Lincoln in charge. By extension, this meant they would now lose control of the federal judiciary. To lose the control which they so long wielded over national affairs was an affront to Southern dignity and a profound threat to the source of Southern wealth—human chattel.

Lincoln's election created a chain reaction. All of the Southern frustration over loss of power and fear of economic emasculation crashed forward into secession. First South Carolina and then six other states (Mississippi, Florida, Alabama, Georgia, Louisiana, and Texas—in that order) passed ordinances of secession. After the attack on Fort Sumter and Lincoln's call for seventy-five thousand volunteers to protect Washington, recapture federal forts in the South, and preserve the Union, the upper South departed. Led by Virginia, the states of Arkansas, North Carolina, and Tennessee helped round out the new Confederate States of America. Ironically, even the widely-acknowledged-as-weak President James Buchanan joined Abraham Lincoln in not recognizing the Confederacy as anything but a rebellion against legitimate national authority that required, if necessary, military action to suppress.

ABRAHAM LINCOLN: WAR

In the gloom surrounding his first inauguration, Abraham Lincoln tried to reassure the South of his intentions. He was opposed to slavery, but he had no intention or legal right to "interfere with the institution of slavery in the states where it exists." All congressional attempts at peace failed. None of the states who had already seceded gave any indication they would rejoin the Union under any terms. Already, a convention in Montgomery, Alabama, had formulated the Confederate Constitution and elected Jefferson Davis as provisional president (February 1861).

Before and after his inauguration, Lincoln maintained a public posture of openness to reconciliation—in hopes of restoring the Union and avoiding military conflict. Whatever his public posture, he probably suspected war was on the way but was determined not to strike the first blow. If there was going to be war, it would be the South that initiated it. Southerners played right into Lincoln's strategy.

Lincoln was determined to hold possession of federal forts in the South, and one of the few such strongholds remaining in Union hands was Fort Sumter at the mouth of Charleston harbor in South Carolina. At 4:30 a.m., April 12, 1861, Confederate batteries opened fire on Fort Sumter. Major Robert Anderson surrendered Fort Sumter on April 13, 1861, and evacuated his command and the Fort Sumter flag. News of the encounter spread, and Lincoln's call for volunteers to suppress the rebellion proved sufficient to shift sentiment in the upper South toward secession. The war had begun.

ABRAHAM LINCOLN:
TEAM OF RIVALS

In *Team of Rivals*, historian Doris Kearns Goodwin examines Lincoln's leadership style and describes how the new president eventually drew to himself as close advisors all his fierce adversaries in the contest for the Republican nomination. Lincoln did not appoint friends to the Cabinet. He appointed leaders of divisions within the Republican coalition. He played a balancing act, drawing in former Whigs and former Democrats in an effort to expand his party and personal appeal. They did not always agree on economics, but they unified in supporting the Republican hostility to slavery's spread into the western territories.

The premier Cabinet-level post was secretary of state, and for that he chose William H. Seward of New York. Eventually, Seward became a close social companion and admirer of the President. Lincoln picked Simon Cameron of Pennsylvania as Secretary of War, but rumors of personal corruption and clear administrative incompetence led the President to replace him with Edwin McMaster Stanton in early 1862. Given the fact they were managing a war, it is not surprising that Lincoln and Stanton worked in close partnership.

For the secretary of the treasury, Lincoln made his most problematic appointment, Salmon P. Chase of Ohio. Chase proved to be Lincoln's most troublesome antagonist almost from the beginning, and as the years passed, the relationship between the two began to fray. Finally, they clashed over a staff appointment and Lincoln accepted the Ohioan's resignation. In an act of utmost magnanimity, Lincoln elevated Chase to Chief Justice in December 1864.

ABRAHAM LINCOLN:
DOMESTIC POLICY-I

For a president under whose leadership the federal government acquired a substantial increase in power and reach, Lincoln was surprisingly deferential to Congress—at least on domestic affairs. This, of course, was consistent with his Whig heritage, which was suspicious of executive power and communicated that Congress should take the lead in advancing legislation. Congress, shorn of conservative Southern congressmen and senators, vigorously moved the "Whigish," now Republican, agenda.

Most of Lincoln's predecessors accepted the role of a weak executive. Some, however, were capable of extraordinary eruptions of executive creativity—on national expansion, such as Jefferson's purchase of Louisiana; on social questions, such as Jackson's policy of Indian removal and suppression of the national slavery discussion; on federal/state disputes, such as over nullification; or during times of war, such as James Madison during the War of 1812 and James K. Polk in Mexico. One historian explained the "presidency in 1860 was like an underinflated balloon," awaiting a strong president who—faced with a large enough crisis—would be capable of turning potential into reality.

Of all the observers of Lincoln, Confederates were the most skeptical. They were certain he would rise to the potential of executive power, use his office to block slavery's expansion into the territories, and re-order the judiciary to the South's disadvantage. As it turned out, they were correct. They felt they had no choice but to secede.

ABRAHAM LINCOLN:
DOMESTIC POLICY-II

Freed of the conservative Southern restraint by the departure of congressmen and senators into secession, the Republican Congress elected in 1860, 1862, and 1864 moved to enact laws that, for many, had only been a dream in years past.

Congress passed a flood of legislation affirming the federal government's expanding role in national life. To pay for the war, Congress passed first the Revenue Act of 1861, which instituted the United States's first income tax, and followed it with the Revenue Act of 1862. The Legal Tender Act (1862) authorized millions of dollars of federal (paper) notes without raising taxes, after which paper money depreciated vis-à-vis gold.

The Pacific Railroad Act of 1862 and subsequent revisions established the funding mechanism for the construction of the first Transcontinental Railroad. Additionally, the Homestead Act of 1862 provided free government land to settlers who would improve western lands. In the end, some sixteen million acres, or 10 percent of U.S. territory, was given for free to citizens who would settle and develop the land—pulling the total population of the nation to the west.

This legislation went a long way shaping post–Civil War national life and profoundly advanced the position of the federal government in its relations with citizens and states.

ABRAHAM LINCOLN:
COMMANDER IN CHIEF-I

Abraham Lincoln's understanding of the Constitution may have created ambiguity about his role in domestic legislation, but on national security and the military his sense of role was unequivocal. He was Commander in Chief of the Army, Navy, and state militias, and he acted with vigorous intensity from the moment Confederate forces attacked federal property in Charleston.

When Confederate sympathizers attempted to attack and block troops from getting through Maryland, Lincoln suspended the writ of *habeas corpus*[1] and during the war arrested thousands of persons who threated the war effort. When challenged judicially and otherwise, Lincoln responded that he was following the people's demand, loosely approximating John Locke's doctrine that in an emergency—when the very survival of the state was threatened—the legal system must bend before the necessity of executive action.

As it turned out, executive action was the least of the nation's problems. The country had a leader ready to preserve and protect the Union—one who was slowly developing a strategy for accomplishing just that. Lincoln's difficulty was that he lacked a competent structure of military leadership to implement his plan.

ABRAHAM LINCOLN:
COMMANDER IN CHIEF-II

In the early years of the war, Lincoln was faced with a military establishment that was reluctant, if not downright passive, in its response to his direction. The President's military experience was limited, but he was a quick learner. Beating the Rebels required the utter defeat of the Confederate war machine—destroying Southern armies.

It took a while for Lincoln to identify the commanders who would execute his orders without hesitation. George McClellan was a typical example. Lincoln elevated him, relieved him, promoted him again, and relieved him again. He relieved Ambrose Burnside and Joseph Hooker after crushing defeats. George Meade defeated Lee at Gettysburg but incurred the President's wrath when he failed to pursue the Confederate back into Virginia and run him to ground, thus losing the last chance to bring the protracted conflict to an early conclusion.

The only theater where there was good news was in the west. There Lincoln found his solution to the "general" problem. In Ulysses S. Grant he found a general who would beat the enemy—"I can't spare this man, he fights." With Grant as General in Chief and Edwin M. Stanton as Secretary of War, Lincoln no longer had to be so personally involved in the direct administration of the war effort and could concentrate on strategy.

ABRAHAM LINCOLN: EMANCIPATION

Almost immediately in 1861, the Republican Congress moved to free slaves. They also acted to hold rebels and their allies as treasonous. This included two major property confiscation laws, which were largely ineffectual because congressional mandates only applied to those states under Union control. Congress also permanently ended slavery in the territories, eviscerated fugitive slave laws, and freed slaves in Washington, DC.

It did not take long for Lincoln to realize his delicate respect for Southern sensibilities about slaves was counterproductive. No amount of assurances about slavery would entice the South back into the Union. This change was in parallel to his changing attitude toward the slaves and black people in general. He did not come to the White House as an abolitionist, but his perspective shifted. Lincoln was constantly evolving and in no subject was this truer than on race relations and emancipation. The war was forcing a change in Lincoln: transforming him from a conservative anti-slavery politician to one favoring abolition.

Sensing an important opportunity, after the Union victory at Antietam, Lincoln moved to free the slaves, but he did so as a military action. Acting as Commander in Chief, he moved to strike at one of the most useful Confederate war resources. Lincoln issued the Emancipation Proclamation. As of January 1, 1863, all slaves in those areas in rebellion against the United States were freed. As they established federal control over the South, Union military officers executed the Proclamation, thus shattering the fetters of over three million slaves.

ABRAHAM LINCOLN: BLACK TROOPS

Lincoln freed slaves in those states under rebel control with the Emancipation Proclamation on January 1, 1863. He directed his military commanders to enforce this ordinance in areas they occupied, and they began freeing millions of slaves.

Until the Civil War, blacks were not officially permitted to serve in the Army. As the body count escalated in 1862 and 1863, and as the need for manpower in the Union Army became more pressing, Northern whites became more willing to accept black troops. The President was ready to take full military advantage of this rich source of manpower—newly emancipated slaves. No longer hesitant, by spring 1863 he began aggressive recruitment of African American troops. Unfortunately, they fought just as hard for less pay.

Initially, the federal government did not have a national plan for organizing Negro enlistees. In response, the government created The Bureau of Colored Troops to streamline the process of activating black units. Only white men were permitted to command black troops. To prepare these officers, a school was established in Philadelphia. After an intensive thirty-day curriculum, applicants could present themselves for examination in Washington. More than six thousand officers commanded 179,000 African American troops during the Civil War.

At first, because of racial prejudice in the North and fears of Southern retribution, black soldiers were not used in combat situations as extensively as their white counterparts. As the effusion of blood became a torrent, blacks increasingly were asked to stand as equals in the line of fire.

ABRAHAM LINCOLN: LEADERSHIP IN DARK TIMES

No president before or since has faced the challenges that Lincoln did. With the future of the republic literally hanging in the balance, he steered the ship of state through perilous waters. He did so with a combination of grim determination and cautious optimism, always willing to shift strategy in his search for a better outcome.

After the terrible, bloody Union victory at Antietam, Lincoln evidenced growing optimism until caught up in the gloomy aftermath of the crushing Union defeat by Robert E. Lee at Fredericksburg. With little more than shear willpower, the President sought again to find a winner, promoting the daring and aggressive Joseph Hooker to lead the Army of the Potomac.

At Chancellorsville, "Fighting Joe" divided his forces into three columns. General Lee—in a brilliant display of tactical audacity, in this, his most "perfect battle"—split his Army once and then a second time and battered Hooker into retreat. Tempted by his success, Lee began his (ultimately fatal) second invasion of the North toward Gettysburg.

Those surely must have been dark days for Lincoln, but they illustrate his unwavering leadership style. He labored on and eventually found the right combination of military leadership and strategy that made good use of the overwhelming Union advantages in population, financial strength, and industrial capacity. This brought the South to heel and restored the Union.

ABRAHAM LINCOLN:
GETTYSBURG ADDRESS[2]

At Gettysburg, the casualties on both sides were enormous. Over the three-day period, in excess of fifty thousand were killed, wounded, missing, or captured. With contributions from eighteen Union states, seventeen acres were purchased near the center of the Union line for a "national cemetery." Dedication was set for November 19, 1863.

The principal speaker was to be Edward Everett, orator, statesman, and president of Harvard College. President Lincoln would make a few remarks. After Everett's two-hour oration, Lincoln stood in his black frock coat and white gloves and delivered his 272-word, three-minute speech.

His simple yet eloquent words defining the purpose of the war were a moving tribute to the fallen. They are recognized by many as perhaps the most profound expression of freedom and the democratic spirit in the English language. The next day, Everett wrote Lincoln, "I should flatter myself that I came as near to the central idea of the occasion in two hours as you did in two minutes."

ABRAHAM LINCOLN: RE-ELECTION

Abraham Lincoln did not think he was going to be re-elected. The news from the battlefield in mid-1864 was not good. The war was grinding along with horrific casualties. In the Overland Campaign, the losses on both sides were dreadful—particularly at Cold Harbor. But Grant refused to retire, instead engaging in a series of flanking maneuvers that eventually smashed Lee onto the defenses of Richmond.

Politically, Lincoln wielded considerable patronage power. He systematically replaced Democrats in the government with loyal Republicans. At the Convention, the President was re-nominated by near acclamation. In an effort to broaden his coalition, he ran under the Union Party label so as to embrace many War Democrats, such as War Secretary Edwin Stanton and Lincoln's Tennessee running mate, Andrew Johnson. The Democratic Party was seriously divided. Their candidate, General George B. Mc-Clellan, refused to run under the peace platform adopted at the Democratic Convention, and the party had to fend off Republican attacks against the party as harboring disloyal Copperheads.[3]

Lincoln and Stanton cleverly allowed many Union troops go home on leave so that they could vote; and in the end, 78 percent of Union troops—Republican and Democrat alike—voted for their Commander in Chief. Lincoln won in a landslide.

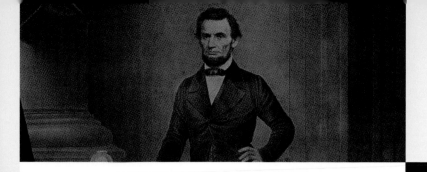

ABRAHAM LINCOLN: THIRTEENTH AMENDMENT

Lincoln's journey from anti-slavery to abolition was complete with the passage of the Thirteenth Amendment. A version passed the Senate in April 1864, but it failed to achieve the requisite two-thirds House vote in June of that year. The President was fearful that the slaves he freed with the Emancipation might still be in legal jeopardy by the judiciary. Lincoln supported an abolition amendment in accepting the Republican/Unionist nomination. He made it a campaign issue and then vigorously pursued passage in the House in the weeks following his re-election.

The debate was a heated one, with Democrats—led by Representative George H. Pendleton, the 1864 Democratic vice-presidential nominee—basing their opposition on the issue of federalism and states' rights. Unsure of the outcome, Republicans toned down their rhetoric, avoiding any reference to advancing black equality and promising only that required under the law. Floor managers postponed the vote and the President engaged in personal lobbying to get the necessary votes to secure passage. There is some evidence that promises of federal jobs were made to secure the votes of lame-duck Democrats, and their votes proved to be crucial to the passage of the Amendment; it passed on a close vote of 119 to 56—barely two-thirds—on January 31, 1865.

ABRAHAM LINCOLN: SECOND INAUGURAL ADDRESS-I⁴

In his second inaugural address, Abraham Lincoln gently celebrated the emerging Union triumph and then pointed the way to national reconciliation. In the summer, he had been resolved to serving only a single term. The horrendous casualties of the Wilderness Campaign had sent Northern public morale spiraling downward. The capture of Atlanta in September, however, restored national confidence in Lincoln's leadership.

As he stood to be sworn in, he spoke confidently of the brightening prospects of a reunited America. Frederick Douglass said "the address sounded more like a sermon than a state paper." Lincoln's normal concision yielded a speech of 703 words in twenty-five exquisitely crafted sentences. He considered it his greatest speech.

> Lincoln remembered the gloomy spirit under which the capitol labored four years before, with two circling antagonists, one of which would make war rather than let the nation survive and the other which would accept war rather than let it perish. The war was fought to resolve the issue of slavery, revealing his own struggle to see its purpose as bringing freedom to the African Americans as a divinely inspired mission.

ABRAHAM LINCOLN: SECOND INAUGURAL ADDRESS-II[5]

Lincoln eschewed judgment against Southerners, recognizing that they, too, had sought God's blessing on their own crusade. In the end, though, both prayed to the Almighty for success, and neither side had had their prayers fully answered. North and South had conspired over the decades through their complicity in slavery to bring this terrible scourge of war on the land. Author Ronald White says Lincoln is here speaking against any "God bless America" notion that does not recognize evil and hypocrisy in its own house.

His vision and path to understanding emerged in the final words. Though he would not preside over that reconciliation, his spirit insured that the Union, re-forged in the bloody crucible of battle, would never again be threatened by sectional animosity:

> With malice toward none; with charity for all; with firmness in the right, as God gives us to see the right, let us strive on to finish the work we are in; to bind up the nation's wounds; to care for him who shall have borne the battle, and for his widow, and his orphan—to do all which may achieve and cherish a just and a lasting peace among ourselves and with all nations.

ABRAHAM LINCOLN:
ASSASSINATION

Though Andrew Jackson had suffered physical assault on one occasion and survived an assassination attempt at another, no president had yet been assassinated. That changed on Good Friday, April 14, 1865, shortly after the collapse of the Confederacy. President and Mrs. Lincoln and their guests were attending the comedic performance of *Our American Cousin* at Ford's Theater. Actor John Wilkes Booth quietly entered the presidential box and shot Lincoln in the back of his head. Booth struggled with one of Lincoln's guests and leapt out of the box onto the stage shouting, "*Sic Semper Tyrannis*, thus always to tyrants" (the Virginia state motto, and said to have been uttered by Brutus at the assassination of Julius Caesar).

The wounded President was taken to the Peterson house just across the street and—despite heroic efforts by his physicians—died the next morning at 7:22 a.m. His body was carried to the White House and then lay in the Capitol Rotunda for three days. The caskets of Lincoln and his son Willie were then placed in a special coach that wound its circuitous way through the North to bring Abraham Lincoln home to Springfield, Illinois. Many attended memorial services in cities on the route. After four bloody years of war yielding over seven-hundred thousand casualties, Lincoln's assassination unleashed a torrent of grief and anguish. For many, his death served as a cathartic release after so much suffering and sacrifice.

ABRAHAM LINCOLN: LEGACY

Given the circumstances surrounding his presidency, Lincoln's determination to preserve the Union, and his successful management of the war effort, it is small wonder that he is uniformly included by historians and other observers in the top rank of American presidents. No president before or since faced the challenges Lincoln did, and he executed his responsibilities with remarkable felicity, though at times he experienced a darkness of spirit.

His rhetoric helped define the American Republican experiment into the future. Before the war, "These United States" were a federation of sovereign entities where the focus of power was indigenous. After Lincoln, the country was known as "The United States," where what the people do together as a nation is stronger and more important than what they do as individuals or as individual states. This shift—however seemingly slight—was permanent and inviolate.

Lincoln set in motion the completion of the nation's business left unfinished by the framers of the Constitution. With the defeat of the South and the passage of the Thirteenth Amendment, slavery was done. Period. Despite future attempts at re-establishing white supremacy, no person in the United States could legally ever be dragged back into human bondage. Lincoln also helped settle the issue of federal/state relationships. Abraham Lincoln's presidency—in the name of all the people—permanently curtailed the power of mediating institutions in favor of a rising federal enterprise.

17

ANDREW JOHNSON

ANDREW JOHNSON: LIFE PAGE

Born: December 29, 1808, Raleigh, North Carolina

Married: Eliza McCardle, 1827

Member, U.S. House of Representatives: 1843–1853

Governor of Tennessee: 1853–1857

United States Senator: 1857–1862

Military Governor of Tennessee: 1862–1865

Sixteenth Vice President of the United States: 1875

Seventeenth President of the United States: 1865–1869

United States Senator: 1875

Died: July 31, 1875, Elizabethton, Tennessee

Additional resources available for this president at www.amomentintime.com.

ANDREW JOHNSON:
SOUTHERN UNIONIST

Andrew Johnson was one of the most successful and accomplished politicians in nineteenth-century America. Born in North Carolina, he eventually settled in Greeneville, Tennessee, where he established a successful tailoring business. Using Greeneville as a foundation, he began his political rise aided by his shy, retiring wife, Eliza McCardle; she raised their five children, supported his political work, and quietly helped him improve his math and writing skills.

From his political base in Greene County, he served in the Tennessee legislature, the U.S. House, and U.S. Senate; was elected Governor; and was then chosen by President Abraham Lincoln as Military Governor of Tennessee when Union forces re-took the state during the Civil War. When states—including Tennessee—seceded, Johnson was the only Southern Senator to remain loyal to the Union.

Lincoln chose Southern Democrat Andrew Johnson as his running mate in the 1864 election, and they won an overwhelming victory. At a party in his honor the evening before his inauguration, the Vice President–elect may have imbibed a little too much alcohol; his inaugural speech was a rambling, incoherent, embarrassing disaster. Within a month, Lincoln's assassination had placed Andrew Johnson in the White House. How he would convey the legacy of Lincoln was a matter of concern to many—including those who were to serve with him in Congress and the new administration.

ANDREW JOHNSON:
PRESIDENTIAL RECONSTRUCTION

Given the sad circumstances of his inauguration, Johnson stayed out of public view for his term as vice president. Called upon to lead the country in mourning, Johnson rose to the occasion and earned credit for the dignified and sympathetic execution of his duties during Lincoln's state funeral.

The great issue of Johnson's presidency would be restoration of the Union. To be effective, Johnson had to deal with three groups in Congress: (1) democrats who were a minority in both houses, (2) moderate Republicans who constituted part of the majority in Congress and, with the President's careful cultivation, could have become his allies, and (3) so-called Radical Republicans who were determined to improve the lot of the former slaves. The Radicals proved to be his most intractable foes, as Johnson did not believe the federal government could insert itself between the states and their citizens in the matter of social relationships, civil rights, and voting rights (the franchise).

In 1865, Johnson attempted what has been called Presidential Reconstruction. He offered amnesty, pardon, and the franchise to Southerners who swore a loyalty oath to the United States and accepted black emancipation. White Southerners then held elections. The new legislatures passed the infamous Black Codes, which basically restored the antebellum social and economic status quo. Blacks were effectively returned to the plantations and made to work there in circumstances almost indistinguishable from slavery.

ANDREW JOHNSON: CONGRESSIONAL RECONSTRUCTION

In 1865, word began to filter out of the South that white Southerners were systematically abusing former slaves and white Unionists so as to re-establish the antebellum status quo. The white majority began electing only lightly re-constructed former rebels to Congress, such as former Confederate Vice President Alexander Stephens. Congress refused to seat these Southerners and embarked on Congressional Reconstruction.

In early 1866, Congress passed two bills. The first extended the life of the Freedman's Bureau and the second was a Civil Rights bill, which affirmed the citizenship of all persons born in the United States. Johnson vetoed both—a huge political mistake. It was his biggest political mistake. Congress then figured a way to keep the Freedman's Bureau in business and passed the Civil Rights bill over the President's objections—the first major bill in American history to overturn a presidential veto.

Next on the Congressional agenda was the Fourteenth Amendment. Then Congress passed the 14th Amendment which would block any state law designed to deprive citizens of "life, liberty or property, without due process of law." After this, Johnson pretty much declared political war on Congress, and the battlefield was the mid-term elections of 1866. The North awarded the Republicans an enormous victory in the election. From that point, Andrew Johnson's presidency collapsed.

ANDREW JOHNSON:
TENURE OF OFFICE ACT

Johnson was facing an almost intractable situation in Congress. He was checked at every turn by overwhelming Republican majorities in both Houses who were dismantling presidential reconstruction and putting in place a plan of their own. To prevent Johnson from removing Cabinet secretaries who worked against his policies or were allied with Congress, the House and Senate passed the Tenure of Office Act. The law permitted presidential appointees who had been confirmed by the Senate and subsequently fired by the President to remain in office until their successor had been approved by the Senate. (The Tenure of Office Act was later revised and, in the 1880s, repealed.)

The President was particularly estranged from Secretary of War Edwin McMaster Stanton. Johnson appreciated his service during the Civil War, but it was clear that Stanton was a strong ally of Congress and was working both to undermine the President's plan for the South and to advance the Radical Republican agenda. The Tenure of Office Act allowed the President to suspend Stanton and replace him temporarily with a reluctant General Grant. When, in February 1867, the Senate failed to approve Stanton's removal, the President decided to test the constitutionality of the Tenure of Office Act by permanently replacing Secretary Stanton. Johnson fired Stanton. Congress by then had had enough and began impeachment proceedings against Andrew Johnson.

ANDREW JOHNSON:
IMPEACHMENT AND TRIAL

Despite the hostility between the congressional majority and President Johnson, his removal was by no means assured. Impeachment[1] of an American president had been threatened but never officially attempted. In late February 1868, the House impeached the President for deliberate violation of the Tenure of Office Act. The vote was 128 to 47. Eleven articles of impeachment were transmitted to the Senate, and the three-month trial began on March 5.

Chief Justice Salmon P. Chase presided over the trial and forced the proceedings onto the narrow legal grounds of the President's violation of law—thus preventing the House managers from presenting a case based on Johnson's character and leadership abilities. The defense argued that the President believed the Tenure of Office Act was illegal and had a right to test its constitutionality. The President did not play a public role in his defense but passed word that he would no longer oppose congressional reconstruction and would appoint the widely respected John Scofield to replace Edwin McMaster Stanton as War Secretary.

On May 16, the Senate took the decisive vote on the eleventh article. The vote was thirty-five guilty and nineteen not guilty, one vote short of the two-thirds necessary for conviction. Votes on an additional three articles came later with the same result. Johnson's opponents gave up, Stanton left office, and Scofield was confirmed by the Senate. The nation's first foray onto the field of presidential impeachment was over.

ANDREW JOHNSON: LEGACY

From his veto of the Civil Rights Bill (1866) and accompanying harsh message, President Johnson was locked in a death struggle with the congressional majority. That he was spared the humiliation of removal was not due to his actions or what residual respect or affection that remained for Johnson himself. The Republican senators that voted not guilty were uncertain what the radical step of presidential removal might create.

After his brush with political ruin, Johnson pursued the Democratic nomination for president in 1868. The Democrats understood the steepness of that electoral challenge and were not about to nominate such a toxic candidate. He attempted a return to the U.S. Senate in 1869, but lost in a closely held legislative election.[2] He tried again in 1875 and won with a single vote margin.

On the issue of slavery, Representative Johnson opposed the provision of the Compromise of 1850 that abolished slavery in the District of Columbia. With the nation reeling from news of John Brown's raid on the Harper's Ferry federal arsenal, in December 1859 he stated on the Senate floor that the "all men are created equal" from the Declaration of Independence did not apply to African Americans. In the White House, Johnson's racist attitudes shaded his policies, but he understood that slavery was a dead issue.

18

ULYSSES S. GRANT

ULYSSES S. GRANT: LIFE PAGE

Born: April 27, 1822, Point Pleasant, Ohio, as Hiram Ulysses Grant

Education: United States Military Academy, BS

Married: Julia Dent, 1848

Military Service:

Mexican War: 1839–1854

      American Civil War: 1861–1869

      Commanding General of the United States Army

Eighteenth President of the United States: 1869–1877

Died: July 23, 1885, Wilton, New York

Additional resources available for this president at www.amomentintime.com.

ULYSSES S. GRANT:
CIVIL WAR LEADERSHIP

Born Hiram Ulysses Grant, the future president acquired the name Ulysses S. Grant when the congressman who nominated him for admission to West Point confused his name, recalling his mother's maiden name was Simpson. The recommendation was sent to the Academy as Ulysses S. Grant—the name by whom he is known to history.

Lieutenant Grant served with distinction in the Mexican War, but he began a long struggle with alcohol consumption and, as a result, was forced from the Army. In 1861, he returned to the military first as a leader of volunteers and then regular army service. He was an instinctive leader and rose quickly in the ranks. He led his army up the Tennessee River in early April 1862 to engage the rebels around Shiloh Church at Pittsburg Landing. The bloodletting was horrendous on both sides, but Union forces carried the day. When critics went after Grant's aggressive, seemingly pitiless tactics, President Abraham Lincoln came to his defense. "I can't spare this man; he fights."

After the Emancipation Proclamation, Grant began incorporating freed slaves into those units he commanded, which aided in his investiture and capture of Vicksburg on July 4, 1863. After Vicksburg, President Lincoln brought Grant back east and placed him in charge of all Union forces. Ulysses Grant had risen in just four years from his disappointing civilian pursuits to the top of the Union Army. In 1866, he was awarded the unprecedented four-star rank of General of the United States Army.

ULYSSES S. GRANT:
ELECTION OF 1868

At the conclusion of the Civil War, Grant was elevated to the rank of General of the Army. His relations with President Andrew Johnson were cordial at first, with the president taking him on his ill-fated "swing around the circle" speaking tour through the North and Midwest. President Johnson hoped Grant's popularity would give luster to his purpose for the trip, securing Northern support for his lenient policies toward the defeated South. Grant gradually became disgusted with Johnson's words and demeanor and left the tour early. From that point their relationship became increasingly icy.

Grant was caught up in the controversy over the Tenure of Office Act when Johnson appointed him acting Secretary of War in an effort to remove Radical Republican ally Edwin McMaster Stanton. In early January 1868, Grant turned the physical office of Secretary of War back over to Stanton, who had been restored to his position by the Senate. From that point, Grant and President Johnson were thoroughly estranged.

By the end of President Johnson's impeachment trial, Grant had received the Republican nomination for president and ran a campaign by "waving the bloody shirt"—emphasizing his war record and the Republican record of restoring the Union. Thanks to the votes of newly enfranchised former slaves, Grant won 52.7 percent of the popular vote and carried the Electoral College by 214 to 80. Ulysses S. Grant was forty-six years of age when he won the White House, the youngest president elected to date.

ULYSSES S. GRANT: RECONSTRUCTION

At the beginning of the Grant administration, there was cautious optimism that, with the departure of Andrew Johnson from the White House, the resistance to serious efforts at Reconstruction would dissipate. The three great Reconstruction amendments were in place.[1] President Grant was at the peak of his power and respect, to a degree even in the South. President Abraham Lincoln had appointed the majority of justices of the Supreme Court. The Republican majority in both Houses of Congress was firmly in control of the legislative process. So why is it that Reconstruction largely failed?

First, the vast majority of whites in the South conspired through state legislation or violence to suppress the civil rights of black citizens. When blocked by the presence of federal troops from such tactics, whites formed groups such as the Ku Klux Klan and used intimidation, murder, lynchings, and assassinations of black officials and allied whites.

President Grant tried to enforce the law and largely failed. He was willing to use the courts to aid in enforcement, but he was unwilling to reinvade the South with a large military commitment to enforce essentially a civilian policy. His Southern opponents sensed his indecision and took advantage of it. In the end, Grant's timorous on-and-off execution undermined his good intentions. And in the South, white majority pressure against the unprotected freedmen—whether with the whip, the rope, or the vote—was relentless and overwhelming.

ULYSSES S. GRANT: INDIAN POLICY

President Grant was sensitive to the plight of Native Americans, as nearly everywhere the tide of white civilization was overwhelming the indigenous population. He learned to empathize with the sad circumstances of displaced Indian clans when he was stationed in the Pacific Northwest as a young Army officer. He did believe, however, that Indians—for their own good—should give up their nomadic existence and assimilate into the wider white culture.

The biggest problem was that the Indians fundamentally disagreed with the notion of assimilation.

Conflict escalated when gold was discovered in the Black Hills of South Dakota, land considered to be sacred by many tribes. The Indians started attacking the miners in the region who were exploiting this new source of mineral wealth. Indian clans led by Sitting Bull and Crazy Horse fled the reservation and gathered for protection on the banks of the Little Bighorn River. Sent to scout out the Indian camp, the ever-ambitious General George Armstrong Custer attacked the camp. He and all of his men were wiped out. President Grant condemned Custer's actions as "wholly unnecessary" and negotiated a settlement with the various tribes in which they abandoned their claims to the Black Hills and returned to reservation life. Relations between white culture and American Indians continued to deteriorate until the climax of Indian Wars—the massacre at Wounded Knee on December 29, 1890—ended any effective Native American resistance.

ULYSSES S. GRANT: PANIC OF 1873

President Grant was a superb military tactician and a journeyman politician, but he was clearly an economic illiterate. Grant depended for advice on the creditor class—financiers and bankers. The advice they gave the president was very conservative—low taxes, reduced budgetary deficits, and the use of gold dollars or dollars backed by gold. Following this advice, Grant was determined to swiftly wrestle the federal budget into balance and reduce the national debt that lingered from the wartime expenditures of the early 1860s.

In his effort to pay down the national debt, Grant was periodically selling off U.S. gold stocks. These sales kept the price of gold low. In 1869, the economy had a brief severe shock due to the corrupt attempt of two New York financiers, Jay Gould and James Fisk, to "corner" or manipulate the gold market. When Grant realized what they were up to, he had Treasury Secretary George Boutwell resume selling gold. This broke the price and the conspiracy. Unfortunately, as a result, many banks collapsed and businesses went bankrupt.

The President had such confidence in gold as a way of backing U.S. currency that he ended the use of silver as money. Grant signed the Coinage Act of 1873, which terminated minting of new silver dollars. This made it harder for farmers to pay their debts and created severe deflation. As commodity prices collapsed, this set the stage for the major economic crisis of the Grant administration—the Panic of 1873.

ULYSSES S. GRANT: LEGACY

Not every president has come to office having served in the military. Like Grant, twenty-one of the forty-five presidents experienced military service prior to the White House.[2] Ulysses S. Grant, along with Abraham Lincoln, can be said to have saved the Union. Grant's skillful military leadership and tactical shrewdness helped rationalize and focus the national war effort so as to break the back of Confederate resistance and hammer the rebellion to its end.

Grant found the transition to political leadership a difficult one. He found it problematic in selecting honest subordinates, and his presidency is noted for a level of corruption and scandal that few equal.

The great failing of Grant's time as president involved not his intent, but his failure to follow through on his greatest challenge—civil rights for blacks. His failure and that of his successors doomed the former slaves and their descendants to generations of humiliation, suffering, and second-class citizenship.

Financial setbacks in his latter years left the Grant family in need. At the suggestion of his friend Mark Twain (Samuel Clemmons), Grant embarked on writing the story of his life. Diagnosed with throat (esophageal) cancer in summer 1884, with great intensity Grant pursued the memoir project. Former President Grant finished the final proofs of *The Personal Memoirs of Ulysses S. Grant* just days before his death.

19

RUTHERFORD B. HAYES

RUTHERFORD B. HAYES: LIFE PAGE

Born: October 4, 1822, Delaware, Ohio

Education:

Kenyon College, BA

       Harvard University, LLB

Vocation: Attorney

Married: Lucy Webb, 1852; she died 1889

Military Service: Major General, United States Army: 1861–1865

Member, U.S. House of Representatives: 1865–1867

Twenty-ninth and thirty-second Governor of Ohio: 1868–1872; 1876–1877

Nineteenth President of the United States: 1877–1881

Died: January 17, 1893

Additional resources available for this president at www.amomentintime.com.

RUTHERFORD B. HAYES:
TROUBLED ELECTION

Rutherford B. Hayes entered the White House after one of the most controversial—indeed perhaps the most corrupt—presidential elections in U.S history. Previously he had been elected to the U.S. House. Hayes then returned to Ohio and was the first person to be three times elected Governor.

From the beginning, it became clear the election of 1876 was going to be very close. The final result would depend on the distribution of electoral votes in three Southern states: Florida, Louisiana, and South Carolina. Because of the presence of Army troops in these states, the Republicans controlled the election process and used it to certify Hayes's election in all three states by disqualifying Democratic votes.

Neither party was guiltless. The Democrats in these and other states had used violence and intimidation to suppress the votes of thousands of African Americans who would have voted for Hayes. Representatives of the Democratic National Committee actually promised a large bribe to officials in Louisiana to secure that state's electoral votes, but the cash payment was too long in coming and they accepted a Republican bribe even though it was less money. So egregious was the fraud in this election that it forever tainted the person, election, and administration of Rutherford B. Hayes.

RUTHERFORD B. HAYES: COMPROMISE OF 1877 AND THE DEATH OF RECONSTRUCTION-I

As the weeks dragged by following the disputed election of 1876, no resolution of the deadlock seemed forthcoming. Democrat Samuel J. Tilden had won the popular vote and was one vote short in the Electoral College. Republican Rutherford B. Hayes needed every electoral vote in contention. There were disputed Electoral votes from South Carolina, Florida, and Louisiana. The Democratic House and GOP Senate could not decide who would count the votes.

The President and Congress agreed to an Electoral Commission. Hayes needed every disputed vote; Tilden only one. The Commission had five Republican Senators, five Democratic Representatives and five Supreme Court Justices, two Democratic justices, two Republican, and an Independent, David Davis. When the Commission met in February 1877, it decided all votes on a party line basis. Hayes received all disputed electoral votes. Why would Democrats vote for a Republican candidate?

RUTHERFORD B. HAYES: COMPROMISE OF 1877 AND THE DEATH OF RECONSTRUCTION-II

When the crucial vote came to accept the Electoral Commission's report that gave the election to Hayes, astonishingly a large number of Southern white Democrats voted to support Hayes. This political "miracle," the so-called Compromise of 1877, was wrought at Wormley's Hotel, 1500 H Street NW in Washington, DC. Southern Democrats extracted promises from Republicans that Hayes would withdraw federal troops from the three states in contention and that federal money would be used to help the South rebuild its shattered economy, develop railroads, and do other infrastructure projects.

All of Hayes hopes were dashed. The Southern Republican Party faded away. Like Ulysses S. Grant before him, Rutherford B. Hayes failed Southern blacks. He turned them over to the gentle mercies of white Democrats—who had no intention of respecting their rights and every intention of abusing them and hammering them into second-class citizenship. With no hope of prospering in the region of their birth, blacks despaired of Hayes and the South and began the long Great Migration out of the South to the West and North. The so-called Compromise of 1877 meant the birth of Jim Crow.[1]

RUTHERFORD B. HAYES: LEGACY

Given the corrupt bargain that lay at the foundation of the Hayes presidency, it is remarkable that Hayes was able to accomplish much of anything. He was fundamentally a decent human being and had a commitment to a moral, just society. This made even more distressing his having to endure slurs like "His Fraudulency" or "Rutherfraud." Honoring his inaugural pledge, he did not seek re-election and it is not certain he could have won if he had.

Hayes and his wife, Lucy, were strongly influenced by evangelical Christianity, advocated "traditional" family values, and supported the post office's anti-obscenity campaign of investigator Anthony Comstock. While Hayes was not opposed to women working outside the home, he and his wife were strongly skeptical of women's suffrage, feeling that marital duties were irreconcilable with political activity.

Late in life—long after he had power at the state or federal level with which he could actually do something about it—he privately awakened to the scandal of inequality between wealthy and deprived Americans—between rich and poor.[2]

He took leadership roles in veterans' groups and continued his advocacy of federal and state funding for education as the panacea for society's advancement. Hayes died in 1893.

20

JAMES A. GARFIELD

JAMES A. GARFIELD: LIFE PAGE

Born: November 19, 1831, Moreland Hills, Ohio

Education: Hiram College and Williams College, 1856

Vocation: Attorney

Married: Lucretia Randolph Garfield, 1858

Military Service: Major General, U.S. Army, 1861–1863

Member, House of Representatives: 1863–1880

Twentieth President of the United States: 1881

Assassinated: July 2, 1881, by Charles J. Guiteau

Died: September 19, 1881

Additional resources available for this president at www.amomentintime.com.

JAMES A. GARFIELD: CAMPAIGN AGAINST CORRUPTION

The election of 1880 had a very close outcome. The ticket of James A. Garfield and Chester A. Arthur prevailed over the Democratic candidate Winfield Scott Hancock, but the margin of victory was less than ten thousand votes. Voting in the Electoral College was more decisive (214–155).

Agreeing with former Presidents Rutherford B. Hayes and Ulysses S. Grant, Garfield believed that the government hiring was corrupt and needed serious reform, but he contributed to this crusade in a way no one could conceive in the early days of his term. Garfield was determined to appoint his own slate of Cabinet members and sub-Cabinet federal appointments nationwide, and he defied Senator Roscoe Conkling of New York, who wished to control federal appointments in New York State. When Garfield's appointments prevailed, in a fit of spite, Conkling resigned his Senate seat in protest and was shocked when the New York legislature refused to re-appoint him. Garfield had emerged triumphant.

Garfield was also concerned that African Americans in the South were seeing civil rights abridged by a racist white majority determined to reclaim the social arrangements of the pre–Civil War era. Garfield continued to appoint African American and white Southern Republicans to prominent government positions.

JAMES A. GARFIELD:
ASSASSINATION

In the aftermath of his victory over the Stalwart Republican faction of former Senator Roscoe Conkling and Vice President Chester A. Arthur, President Garfield planned a political trip to shore up his political support in New England. On July 2, 1881, the president was chatting with Secretary of State James G. Blaine as he awaited his train on the concourse of the Baltimore and Potomac Railway Station. Suddenly, he was approached by a disillusioned federal office-seeker, Charles J. Guiteau, who then shot the president twice. As he was led away, the would-be assassin said, "I did it. I will go to jail for it. I am a Stalwart and Arthur will be president."

As Secretary of War Robert Todd Lincoln watched in horror, the nation began to relive the tragedy of his father's assassination sixteen years earlier. The President's first wound was superficial, but the second lodged itself in his abdomen. Repeated attempts to probe the wound to find the bullet were unsuccessful. The doctors examined the president with unwashed hands and unsterilized instruments, undoubtedly contributing to the infections which ultimately took his life. After months of struggle, President Garfield succumbed to pneumonia, and perhaps heart difficulties related to his deteriorating condition, on September 19, 1881.

Guiteau was a religious fanatic who considered himself deserving of a federal appointment because of his political support for the Republican Party. He has been variously diagnosed as a "narcissistic schizophrenic" or a "clinical psychopath." He may also have suffered from neurosyphilis, which causes severe mental deficiency. Guiteau was convicted of murder and executed in June 1882.

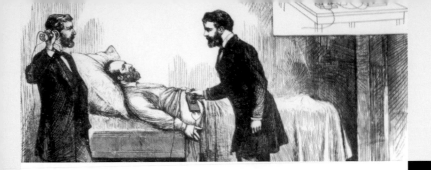

JAMES A. GARFIELD: LEGACY

It is one of the ironies of Garfield's only-too-brief term in office that his removal spurred the movement to bring an end to the spoils system. The federal appointment system was rife with corruption—due in part to the way in which people were hired. If you wanted a government job, you had to give your support to one of the political parties which then rewarded its loyalists. Often jobseekers were required to make donations in the form of campaign contributions to secure party support in their pursuit of government employment.

Garfield's assassination by a disgruntled, albeit mentally disturbed, religious fanatic who believed he was owed a government position spurred the civil service reform movement. The President was a moderate advocate of this reform and other anti-corruption initiatives. One could say his tragic death, and the preliminary steps in the direction of cleaner government, made him martyr to the cause of executive reform.

He is often not included in the rankings of presidents by historians because of the brevity of his time in office. It is interesting to speculate, however, how his generally ethical behavior in his years as a legislator and his early presidential initiatives might have dictated the positive direction he could have taken the country in.

21

CHESTER A. ARTHUR

CHESTER A. ARTHUR: LIFE PAGE

Born: October 5, 1829, Fairfield, Vermont

Education: Union College

Vocation: Attorney, Public Servant

Married: Ellen Herndon, 1859; she died in 1880

Military Service: Administrative posts within the Civil War New York Militia

Customs Collector for the Port of New York: 1871–1878

Twentieth Vice President of the United States: 1881

Twenty-first President of the United States: 1881–1885

Died: November 18, 1886

Additional resources available for this president at www.amomentintime.com.

CHESTER A. ARTHUR:
CIVIL SERVICE REFORM

In the 1880s, the Republican Party was divided on the issue of civil service reform. Conservatives—the "Stalwarts"—wanted to keep the corrupt spoils system, which required federal appointees to support the Party with loyalty and contributions. Chester A. Arthur was the bewhiskered political creation of the Stalwart faction. Supporters of reform were fearful that Arthur would thwart their efforts. Arthur surprised them.

As president, Arthur faced a political landscape significantly altered by the assassination of his predecessor by a frustrated office seeker. Astonishing his critics and friends alike, soon after taking office the new President called for a reformed civil service. In response, Democratic Senator George H. Pendleton of Ohio re-introduced the Civil Service Act. Originally, the new bill met the same fate as had previous similar legislation, but Arthur and Pendleton persisted. In late 1882, after losing badly in the mid-term elections, a chastened Republican Congress passed the Pendleton Civil Service Reform Act, which the president later signed on January 6, 1883.

Henceforth, those federal jobs covered by the Act would be chosen through merit—as demonstrated by performance on written examinations.

CHESTER A. ARTHUR: LEGACY

Often there is a salutary transformation when a politician or candidate takes the oath of office as president. Overnight this individual no longer feels solely obligated to dutifully represent a narrow constituency or regional or political bias. Remarkably, the president recognizes that he represents the entire country and is president for all.

No one would have considered Chester A. Arthur to be a candidate for this transformation. He was of the Stalwart inclination within Republican ranks, but once in office, Arthur defied expectations. He enthusiastically and persistently pursued a policy of civil service reform that challenged the position and dogma of those who sponsored his rise to power.

He valued the good life and "loved the pleasures of the table," and was a genial and pleasant politician who sought and often received the love of his constituents. His stewardship of the White House was balanced and competent. Nevertheless, as the 1884 election approached, none of the Republican factions—Stalwart (pro-spoils system), Half-Breed (moderates), or reformers—were committed to his nomination for re-election. Perhaps it was his perception of declining health that convinced him not to press the issue.

After leaving office in 1885, he returned to New York City to resume his legal practice, but ill-health prevented a full embrace of his work. His condition worsened and, in November, he suffered a cerebral hemorrhage. Former President Chester A. Arthur died on November 18, 1886.

22

GROVER CLEVELAND

GROVER CLEVELAND: LIFE PAGE

Born: March 18, 1837, Caldwell, New Jersey

Vocation: Attorney

Marriage: Francis Folsom, 1886

Sheriff of Erie County, New York: 1871–1873

Thirty-fourth Mayor of Buffalo, New York: 1882

Twenty-eighth Governor of New York: 1883–1885

Twenty-second President of the United States: 1885–1889

Twenty-fourth President of the United States: 1893–1897

Died: June 24, 1908

Additional resources available for this president at www.amomentintime.com.

GROVER CLEVELAND:
PRO-BUSINESS REFORM DEMOCRAT

Grover Cleveland's convictions and policies as a candidate, public servant, and president demonstrated strong pro-business inclinations. He was a Bourbon Democrat. Bourbon Democrats were political conservatives who, with stubborn intensity, supported the economic principles of Thomas Jefferson and Andrew Jackson, *laissez-faire* liberalism, states' rights, and the absolute gold standard.

As a self-educated attorney, he rose to power in the city of Buffalo, where he served as sheriff and then as mayor. Leading the city, he gained a reputation for clean government. When the Democrats began searching for a candidate for New York governor, Cleveland's sterling reputation helped carry the day, and the Party took over complete control of the state government.

In Albany, Cleveland almost immediately began enhancing his political brand, offering up eight vetoes in just a few weeks in office. One of his most notorious was the veto of an extremely popular reduction in New York City's elevated-train fares. His principled stand convinced reformers, including Theodore Roosevelt, and they changed their minds and sustained his veto. By this time, his reputation for honest, tight-fisted government was being discussed nationally. In 1884, Cleveland went to the Democratic Convention with the hopes of influencing the nomination choice in what was shaping up to be the best Democratic year since before the Civil War.

GROVER CLEVELAND: SCANDAL, ELECTION, AND MARRIAGE

The election campaign of 1884 was destined to be waged on the issue of public corruption, and Grover Cleveland was not without a juicy scandal of his own—this one personal. While a rising attorney in Buffalo, he had taken to bed Maria Crofts Halpin, a lovely widow who had settled in Buffalo. Cleveland admitted their relationship was intimate and sexual. When Oscar Fulsom Cleveland was born, Cleveland financially supported the boy, who was placed by his mother in an orphanage. During the campaign, a Buffalo pastor made the allegations public. Cleveland did not hesitate. He admitted the truth, told his supporters to tell the truth, and gradually the "scandal" went away.

Since any Democrat was guaranteed the electoral votes of the Solid South, Cleveland only needed to carry four additional states: New York, New Jersey, Indiana, and Connecticut. Cleveland carried all swing states in close votes and went to the White House.

If a personal issue had imperiled his election, a personal issue after he entered the White House only contributed to his growing popularity. During the first two years of his first term, Cleveland courted Francis Fulsom, the daughter of his former law partner. In June 1886, the couple was married in the Blue Room of the White House. Francis Fulsom Cleveland, at twenty-one years of age, was the youngest First Lady in history. She certainly transformed the president's public persona and guaranteed favorable headlines in the years remaining in his first term.

23

BENJAMIN HARRISON

BENJAMIN HARRISON: LIFE PAGE

Born: August 20, 1833

Education: Miami University, BA

Married: Caroline Scott, 1853; she died in 1862

       Mary Scott Lord, 1896

Vocation: Attorney

Military Service:

American Civil War: 1862–1865

Union Army of the Cumberland

Brevet Brigadier General, Union Army

1st Brigade, 1st Division, XX Corps

United States Senator: 1881–1887

Twenty-third President of the United States: 1889–1893

Died: March 13, 1901

Additional resources available for this president at www.amomentintime.com.

BENJAMIN HARRISON: ELECTION OF 1888, TARIFF, AND ANTI-TRUST LEGISLATION

After distinguished service in the Union Army during the Civil War, Harrison returned to Indianapolis, Indiana, assumed his lucrative legal practice, and became active in Indiana Republican politics. Harrison came from behind at the 1888 Republican Convention to secure the presidential nomination. He went on to lose the popular vote but defeated incumbent President Grover Cleveland in the Electoral College, 233 to 168, primarily on his ability to carry Cleveland's home state of New York.

As president, he was only a restrained supporter of Civil Service reform. He demonstrated his enthusiasm for higher tariffs by signing the higher McKinley Tariff, designed to protect U.S. commercial interests. The flood of revenue thusly created increased the already exorbitant government surplus and made possible the unpopular, first billion-dollar U.S. budget.

While Harrison demonstrated his strong pro-business bias, he was sympathetic toward mild efforts to curb the domination of big business. The president signed the Sherman Anti-Trust Act, which was intended to curb monopolies and the tendency of big business to engage in vertical integration (controlling all the means of production and distribution within an industry).

BENJAMIN HARRISON: CIVIL RIGHTS LEGISLATION AND NATIVE AMERICAN POLICY

As a prominent Civil War veteran, Harrison moved from the Whig Party to the Republicans. He was a strong opponent of slavery and was emotionally connected to the newly enfranchised African Americans in the former Confederate states. As president, he spoke forcefully in support of civil rights and pushed major legislation in Congress to help African Americans overcome the resistance of the white majority to their voting and to provide federal financial support for education to schools—regardless of the race of students. Both attempts failed, as Southerners flexed their muscle in the Senate and defeated his efforts.

Harrison's time in the White House marked the effective end to Native Americans' resistance to white encroachment on their treaty-assigned territory. When a spiritual movement known as the Ghost Dance was incorrectly perceived by Washington to be a belligerent movement, the Army was ordered to suppress it. Troopers from the Seventh U.S. Cavalry surrounded and then attacked a Lakota Sioux encampment at Wounded Knee in South Dakota. The resulting massacre—upwards of 146 men, women, and children—is considered a moral outrage. Harrison's policy toward the Indians was to encourage assimilation into white society—though the allotment system he developed ended in disaster, as many Indians unknowingly sold their property to cold-blooded white land speculators.

BENJAMIN HARRISON: MONETARY POLICY

One of the most explosive issues in late nineteenth-century American politics was whether the U.S. should underwrite its paper currency with gold, silver, or a combination of both precious metals. Westerners and Southerners of both parties wanted increased coinage of silver with which voters could pay their taxes and debts. Congressmen from the Northeast wanted to retain the more conservative gold standard.

Harrison was a bimetallist—he favored striking coins in both precious metals—but he attempted to thread a compromise position. When Senator John Sherman of Ohio advanced the Sherman Silver Purchase Act, which would put more currency in circulation, the president signed it with the provision that the value of silver and gold should float rather than be in some government-determined fixed ratio.

Under the president's plan, there would still be more money in circulation, but not as much as when the gold-to-silver value was fixed; but then the value of silver collapsed. Speculators bought silver coins at the market rate (say, $1.16/ounce), sold it at the government fixed rate ($1.30/ounce), bought gold coins with the profits (at $1.45/ounce), sold the gold coins at the new inflationary rate ($1.55/ounce), bought silver coins at a new deflated price ($1.05/ounce), and then repeated the process over and over. By 1894, the price of silver was $0.60 per ounce.

International banks and governments demanded payment in gold not silver, and so America's gold supply began to shrink—a problem that would await future years for resolution.

BENJAMIN HARRISON: LEGACY

Benjamin Harrison's accomplishments are largely ignored by historians. He epitomized the era of pigmy presidents—between the greatness and challenge of Abraham Lincoln and the modern presidency represented by William McKinley and Theodore Roosevelt. Harrison was generally regarded as a competent Chief Executive with impeccable moral values and behavior. Harrison emerged from his White House experience with reputation intact. He was a faithful and devout Presbyterian and filled his Cabinet with those who shared that sectarian distinctive.

His robust advocacy for black civil rights and universal federally funded education for all races is a strong indication of his moral compass. Though these initiatives failed, largely because of Southern congressional opposition, it does indicate that many in the Northern political nexus were resisting the decline in national support for African American rights and well-being. After his failed efforts, not until the 1930s was the conscience of the nation sufficiently attuned to the need for racial reform.

With the looming threat of economic instability leading eventually to the Panic of 1893, Harrison faced a challenge within his party when he sought re-nomination and was defeated by the man he defeated, Grover Cleveland. The Electoral College vote was a reverse of the previous election. Harrison had an active life of service in his post-presidency in the national and international arenas.

GROVER CLEVELAND

1750   1775   1800   1825   1850   1875

After the Benjamin Harrison inauguration, the Clevelands settled in New York City and started a family. The former president relaxed into a moderately engaged legal practice and spent much time fishing at the couple's vacation home out at Buzzards Bay in Massachusetts.

Cleveland remained an acute observer of the national scene and watched with concern the Harrison administration enact an ambitious economic program and then politically implode. The Republicans passed the McKinley Tariff and the Sherman Silver Purchase Act, and Cleveland opposed both of these economic measures. Finally, in 1891, he spoke out against both in a letter to New York state reform activists. Cleveland's outspoken opposition to the Republican program reawakened enthusiasm in the party for Cleveland, and at the Democratic National Convention he was nominated on the first ballot.

The Republicans suffered because many voters could directly attribute rising prices for imported goods to the McKinley Tariff, and because their campaign was less intense and poorly organized this time around. Cleveland was re-elected in a landslide, winning his third popular vote majority with a margin of over four-hundred thousand—but this time winning the Electoral College in a wipeout, 277 to 145.

GROVER CLEVELAND:
PANIC OF 1893

Having achieved restoration to the White House, within weeks Grover Cleveland faced a serious economic crisis. The so-called Panic of 1893 ushered in the most serious depression of the century, a four-year-long business contraction that crushed Cleveland's hopes for his second term.

Cleveland was unable to respond to the growing crisis because he shared the prevailing common political and economic wisdom that the government was unable and incapable of applying fiscal or monetary measures to improve the economy—and what he did do made matters worse. At the very time the government should have been working to counter deflation, Cleveland embarked on a plan to restrict the money supply.

He called Congress into session to repeal the Sherman Silver Purchase Act, by which the government was required to purchase large amounts of silver. President Cleveland also tried to repeal the McKinley Tariff. It had raised rates significantly, but he was unable to do much more than nibble around the edges of tariff rates.

When the economy did not improve and, in fact, got worse, the voters blamed Cleveland and the Democrats. The electorate delivered to the Republicans a historic victory in the 1894 mid-term election. The Party gained 117 seats, the most crushing political reversal in the nation's history. Cleveland labored on through his last two years, hoping that his reliance on the gold standard and parsimonious government would bring the country out of the depression. He failed.

GROVER CLEVELAND: CANCER AND THE SECRET OPERATION

With the nation in financial meltdown due to the Panic of 1893, the president's personal life took an ominous turn during that summer of conflict over the repeal of the Sherman Silver Purchase Act. Cleveland began to note a soreness on the surface of his hard palate. Doctors agreed that the presentation was cancerous.

Cleveland faced a dilemma. He and his doctors felt he needed to have this condition treated, but a major operation under sedation might create anxiety in the country and further jeopardize an already unstable economy. Also, word that the president might be incapacitated would place focus on Vice President Adlai Stevenson, who was known to disagree with President Cleveland on the issue of silver purchases. This might undermine Cleveland's efforts to repeal the Sherman Act.

The solution was a secret operation. Cleveland borrowed *Oneida*, a yacht owned by one of his friends. The procedure was conducted on deck in the open air while cruising off the shores of Long Island. The team of surgeons removed a large section of Cleveland's upper left jaw and the palate. Since this would have caused a serious disfigurement of the presidential face, a hard rubber prosthesis was inserted to restore his normal appearance.

The White House concocted a story about a fanciful removal of two teeth and was in full denial mode when reports surfaced about the true nature of the operation. Cleveland enjoyed a complete recovery and lived for many years following the tumor extraction.

GROVER CLEVELAND: *THE CROSS OF GOLD AND THE DEATH OF BOURBON DEMOCRACY*

Grover Cleveland was an inept party leader. The difficulty was that he was antagonistic to many of the ideas held by members of his party. As a Bourbon (pro-business) Democrat, on some issues he had more in common with Republicans than his fellow partisans. His strong support of civil service reform and the gold standard resonated with conservative congressmen and voters. His hostility to the labor movement and willingness to use federal resources to break strikes that he deemed to be detrimental to the national interests or not beneficial to big business alienated the growing populist impulse in his party.

At the Democratic Convention of 1896, Congressman William Jennings Bryan, the articulate, inspiring firebrand from Nebraska, captured the nomination and the Party's imagination. Bryan was nominated for president (three times as it turned out) and support for Cleveland's pro-business doctrine among Democrats collapsed. Cleveland's political ineptitude, his myopic pursuit of a seemingly mean-spirited conservative economic agenda, his stubborn determination to have his way on matters of policy, and growing isolation during his second term gave his Democratic opponents a chance to steal control of the party from the president and his allies. This reduced Cleveland's influence on the future of national and Democratic politics.

GROVER CLEVELAND: *PLESSY* AND THE DECLINE OF CIVIL RIGHTS PROTECTIONS-I

Securing African American rights was a decades-long process following the American Civil War. The passage of the three great Reconstruction amendments ending slavery (thirteenth), providing equal protection (fourteenth), and securing voting rights (fifteenth) were thought by the victors in the war to have opened the door to full participation in the rites of citizenship for freedmen. This overly optimistic assessment did not take into consideration the intensity of racial animus still remaining in the entire country, most particularly in the South.

Taking full advantage of the prevailing legal theory, which gave to the states the power to orchestrate the rites of citizenship, Southern states devised an extensive repertoire of repressive techniques to keep blacks in their place. Violent intimidation, economic coercion, personal threats, poll taxes, literacy requirements, grandfather clauses, and confusing regulations kept blacks and poor whites from voting or even seeking common cause in bettering their existence. In addition, a regime of humiliating restrictions in public accommodations and transportation sapped the morale and resistance of those being suppressed. Unfortunately, as the decades passed, there was a diminishing inclination and outright weariness on the part of Northerners to provide a counterweight to this vicious system of apartheid to help the freedmen and their children in their plight.

GROVER CLEVELAND: *PLESSY* AND THE DECLINE OF CIVIL RIGHTS PROTECTIONS-II

As they flooded back into Congress following Reconstruction, Southerners did everything to block legal moves to help blacks vote. Yet the most destructive force abridging African American civil rights was the Supreme Court. The Court eviscerated the Civil Rights Bill of 1875 in *Civil Rights Bills* (1883), saying the Fourteenth Amendment only forbade discrimination by federal and state governments, not by individuals. In *Giles v. Harris* (1902) and *Giles v. Teasley* (1904), the Court held that discrimination was not "intended" by laws governing voting in the South since they applied to whites as well.

The final and most destructive ruling by the Court, which firmly established the Jim Crow era, was *Plessy vs. Ferguson* (1896)—which enshrined the principle of "separate, but equal." Along with *Dred Scott vs. Sanford*, it is regarded as one of the worst rulings in Supreme Court history. This misguided decision allowed states to engage in discrimination in education, transportation, and public accommodations if these were deemed to be equal in quality. Of course they were never equal, and by its actions, the Court blocked for six decades the chance African Americans had to appropriate their share of the American dream or participate in the rites of citizenship.

GROVER CLEVELAND: LEGACY

Grover Cleveland was the only president to serve two non-consecutive terms. His political rise was surprisingly swift, serving less than a year as Mayor of Buffalo and less than a full term as Governor of New York. As president during the Gilded Age—an era noted for corruption—he arrived at the White House with a reputation for personal rectitude and fiscal parsimony in government.

His courageous support for the gold standard has won him the praise of some historians, but others believe his stubborn opposition to any bi-metallic compromise, hostility to labor unions, and unwillingness to lead a compassionate government response to the Panic of 1893 spelled electoral doom for the Democratic Party for a generation.

Yet, perhaps the most profound moral failure of President Cleveland was his open hostility to African American civil rights. He opposed federal intervention to aid African Americans secure their rights, secured the repeal of the Enforcement Act (1871), and put the weight of his office behind opposition to the Lodge Force Bill—which would have empowered the federal government to vigorously enforce the Fourteenth and Fifteenth Amendments.

After leaving office, the Clevelands moved to their estate in Princeton, New Jersey, and he died of a heart attack in late June 1908.

WILLIAM McKINLEY

WILLIAM MCKINLEY: LIFE PAGE

Born: January 29, 1843, Niles, Ohio

Education:

Allegheny College

Mount Union College

Albany Law School

Vocation: Attorney

Married: Ida Saxton, 1871

Member, U.S. House of Representatives: 1877–1884 and 1885–1891

Thirty-ninth Governor of Ohio: 1892–1896

Twenty-fifth President of the United States: 1897–1901

Died by assassination: September 14, 1901

Additional resources available for this president at www.amomentintime.com.

WILLIAM MCKINLEY:
DEPRESSION AND ELECTION

The presidency of William McKinley has often paled in memory by being compared to his more ebullient and colorful successor, but McKinley's five years in office marked a dramatic shift in the position of the United States. When he took power, the nation was mired in the greatest depression of the century. Bloody demonstrations, labor management disputes, and public despair were the order of the day. By the end of his term, the nation had been transformed economically, internationally, politically, and—to a degree—socially.

After a stellar war-time record, McKinley was elected to the U.S. House and then, as Ohio Governor, watched the nation's economy collapse in the Panic of 1893, made even worse by the paralysis and ineptitude of the Cleveland Administration.

Under the tutelage of his friend and mentor, businessman Mark Hanna, in 1896 McKinley began to campaign for the Republican nomination. By the national convention, he had it locked up. In the end, the depression—which voters clearly laid at the feet of the Demo-crats—carried the Republican into office. McKinley won the Northeast and Midwest and carried most urban areas. His popular vote was 51 percent, and he won a strong majority in the Electoral College.

WILLIAM MCKINLEY: SPANISH-AMERICAN WAR AND IMPERIALISM

In the early years of the McKinley administration, tensions gradually increased between Spain and the United States. The primary flashpoint of conflict was the island of Cuba, where for years rebels had been conducting a low-grade insurgency. Support for Cuban independence was widespread in the U.S. and public opinion was aroused after the destruction of USS *Maine* in Havana Harbor in February 1898. After the USS *Maine* exploded in the Havana harbor on April 20, 1898, Congress declared war against Spain.

A combined force of Army troops and volunteers landed at Santiago de Cuba and scored a major victory at the Battle of San Juan Hill on July 2. There, the Rough Riders—under a young Theodore Roosevelt—led a day-long, bloody but decisive battle. When the Spanish Caribbean fleet tried to escape but was destroyed by naval forces led by Rear Admiral William Sampson, southern Cuba—indeed the whole island—was effectively under U.S. control. America then invaded Puerto Rico. When all resistance collapsed, Spain sued for peace. In the Treaty of Paris (1898), Spain ceded the Philippines, Guam, and Puerto Rico to the U.S. and gave up its claim to power in Cuba.

With the annexation of Hawaii (1898), the president and U.S. leaders realized the difficulty of managing a world-wide naval conflict if there was no easy access from the Atlantic to the Pacific Oceans. Therefore, he re-negotiated a treaty with Britain, revising previous agreements and permitting the U.S. to have sole control of any canal it cut across Central America.

WILLIAM MCKINLEY: RE-ELECTION AND ASSASSINATION

The election of 1900 was a replay of the 1896 contest. Again, William Jennings Bryan hit the hustings while McKinley only made a single speech accepting the nomination. This time, however, Bryan was challenged on the road by the bright, enthusiastic, Republican vice-presidential candidate—former New York Governor and war hero Theodore Roosevelt. McKinley won in a landslide, even carrying Bryan's home state of Nebraska.

Shortly after his second inaugural address, the McKinleys embarked on a long tour of the country, going in a wide circle south, west, north, then back east. Due to Ida McKinley's ill-health, they had to delay a visit to the Pan American Exposition in Buffalo. The president did go to the Exposition in September and was there assassinated by Leon Czolgosz, an adherent to anarchism. Czolgosz shot the president twice in the abdomen, but doctors were not able to find and remove the second bullet. Doctors were optimistic about his recovery, but after several days, gangrene infected the walls of his stomach. He died in the early hours of September 14, 1898.

Vice President Theodore Roosevelt had rushed back from a camping trip in the Adirondack Mountains and took the oath of office in the morning. The president's assassin, Leon Czolgosz, was tried and convicted of murder in September 1898 and electrocuted a month later.

WILLIAM MCKINLEY: LEGACY

Compared in the white-hot reflection of his successor's brilliance, William McKinley has frequently been ignored and his accomplishments devalued. Yet, much of what we know as modern presidential style originated with McKinley. His domination of the media and his expansion of the presidential role of commander-in-chief laid the groundwork for the modern executive office—often described as the "imperial"—presidency.

Some historians see McKinley's 1896 victory as a realignment election, but if it was, it was a gradual process. Without question, his term aided in the transformation of America from a rural, agricultural nation to one dominated by business, industry, and mass politics. McKinley's impact was greatest in foreign affairs. In the span of four years, America's power and presence took on global dimensions, acquiring the Philippines, Puerto Rico, Guam, and Hawai.

During his lifetime, William McKinley was one of the most popular U.S. presidents, but he has been accused by some observers as following rather than leading the public. Nowhere is that more tragically demonstrated than in his almost complete acquiescence in the face of white bigotry and his abandonment of African Americans in their struggle against discrimination and abuse.

Nevertheless, from being mired in a wrenching depression in 1896, the United States under William McKinley leapt up and forward into a new role as a world-wide economic, diplomatic, and military powerhouse.

THEODORE ROOSEVELT

THEODORE ROOSEVELT: LIFE PAGE

Born: October 27, 1858, New York, New York

Education: Harvard University

Vocation: Author, Politician, and Soldier

Married: Alice Lee, 1880; she died in 1884

       Edith Carow, 1886

Member, New York State Assembly: 1882–1884; Minority Leader: 1883

President of New York City Board of Police Commissioners: 1895–1897

Assistant Secretary of the Navy: 1897–1898

Governor of New York: 1899–1900

Twenty-fifth Vice President of the United States: 1901

Twenty-sixth President of the United States: 1901–1909

Nobel Peace Prize: 1906

Congressional Medal of Honor (posthumously): 2001

Died: January 6, 1919

Additional resources available for this president at www.amomentintime.com.

THEODORE ROOSEVELT: OVERCOMING ADVERSITY

Theodore Roosevelt was the second of four children born to Theodore Roosevelt Sr. of New York City and Martha "Mittie" Bulloch of Roswell, Georgia. He was the uncle of First Lady Eleanor Roosevelt and a distant cousin of his successor in the White House, Franklin Delano Roosevelt. Young Theodore was a sickly, asthmatic child whose father encouraged him to battle his physical inadequacies with a program of hard vigorous exercise—hunting, hiking, and boxing.

Schooled by tutors, Roosevelt entered Harvard in 1876. Theodore Sr. died midway through his son's college years, and Roosevelt felt deep distress at the loss of his namesake. But the younger Roosevelt recovered his focus, was inducted into Phi Beta Kappa, and graduated *magna cum laude* in 1880. He attended Columbia Law School but declined to pursue his degree or the practice of law. Instead, he began writing his first book, *The Naval War of 1812*, and published it in 1882. That same year he was drawn into New York City Republican politics, defeated a machine candidate, and took a seat in the New York state assembly.

After his mother and his wife, Alice, died on the same day from different diseases, Roosevelt poured himself into his work in Albany. There, in three terms he gained the reputation as a reform politician focusing on government and corporate corruption. In the presidential election of 1884, he offered only lukewarm support for the Republican nominee James G. Blaine, diminishing his support among reformers.

THEODORE ROOSEVELT: PROGRESSIVE POLITICIAN

After the death of his first wife, Alice, and mother, Mittie, and with a decline in his political influence during the presidential election of 1884, Theodore Roosevelt retired from the early phase of his political career and left for his ranch in North Dakota. There, he worked hard at the tasks associated with a class of people far from those with whom he had grown up. He earned their respect and absorbed an understanding of the common people of the West.

He marked his return to public life with his marriage to Edith Kermit Carow, and together they raised his daughter, Alice, and produced a prodigious brood of their own. In 1888, Benjamin Harrison surprisingly took the White House and appointed Roosevelt to the United States Civil Service Commission. There Roosevelt earned a reputation as a vigorous reformer—the proverbial "bull in the china shop"—demanding an end to patronage appointments and loudly insisting on full enforcement of civil service laws. In 1883, President Grover Cleveland re-appointed Roosevelt upon his return to the presidency.

Roosevelt declined the offers of support should he wish to run for Mayor of New York, but he did accept appointment to the Board of Police Commissioners. He became President of the Board and drastically transformed police service in the city. To whatever position Roosevelt chose to serve, he brought ebullience, energy, reform, and transformation. This service enhanced his reputation as a reform-minded progressive and built a growing popularity among the voters.

THEODORE ROOSEVELT:
ROUGH RIDER

President William McKinley appointed Roosevelt as Assistant Secretary of the Navy, where Roosevelt flowed into the power vacuum and made most of the major decisions. Inspired by the writings of naval historian Rear Admiral Alfred Thayer Mahan, he began to push for augmented naval power, including the construction of a new class of battleships. As tensions grew in 1898, Roosevelt quietly began urging President McKinley to provoke a war with Spain. When the USS *Maine* was blown up in Havana Harbor on February 15, without approval Roosevelt ordered naval squadrons to prepare for war. When Congress finally declared war, Roosevelt's quick actions insured that the Navy was prepared and scored important early victories—such as that by Commodore George Dewey at Manila.

With the coming war, battle beckoned to Roosevelt. He resigned from his political post and formed the First U.S. Volunteer Cavalry. Professional and amateur athletes, cowboys, hunters, miners, college students, and upper-class gentlemen clamored to join the unit soon to be press-christened "Rough Riders." After training in San Antonio, Texas, the Riders were shipped to southern Cuba and were involved in a minor clash at Las Guasimas and the major encounter outside Santiago de Cuba along the San Juan Heights. Colonel Roosevelt led his men with bravery and distinction, and for this leadership, he was posthumously awarded the Congressional Medal of Honor (2001). His foray onto the battlefield fixed permanently his fame and secured his political fortunes.

THEODORE ROOSEVELT: GOVERNOR AND VICE PRESIDENT

Forged on the range, the battlefield, and the campaign trail, Roosevelt resonated with the aspirations of people other than his upper-class contemporaries. On occasion, Roosevelt acted vigorously to fulfill the dreams of common citizens. Additionally, Roosevelt perceived—and indeed embraced—the political opportunities afforded by the shift in national politics away from the legislative branch toward the executive. This shift fit perfectly into his leadership style, as he preferred to act with little restraint or deference to other branches of government. The breath of his intellectual understanding represented by his extensive writings prepared him for engagement and action on a broad vista.

The hero of San Juan (Kettle) Hill returned to great acclaim. Exploiting his war record, he promptly jumped back into politics. He stood for the Republican nomination for Governor of New York; he won handily in the party caucus but only won the election by the barest of margins. Roosevelt began to express a philosophy about corporate responsibility, which he articulated in his support for the Ford Franchise-Tax Bill.

When the opportunity came to step onto the national stage as vice-presidential nominee in 1900, he seized it and enthusiastically campaigned for the ticket. The passive role of vice president was, of course, totally inconsistent with his activist temperament, but Roosevelt was soon thrust into a role of much greater consequence.

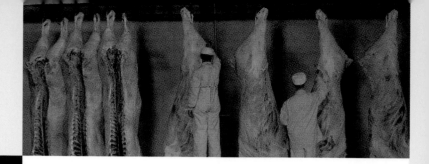

THEODORE ROOSEVELT: SQUARE DEAL AND BUSINESS RELATIONS

The heart of Roosevelt's domestic program was what he called a "Square Deal" for the American people. His target: giant corporations (often called trusts at that time) who were engaged in vertical integration of particular industries, thus controlling supply, fabrication, and marketing.

The primary cudgel Roosevelt used was the Sherman Anti-Trust Act of 1890. He broke up the Northern Securities Company, a huge railroad monopoly, and regulated Standard Oil. When Upton Sinclair's *The Jungle* appeared in 1906, the public was transfixed by this story of abuse in the meatpacking business. The book stimulated support for Roosevelt's Meat Inspection Act of 1906, which forbade the use of harmful preservatives and deceptive labeling in the production, packaging, and distribution of meat products. On the same day, he signed both the Meat Inspection Act and the Pure Food and Drug Act, these last two designed to reign in the out-of-control patent medicine business. This law, among others, led to the establishment of the consolidated Food and Drug Administration in the 1930s.

Roosevelt created the Department of Commerce and Labor, which would house the Bureau of Corporation. In addition, Roosevelt supported passage of the Hepburn Act (1906), by which the Interstate Commerce Commission began setting the prices that railroads could charge customers and regulate other features of railroad operations.

Everett Historical / Shutterstock.com

THEODORE ROOSEVELT: CONSERVATION PRESIDENT

From childhood, Theodore Roosevelt demonstrated a fascination with wildlife, nature, and the environment. Bolstered by his experience as a rancher in North Dakota and emboldened by growing public concern about the destruction of natural resources in the service of economic growth, Roosevelt transformed himself into the nation's first conservation president.

Using legislation and executive orders, the president allied himself with the growing environmental movement and aggressively pursued some but not all parts of their agenda. His first strategy was a legislative one. Roosevelt established the U.S. Forest Service and then worked with its chief, Gifford Pinchott, and Interior Secretary James R. Garfield to set up programs to enhance the environment. He sought passage of a law creating five new national parks and signed the Antiquities Act (1906), which established a number of new national monuments. The total amount of land this conservation president secured under national protection was about 230 million acres—including 150 million reserved forest lands. Some of the most passionate environmentalists were disappointed in Roosevelt's record, but his program angered conservative businessmen and those with land interests in the Western states. They felt that he was taking advantage of constitutional ambiguity about executive power and restricting economic freedom.

THEODORE ROOSEVELT: FOREIGN POLICY

From the 1890s, Theodore Roosevelt proudly accepted the mantle of imperialist. He wanted the U.S. to acquire overseas territory. He fought in Cuba to wrest that island from Spain and supported the acquisition of the Philippines. As the U.S. economy grew and extended its international reach, U.S. commercial and military involvement in foreign affairs was almost inevitable. At the same time, most Americans were isolationists, uncomfortable with the loss of the nation's moral statute if it became an imperialist power.

Roosevelt was primarily concerned with expanding U.S. influence and power projection. He helped broker the Treaty of Portsmouth (1905) between Russia and Japan, which ended their conflict. For that he received the Nobel Peace Prize.

But Roosevelt's obsession was in the Caribbean, particularly Panama—a politically restive province of Columbia. He wanted to build a shipping canal across the Isthmus of Panama. When Columbia rejected a treaty permitting the construction of the canal, Roosevelt signaled to Panamanian rebels that they had his support. U.S. backing and recognition was crucial to the outcome. In a treaty with the new Panama, the U.S. secured permission to construct the canal. Roosevelt's high-handed imperialist actions in the Panama affair won for him substantial criticism both in and out of the press.

THEODORE ROOSEVELT: LEGACY

Theodore Roosevelt bridged the gap between the nine-teenth-century paradigm of impassive chief executives and the so-called modern presidency. He placed the U.S. President at the center of national affairs and, because of his robust personality, made the president's character a key part of future presidential leadership. Nevertheless, his legacy was a decidedly mixed one. He has been consistently placed in the top rank of presidents by historians, but many observers admit to reservations.

He understood the value of public relations and maintained close connections with the media. The result was spectacular, consistent, and widespread popular support. His conservation initiatives laid the foundation for the modern environmental movement. His emphasis on corporate responsibility as demanded by public opinion foreshadowed the modified capitalist system and laid the groundwork for the liberal welfare state of the future. Corporations (trusts) were now expected to enter into a business–government partnership that sought the public good.

Perhaps the darkest part of Roosevelt's legacy was on the issue of race. African Americans, Native Americans, and Asian Americans all felt the sting of exclusion within white-dominated society, unfortunately beginning in the White House. The president demonstrated consistent support for segregation. He did little to challenge the prevailing white attitude toward blacks and, on the whole, supported social injustice as befitted the president presiding over the inauguration of the Age of Jim Crow.[1]

27

WILLIAM HOWARD TAFT

WILLIAM HOWARD TAFT: LIFE PAGE

Born: September 15, 1857, Cincinnati, Ohio

Education: Yale University, BA

University of Cincinnati, LLB

Vocation: Attorney

Married: Helen Herron, 1886

Sixth Solicitor General of the United States

Judge of the United States Court of Appeals of the 6th Circuit: 1892–1900

Governor General of the Philippines: 1901–1903

Provisional Governor of Cuba: 1906

Forty-second Secretary of War: 1904–1908

Twenty-seventh President of the United States: 1909–1913

Tenth Chief Justice of the United States: 1921–1930

Died: March 8, 1930

Additional resources available for this president at www.amomentintime.com.

WILLIAM HOWARD TAFT:
EARLY SERVICE

William Howard Taft was a sober; careful, if conservative, jurist; excellent administrator; cautious and successful bureaucrat; and loyal subordinate, but—as events later revealed—he demonstrated the validity of the Peter Principle.[1] Taft always achieved success within a structure set by those he served, but he was ill-equipped to lead a vast nation, particularly in times of acute political stress. Instead of being the zenith of his life's achievement, his single term as U.S. president was the nadir of an otherwise brilliant career.

Born to a prosperous, upper-class Ohio family, he sailed through his Yale education and legal training and embarked on a career as an attorney. He married well and, ironically, sought political office with less ambition than his wife, Helen, did. Taft served as U.S. Solicitor General then settled into service on the U.S. Appeals Court of the 6th Circuit.

In 1903, President Theodore Roosevelt nominated Taft to be Secretary of War and the two developed a close working relationship. Toward the end of Roosevelt's term, it became clear the president was going to fulfill his promise to not seek a second term. Taft was Roosevelt's candidate to succeed him. Taft was reluctant because his deep desire was service on the Supreme Court, but he was constitutionally incapable of resisting a call to duty issued by one so important in his life.

Everett Historical / Shutterstock.com

WILLIAM HOWARD TAFT: PARTY DISINTEGRATION

The Republican Party that had begun the Taft era united, and with high expectations, was hopelessly divided as the 1912 election approached. The party divisions were complicated by the gradual worsening of the relationship between President Taft and his predecessor. Theodore Roosevelt had spent the first fifteen months of the Taft presidency out of the country. When he returned, the former comradery was gone, replaced by a formal connection that bordered on the frosty.

In a series of speeches, Roosevelt articulated a New Nationalism, a shift leftward in his thinking. He condemned corporate campaign contributions seeking transparency in campaign outlays and advocated regulation of corporations, a commission to set export tariffs, workman's compensation, and a progressive income tax. Taft considered Roosevelt's New Nationalist program to be ill-advised and began to move in a more conservative direction.

It was clear that Roosevelt was moving toward challenging Taft for the Republican nomination. He ran in the primaries and carried most of the delegates, but Taft controlled the Party apparatus and, in the end, triumphed. Roosevelt accused Taft and the Party of "stealing" the nomination. He and his followers bolted from the Republicans and formed the Progressive Party, virtually guaranteeing Taft would be a one-term president.

WILLIAM HOWARD TAFT: DEFEAT AND SERVICE AS CHIEF JUSTICE

By the beginning of the election season of 1912, President William Howard Taft was resigned to the fact that he was going to lose. Badly. Unwilling to step aside for Theodore Roosevelt, he doomed his party to defeat and himself to the most inglorious and profound rejection of an incumbent president in U.S. history. He made a single speech during the campaign. His opponents—Democrat Woodrow Wilson and former President Roosevelt—virtually ignored the president and contested the election on a variety of issues within the progressive agenda.

The results of the election were predictable. Taft won only two states for a total of eight votes. Roosevelt won eighty-eight. Wilson triumphed with 435 votes. Taft quietly left Washington and took a position as Kent Professor of Law and Legal History at Yale University Law School.

Taft remained active in public affairs and was supportive of President Woodrow Wilson's foreign policy, the war effort (during which he led the American Red Cross), and President Wilson's concept of a post-war international organization to enhance dialogue and peace efforts—the League of Nations. In 1921, President Warren G. Harding nominated him to be Chief Justice of the Supreme Court, realizing one of Taft's life-long goals. Taft helped modernize and bring efficiency to the American judiciary and lobbied for the Court to have its own building. He had hoped to lead the Court to its new headquarters, but he died before construction was completed in 1935.

WILLIAM HOWARD TAFT: LEGACY

Considering his lack of ebullience as compared to his predecessor, one historian has described William Howard Taft as "boring—honest, likable, but boring." By the time Taft took office, Americans hungered for a president who led through a combination of character, intellect, and accessible personality. Undoubtedly in possession of the first two, he decidedly lacked the third. He did not like electoral politics and this rendered his term of office largely a failure, because he was simply not cut out for the role of president. In the view of his opponents, Taft was lethargic, much too tied to legalisms, and hesitant to act as a strong, assertive president.

Taft acquiesced in the face of the prevailing racist bias of white Americas and led the Republican Party to continue abandoning its traditional role as defender of African American rights. He refused to appoint blacks to federal positions, such as postmaster, which would arouse white hostility in the South and also to few such positions in the North. This continued the deterioration of relations between his party and the black community, which in later decades would intensify the drift of African Americans toward the Democrats.

During his time as an effective and beloved Chief Justice, Taft's health was declining. He was addressing his obesity with exercise and diet and brought his weight down to manageable proportions, but to no avail. He also began to experience some mental deterioration. William Howard Taft resigned from the Court on February 3, 1930, and died on March 8.

28

WOODROW WILSON

WOODROW WILSON: LIFE PAGE

Born: December 28, 1856, Staunton, Virginia

Education:

Davidson College

College of New Jersey (Princeton)

University of Virginia

Johns Hopkins University, PhD

Vocation: Academic and Politician

Married: Ellen Axson, 1885; she died in 1914

       Edith Bolling, 1915

Professor: Bryn Mawr College: 1885–1888

       Wesleyan University: 1888–1890

       Princeton University: 1890–1902

President, Princeton University: 1902–1910

Governor of New Jersey: 1911–1913

Twenty-eighth President of the United States: 1913–1921

Died: February 3, 1924

Additional resources available for this president at www.amomentintime.com.

WOODROW WILSON: ACADEMIC CAREER AND NEW JERSEY GOVERNOR

Wilson was attracted to the life of the mind and attended Davidson College, the College of New Jersey (Princeton), University of Virginia Law School, and Johns Hopkins University. Wilson was fascinated with the British parliamentary system and, while finishing his PhD at Hopkins, published a well-received examination of U.S. constitutional structures in *Parliamentary Government: A Study in American Politics* (1885). Wilson taught at Bryn Mawr, Weslyan, and Princeton before being elected President of Princeton University in 1902.

While at Princeton, he established academic departments and significant reforms in both curriculum and pedagogy. Students were weekly required to meet in groups of six with teaching assistants called preceptors.

Blocked from enacting key parts of his University program, he moved into politics. He was elected Governor of New Jersey and there demonstrated a strong inclination toward rectitude and political independence. After passage of a strong anti-corruption measure, workman's compensation, and the institution of primaries for all elective offices, the name Wilson was on the lips of Democratic leaders across the country, and the seeds of a national campaign had been planted.

WOODROW WILSON: ELECTION OF 1912

The election of 1912 fielded one of the most impressive group of candidates in American history. With the Democrats requiring a two-thirds majority vote for nomination, Wilson won on the forty-second ballot after besting House Speaker Champ Clark and House Majority leader Oscar Underwood. Clark and Wilson had scored heavily in primaries, but they did not have a majority of delegates. With Clark ahead, he announced the support of New York's political machine, Tammany Hall. At that point, perennial candidate William Jennings Bryan withdrew his support from anyone having Tammany backing, and delegates began stampeding toward Wilson. Southerners joined the trend with support for Wilson, the transplanted son of the South, and Wilson won.

Wilson and Roosevelt campaigned vigorously coast-to-coast. Despite their sharing similar progressive inclinations, the two battled it out on the particulars of the reformist platforms. Wilson prevailed with 42 percent of the popular vote and an enormous Electoral College majority (435 of 531). Roosevelt, William Howard Taft, and Debs followed in succession. Roosevelt's third-party challenge was the strongest in American history. The Democrats retained the House and won the Senate. Woodrow Wilson became the first Democrat since Grover Cleveland to win the White House and the first native Southerner to do so since Zachary Taylor—long before the Civil War.

WOODROW WILSON:
NEW FREEDOM AGENDA-I

In terms of sheer legislative accomplishment, the first two years of Wilson's presidency would only be equaled by Franklin D. Roosevelt and Lyndon B. Johnson. With an aroused Democratic Congress, Wilson plowed through the statutory process with a platform known as the New Freedom. He had four major domestic programs: conservation, reigning in the banks, reducing tariffs, and regulating corporations.

Republicans were strong advocates of high tariffs until the modern era. Democrats, dominated by Southern and western agricultural interests, detested tariffs. They were helped by the passage of the Sixteenth Amendment, which overcame Supreme Court objections and permitted the imposition of a tax on income. The result was the Revenue (Underwood) Act of 1913. Believing that high tariffs were a government-imposed instrument benefitting special interests and damaging those of consumers, Wilson and the Democratic congress had reduced tariffs for the first time since the Civil War and also passed a tax on all incomes above three thousand dollars per year. By the 1920s, federal revenue would largely come from direct taxation rather than from the indirect tax coming from tariffs.

Not since Andrew Jackson's assault on Nicholas Biddle and the Bank of the United States in the 1830s had the U.S. attempted to regulate the banking industry with a central bank. Led by Congressman Carter Glass, the House and, following it, the Senate approved the Federal Reserve Act. The new arrangement went into effect in 1915.

WOODROW WILSON:
NEW FREEDOM AGENDA-II

Wilson began with banking reform and lowered tariffs. He and Congress then turned to corporate regulation by strengthening the Sherman Antitrust Act, so as to prohibit anti-competitive practices such as unfair pricing, tying and exclusive dealing,[1] and interlocking corporate boards. The problem is that businesses are very clever and eliminating all anti-fair-trade exercises requires constant vigilance. Therefore, Wilson pushed for a new organization, the Federal Trade Commission, empowered to guard against anti-trust activities and enforce anti-trust regulations.

Woodrow Wilson's first two years were a stunning success, but the president's re-election was very much in doubt. The Republicans re-united and nominated the talented attorney and well-respected former New York Governor Charles Evans Hughes. To bolster his prospects, in 1916 Wilson appointed Louis D. Brandeis, a renowned liberal and the first justice of the Jewish faith, to the Supreme Court; secured passage of the Keating-Owen bill, which restricted child labor; intervened in a bitter railroad strike and brought it to an end by securing eight-hour workdays for railroad workers; and obtained a federal workman's compensation law and a tax law slanted heavily against large corporations and the rich.

WOODROW WILSON:
NEW FREEDOM AGENDA-III

President Wilson's chances may have been helped by the pleasant transformation in his personal life. Since their marriage in 1885, he had been deeply devoted to his wife Ellen Axon Wilson. The marriage had hit emotional shoals in 1906 when they were on a Bermuda vacation and Wilson met socialite Mary Hulbert Peck; he began a friendship with her that probably had romantic aspects. They weathered that storm, but soon after he became president in 1913, Ellen's health began a steady deterioration. In 1914, she died of what was then called Bright's disease, a sickness of the kidney. Wilson went into a long period of depression—even though in this period he was achieving his breakthrough program of legislation. He began to emerge from this melancholy when he met, pursued, and—despite a bumpy courtship—married Edith Bolling Galt, a widow also from the South. They were married in December 1915. She became his most trusted advisor. His energy restored, he tackled the problem of re-election.

The question remained: Would this second burst of New Freedom reform fervor make Wilson a two-term president?

WOODROW WILSON:
RACIAL INCLINATION·I

Born in the South, Wilson absorbed the social strictures of the antebellum southland early in life. As he matured, he carried those memories and racist tendencies into the personal and professional arena. As President of Princeton, he exhibited an odd juxtaposition of social attitudes. He sought to undermine the influence of the social elite by doing away with the upper-class eating clubs. At the same time, Wilson actively worked to deny blacks admission to the university.

Almost immediately after Wilson entered the White House, he considered the suggestion of Postmaster General Albert Burleson that Wilson segregate the entire federal government. Stung by black criticism and that of liberal Northern newspapers, he relented at first, but then permitted individual department heads to proceed to institute apartheid in their bureaus. Soon the heavy hand of racial separation was felt all over the government—including the Navy, which theretofore had not been segregated.

During World War I, Wilson drafted thousands of blacks into the Army and gave them pay equal to whites, but he separated them into black units with white officers. Outbreaks of race rioting and lynchings directed against African Americans by angry whites broke out all over the North. Wilson forcefully denounced the lynchings, but he refused to send troops to break up white rioters and protect the blacks.

WOODROW WILSON:
RACIAL INCLINATION-II

In response to a request by Thomas Dixon Jr., one of Wilson's classmates at Johns Hopkins, the president permitted the screening at the White House of D. W. Griffith's film *The Birth of a Nation* (1915). The film was cinematically superior but was a racially biased glorification of the Ku Klux Klan during Reconstruction and justified white suppression of black voting rights. Griffith used several Wilson quotes as intertitles in the silent film. Some historians assert that Wilson affirmed the basic narrative of the film. Others assert that the president felt betrayed by Dixon and Griffith. The White House issued a statement denying any approval of the plot. Wilson tried to limit the film's distribution during the Great War, but he never repudiated the sentiments expressed in his writings that the filmmaker used in the movie.

Wilson, like most of the whites of his generation—from both North and South—believed blacks were intellectually inferior, incapable of equal participation with whites in a democratic society. He was a white supremacist and a principled segregationist who believed American apartheid reduced friction between the races. Keeping blacks separate protected them from whites who sought to do them harm. This was the age of Jim Crow.[2] When representatives of the black community criticized his policies in the White House to his face, he practically threw them out. Wilson was unwilling to attack racial bias in the white majority, and he was incapable of challenging it in himself.

WOODROW WILSON: POLICY OF NEUTRALITY AND NARROW RE-ELECTION

Strongly supported by Secretary of State William Jennings Bryan, President Wilson pursued a policy of neutrality between the Allied and Central Powers—who, since late 1914, had been bogged down in slow grinding trench warfare in northeastern France. The U.S. wanted to trade with both sets of antagonists as a sign of its neutral stance, but Wilson had to acquiesce in the reality of the British blockade and did little direct trade with Germany and its allies.

To counter the British blockade, Germany began a deadly submarine operation against allied merchant shipping. Despite Wilson's reticent response, Bryan believed Wilson was preparing the nation for war. He thought he could see the direction U.S. policy was headed and resigned. The president then began to move in the direction of those who favored war against Germany, such as Theodore Roosevelt. He adopted a policy of "preparedness" and began building up the Army and the Navy.

All of this was in the run-up to the election of 1916.[3] Wilson ran on the slogan "He Kept Us Out of War." This, plus his burst of reform legislation, denied to his opponent, Charles Evans Hughes, the campaign hook on which to hang Wilson. Wilson won re-election by a narrow popular majority (49.2 percent to 46.1 percent) and an equally narrow victory in the Electoral College (277 to 254).

WOODROW WILSON:
WORLD WAR I

Having won re-election on the slogan "He Kept Us Out of War," Wilson took the nation to war within a month of his second inauguration. The previous January, Germany renewed unrestricted submarine warfare and began sinking American ships. Germany then encouraged Mexico to join with Germany and declare war on the United States. In response to national outrage, Wilson asked Congress to declare war on Germany. Congress complied with strong majorities from both parties on April 6, 1917. Using recruitment and conscription, by the end of the war the U.S. armed forces had over three million men in uniform.

In the meantime, the stalemate on the French front had shifted in Germany's favor in March 1918. Russia was out of the war and this allowed Germany to shift hundreds of thousands of troops to France. Unfortunately for Germany, the allied lines held—though pressed—and by the middle of 1918 more than ten thousand Americans per day—led by General John J. Pershing—were landing in France.

In late summer, the allies, bolstered by U.S. forces, were on the offensive, hammering the exhausted German Army and defeating it at such battles as Belleau Wood and Château-Thierry. At the end of September, Germany sued for peace. After some reluctance and under considerable pressure from the U.S., France and Britain agreed and the Western war ended on November 11, 1918.

WOODROW WILSON: ESPIONAGE ACT AND SEDITION ACT

During the war, Wilson exercised brilliant organizational leadership. He assembled a "War Cabinet" that met with him weekly to consolidate war planning in the arenas of industry, food, fuel, and trade. To finance the U.S. military build-up and fund large loans to keep the British and French economies afloat, the federal budget exploded. It grew from one billion dollars to nineteen billion dollars in fiscal years 1916 to 1919—an enormous increase. To pay for this surge and keep inflation under control, Congress increased taxes and issued low-interest war bonds, but speculation in bond sales guaranteed that the struggle against inflation was only moderately successful.

To maintain enthusiasm for the war effort, the U.S. engaged in vigorous anti-German propaganda led by the Committee on Public Information. Suppressing anti-war sentiment and agitation was the goal as Congress passed the Espionage Act (1917) and the Sedition Act (1918). Those groups who engaged in anti-war activities—communists, anarchists, and others—were targeted for arrest and imprisonment. After the imprisonment for sedition of Socialist leader and presidential candidate Eugene V. Debs, public opinion began to turn against the administration. For many Americans, it was necessary to build a defense against such violations of free speech traditions. To that end, the American Civil Liberties Union was formed in 1917.

WOODROW WILSON:
PARIS PEACE CONFERENCE
AND TREATY OF VERSAILLES

After extensive preparation by a group of advisors in an effort known as the "Inquiry," President Wilson delivered an important articulation of U.S. post-war aims to Congress. Wilson's speech was known as the Fourteen Points. He called for the elimination of secret treaties, disarmament, freedom of the seas, free trade, an independent Poland, openness to native participation in the government of colonial states, and self-determination of peoples in Austria–Hungary, the Balkans, and areas previously ruled by the Ottoman Empire.

Unfortunately, Wilson had left his progressive coalition untended and this led to the destruction of his post-war dreams. The Republicans ran a super-patriotic, ultra-conservative campaign and triumphed in the 1918 mid-terms.

Secondly, either through carelessness, stubbornness, or bad judgement, Wilson failed to include important Republican senators or even allied Democratic senators in the U.S. delegation to the Paris Conference. These two factors proved to be fatal and probably indicated that Wilson's normally acute political shrewdness was in decline.

WOODROW WILSON: BATTLE OVER THE LEAGUE

Wilson was convinced that though the Treaty of Versailles (1919) was flawed, in it lay the seeds of redemption. The key to correcting the defects in the Treaty regime was the League of Nations. If he could secure passage of the Treaty and gain U.S. participation in the League, perhaps the injustices of Versailles could be rectified. His problem was that ratification required a two-thirds majority in the Senate. At this point, Wilson's mistakes of the previous year came home to haunt him.

Wilson had on his side former President William Howard Taft, former Secretary of State Elihu Root, and most of the Democrats. Among the resistance were the "irreconcilables," those opposed to U.S. participation in the League under any circumstance. Then there were those who were uncomfortable with giving up too much national sovereignty to what would be an international organization. They were willing to accept the Treaty, but with certain reservations designed to protect U.S. independence.

Wilson firmly rejected any reservations and set out on an eight-thousand–mile cross-country quest to win the support of the people. It was a Herculean effort to rescue his vision of a mighty League, which he believed under U.S. leadership would usher in a new era of justice and peace. By the time he reached Pueblo, Colorado, he was near physical collapse. Wilson's doctor called a halt to the trip and rushed him back to Washington to rest and recuperate. It was almost too late.

WOODROW WILSON:
STROKE AND INCAPACITY

On October 2, 1919, Woodrow Wilson suffered a severe, near fatal stroke. He was found unconscious on the floor of his private bathroom in the White House. He was paralyzed on his left side and had lost most of the vision in his right eye. His wife, Edith; aide, Joseph Patrick Tumulty; and doctor, Cary Grayson, kept him isolated, feeding him only selected documents and preventing only select people from connecting with him.

The implications of his incapacity for government operations, future plans, and above all the ratification of the Versailles Treaty (1919) and the accompanying League of Nations Covenant were profound. Some have asserted that by being the conduit through which information flowed to and from the president, Edith Bolling Wilson was the "first female president;" but in reality she was simply the keeper of the body. The real business of the U.S. government was conducted by the heads of departments, as appropriate.

As Woodrow Wilson lay in the White House, isolated and incapacitated, the effort to ratify the Peace Treaty reached a climax. Faced with the choice of passage with reservations, Wilson—whose judgement was probably rendered defective by the aftermath of the stroke—refused any compromise and the Treaty failed.

WOODROW WILSON: LEGACY

Since 1900, the transformation of America into the modern economic and geo-political powerhouse it is today has proceeded with breath-taking rapidity. Several presidents have accelerated this process. Theodore and Franklin D. Roosevelt, Lyndon B. Johnson, Barack Obama, and Woodrow Wilson are at the top of the list. Wilson, often aided by Democratic congressional majorities, made important changes in the relationship between the federal government and those mediating institutions that stand between individuals and Washington. He helped bring rationality to the nation's economic structure through the Federal Reserve, freer trade through reduction of protective tariffs, and the imposition of an income tax to secure a permanent stream of revenue to support government activities.

Perhaps due to his Southern origins, Wilson had a less than salutary record on race relations.[4] He looked the other way when whites engaged in riots directed at black Americans. While this is negative to our modern ears, perhaps Wilson's biggest disappointment was his failure to nurture his progressive political coalition that returned him to the White House in 1916—losing him the debate on the League of Nations.

Despite his failures, observers continue to rank Wilson high among American Presidents. He accomplished so much, only to stumble in the end. Shortly before leaving the White House, still hobbled by the stroke that cut him down, he spoke of his sense of failure to historian William E. Dodd, "What more could I have done?" Actually, he did a lot.

29

WARREN G. HARDING

WARREN G. HARDING: LIFE PAGE

Born: November 2, 1865, Blooming Grove, Ohio

Education: Ohio Central College

Vocation: Journalist, Newspaper Editor

Married: Florence Kling, 1891

Ohio State Senator: 1900–1904

Twenty-eighth Lieutenant Governor of Ohio: 1904–1906

United States Senator: 1915–1921

Twenty-ninth President of the United States:1921–1923

Died: August 2, 1923, San Francisco, California

Additional resources available for this president at www.amomentintime.com.

WARREN G. HARDING:
ELECTION AND APPOINTMENTS

Warren G. Harding grew up in small-town Ohio and made his reputation as a small-town newspaper editor. Harding leveraged the circulation and revenue from his newspaper to build support at home and within Ohio Republican circles.

After a single term as Lieutenant Governor, Harding returned to private life but continued to pursue higher office, eventually securing election as a U.S. senator. Here, Harding revealed his passive tendency to follow rather than lead. He was a skeptic on women's suffrage until it was clear the Nineteenth Amendment would pass; then he supported it wholeheartedly. He was a drinker and was hesitant in his support for Prohibition; but when its passage was assured, he voted to override President Woodrow Wilson's veto of the enforcement mechanism in the Volstead Act.

Since early in his Ohio Senate days, Harding's close friend, political manager, and factotum had been Harry M. Daugherty. As Harding began to circle in on the Republican nomination in 1920, Daugherty calculated that the leading candidates would cancel each other out—leaving a slim but real chance for Harding to secure the nomination. The early votes at the Chicago Coliseum revealed the brilliance of Daugherty's calculation. By the tenth ballot, Harding had his prize. In November, the voters endorsed Harding, giving him 60.2 percent of the popular vote—the largest in U.S. history to that date—and 404 votes in the Electoral College.[1]

WARREN G. HARDING: SCANDAL—
CARRIE PHILLIPS AND NAN BRITTON

Warren and Florence Harding were married in 1891. A divorcee, she pursued the young newspaper editor after she returned home at the end of her marriage. Florence, whom he called "The Dutchess," was a full-partner in the family enterprises and helped turn the *Marion Star* into a prosperous company. They had no children.

Sometime after the turn of the century, Harding began a decade-and-a-half affair with Carrie Fulton Phillips, a resident of Marion. Some historians have concluded, from examination of letters between the future president and Phillips, that their relationship was intimate and sexual. The affair was over by 1920, but the president did not seem to be sexually content, even in the White House.

In 1927, another resident of Marion, Nan Britton, published a salacious book, *The President's Daughter*, which described a torrid affair with Harding. Britton's allegations that Harding was the father of her daughter, Elizabeth Ann Blaesing, were not universally accepted. She had no records of the child-support transactions and had destroyed their love letters at his request. The Harding family countered that the president was sterile and incapable of fathering a child, having suffered mumps when he was young. In 1915, ancestry.com compared DNA samples from the Harding and Blaesing families and concluded a strong possibility that Harding was Elizabeth's father.

WARREN G. HARDING:
SCANDAL — VETERANS BUREAU

At the conclusion of World War One, there were over three-hundred thousand wounded and disabled American veterans who required government assistance with health care, hospitals, and learning job skills. To address this need, in August 1921 Congress created the Veterans' Bureau (since becoming the Cabinet-level Department of Veterans' Affairs). President Harding then appointed his old friend Charles Robert Forbes to head this enormous enterprise. Within two years, the president found that Forbes was using the Veterans' Bureau as his personal bank account and demanded his resignation. Forbes refused to obey and continued the swindle. During his tenure at Veterans', he embezzled about two million dollars.

When President Harding found out that Forbes was still at it, he called him in and asked for his resignation. He let him flee to Europe, from where he resigned on February 15, 1923. The Senate launched an investigation in March. When Forbes returned, he called on President Harding at the White House. The enraged six-foot tall President seized him by the neck and shook him "as a dog would a rat," shouting, "you double-crossing bastard." Forbes testified to senators, but few believed his story. He was indicted and served nearly two years in prison.

The tragedy of this affair was that Harding's fury arose not from Forbes's abuse of the public trust, nor for this travesty of justice, nor from this theft of funds intended for veterans, but because it would be politically embarrassing to the president.

WARREN G. HARDING:
SCANDAL—TEAPOT DOME

The United States created three major oil reserves—giant deposits of crude oil in the ground—specifically for use by the Navy in times of national emergency. One such reserve in Wyoming was the Teapot Dome.

For some time there had been debate as to whether these buried oil reserves should be developed—drilled, brought to the surface, and sold. In 1921, Interior Secretary Albert Bacon Fall began advocating development of the oil reserves, and, acquiescing, President Harding transferred control of the oil reserves from the Navy Department to Interior. Whether or not Fall lobbied for this change so as to profit from it, he certainly came quickly to realize a real opportunity. His two co-conspirators were Harry F. Sinclair, who was given rights of production in the Teapot Dome, and Edward L. Doheny, whose company got the Elk Hills reserve in California. The lease terms were structured to benefit Fall's accomplices at very generous terms. In turn, Doheny gave Fall a $100,000 interest-free "loan" and Doheny and Sinclair gifted their favorite Cabinet member with over $400,000.

Inevitably rumors of this corrupt dealing began to leak out. In mid-April 1922, *The Wall Street Journal* broke the story of a stunning bribery scheme involving oil leases, and the U.S. Senate began an investigation in the Committee on Public Lands. Criminal proceedings eventually landed Fall and Sinclair in jail. Even though the full extent of this scandal broke after Harding's death, his reputation suffered as it confirmed the president's unfortunately poor ability to select competent and honest subordinates.

WARREN G. HARDING:
SCANDAL–JUSTICE DEPARTMENT

In 1920, Harry M. Daugherty and his long-time friend and associate Jesse W. Smith helped put together Warren Harding's nomination and general campaign for the presidency. When Harding made Daugherty Attorney General, Smith came along and was given an ill-defined but influential portfolio at the Justice Department.

As the Teapot Dome scandal was breaking, Smith was selling his influence with the Attorney General to bootleggers who desired protection from prosecution. He was also "liberating" stored government liquor and selling it to crooked alcohol distributors. He and Daugherty split the proceeds of these sales. One of Smith's most notorious scams was to aid in the transfer of the American Metal Company, owned by a German firm, to a group of U.S. investors. Smith was abetted in the scheme by ex-congressman Thomas W. Miller. The two received a half-million-dollar payoff in which, of course, Daugherty participated.

President Harding became aware of Smith's fraudulent operations and ordered Daugherty to get him out of Washington. Smith did not leave Washington, but on the night of May 30, 1923, he was shot in an apparent suicide—though the conditions of his demise attributed his death to more sinister circumstances.

Daugherty and Miller were indicted and twice tried for defrauding the U.S. Miller was convicted in the second trial and served time. Daugherty avoided conviction, but his refusal to defend himself on the stand ruined his political standing. He returned to his legal practice, defiant to the end, forcefully asserting his integrity to increasingly deaf ears.

WARREN G. HARDING: LEGACY

Warren Harding rode to the White House on a wave of euphoria. His call for a return to "normalcy" resonated with an American electorate anxious to move into a new century of promise. He won by an unambiguous number in the Electoral College and the largest popular vote (60.2 percent) in presidential history to that point. Yet at the time of his death, the scandals that engulfed his presidency would destroy his reputation. He is uniformly ranked as the worst president in U.S. history.

Harding's great problem was the marked contrast between his appointments to high office. On one hand, those he chose to run State, Commerce, and Treasury were superb. On the other was the group of associates he brought with him when he inherited the Oval Office—the infamous "Ohio Gang."

There is no evidence that the president personally participated in or profited from their schemes. Harding's tragic legacy is of a man whose flawed personal life carried over into his choice of friends. He gave great responsibility to people undeserving of his trust—or that of the nation.

In summer 1923, as the heart of his presidency was crumbling around him, he left for a long journey to the West Coast and Alaska. He died of a heart attack in San Francisco, knowing that many of his associates had betrayed his trust, sullied his reputation, and brought shame to the nation.

CALVIN COOLIDGE

CALVIN COOLIDGE: LIFE PAGE

Born: July 4, 1872, Plymouth Notch, Vermont

Education: Amhurst College

Vocation: Attorney and Politician

Marriage: Grace Goodhue, 1905

Member, Massachusetts House of Representatives: 1907–1908

Mayor: Northhampton, Massachusetts, 1910–1911

Member, Massachusetts Senate: 1912–1915

Twenty-Sixth Lieutenant Governor of Massachusetts: 1916–1919

Forty-Eighth Governor of Massachusetts: 1919–1921

Twenty-Ninth Vice President of the United States: 1921–1923

Thirtieth President of the United States: 1923–1929

Died: January 5, 1933, Northampton, Massachusetts

Additional resources available for this president at www.amomentintime.com.

CALVIN COOLIDGE:
MASSACHUSETTS POLITICIAN

After graduation, Calvin Coolidge moved to Northhampton, Massachusetts, where he read for the law; after a short time in private practice as a commercial litigant, he began his political career. For his entire adult life, he suckled at the public trough in one political position after another. He served on local boards, in the Massachusetts legislature, and as lieutenant governor while continuing his law practice. In 1918 and 1919, he was elected governor of Massachusetts.

Perhaps the only positive action he took as a state politician was his pivotal action in the face of the Boston Police Strike of 1919. Boston policemen worked long hours in appalling working conditions. To improve their situation, they sought to organize as a union. The Boston police commissioner refused to recognize the union and most of the police force went out on strike. The city degenerated into chaos, rioting, and violence. At that point, Governor Coolidge intervened and sent additional units of the National Guard. Coolidge's decisive action and bold advocacy of law and order caused his national reputation to sky-rocket, and conservatives nationwide had found a new champion.

When the Republican National Convention in 1920 finished nominating the imminently ill-qualified Warren Harding for president, they chose for vice president someone Harding did not want but who all parts of the divided party could accept: Calvin Coolidge.

CALVIN COOLIDGE:
SILENT CAL AND ELECTION

Calvin Coolidge had a naturally retiring personality, but when he stepped onto the national stage he gained the reputation for extreme reticence that alternately captivated and entertained the nation. Soon "Silent Cal" stories were the rage in 1920's Washington society. Social and political etiquette required that he and the ebullient Grace go to endless dinner parties. There, he often remained mute, absorbing, learning, and perhaps enjoying the conversations eddying around him. In one perhaps legendary story, a social doyenne seated beside him told him that she had made a bet that she could make him say more than two words during dinner. To which he replied, "You lose." Whether an elaborate political cultivation or just a reflection of his natural reserve acerbated by sorrow following the death of his youngest son, the reputation of Silent Cal Coolidge entered the pantheon of presidential idiosyncrasies.

After the death of President Warren Harding, the stoic, near-puritanical President Coolidge, whose veracity was irreproachable, walked the nation through the healing process. First, he guided Americans through their mourning at the loss of a truly popular leader. Then, as their appreciation of Harding began to melt away in the face of multiple scandals, Coolidge quickly moved to clean up the mess Harding left behind. In 1924, President Coolidge was nominated by acclamation and led the Republicans to a sweeping victory.

CALVIN COOLIDGE:
DOMESTIC AND FOREIGN POLICY

In office, President Coolidge, consistent with his small government philosophy, slept a great deal and did as little as possible. His only really important pieces of legislation were Revenue Acts (1924, 1926, 1926). These and subsequent corporate tax reductions fulfilled the president's belief that low taxes on the wealthy and reduced government regulation would bring prosperity. For a while, his views seemed to be wise. By the end of his term, the wealthy were almost completely relieved of taxation.

After taking office, he vetoed a bonus to help World War I veterans adjust to peace-time. Congress overrode. He twice vetoed an attempt to help suffering in the farm belt, saying that farms should be run like businesses and that farmers should work their way through price downturns like everyone else. Coolidge's reaction to the Great Mississippi Flood of 1927 was just as frugal.

On race relations, Coolidge accommodated the Republican Party's drift away from its traditional support for African American rights in order to gain the votes of Southern white supremacists. He made rhetorical gestures about black rights in his first speech to Congress but took no actions to bolster their circumstances. While other candidates in 1924 vigorously denounced the resurgent Ku Klux Klan, Silent Cal was utterly silent.

Coolidge knew nothing about foreign policy and did even less, leaving the arena to his subordinates.

CALVIN COOLIDGE: LEGACY

When he received word of President Warren Harding's untimely death in July 1923, Calvin Coolidge took the presidential oath from his justice-of-the-peace father at 2:47 a.m. and then went back to bed. Such apathetic behavior at an event of that import reveals something of the character of the man America came to admire and appreciate. The conclusion of his political career was equally as phlegmatic. While on vacation in 1927, he summoned reporters, lined them up, and handed each in attendance a slip of paper. The message: "I choose not to run for president in 1928."

Within seven months of his departure from the White House, the nation suffered a gigantic stock market crash, the worst economic contraction in U.S. history, and began the long painful decline into the Great Depression. As a result, Silent Cal's reputation and popularity received a well-deserved shock. Most observers have counted Coolidge among the worst presidents.

Four days before his death in 1933, he penned his final thoughts on the state of the Union. With America at the nadir of the greatest downturn in U.S. history, he could not even speak words of comfort into the gloom, writing "in other times of depression it has always been possible to see some things that were solid . . . but . . . I now see nothing to give ground for hope." Fortunately, at that time there was a man elected but not yet in office who understood the people's fear and could speak hope to their despair.

31

HERBERT HOOVER

HERBERT HOOVER: LIFE PAGE

Born: August 10, 1874, West Branch, Iowa

Education: George Fox University

Stanford University, BS

Married: Lou Henry, 1899

Vocation: Geologist and Mining Engineer

Director of United States Food Administration: 1917–1918

Third United States Secretary of Commerce: 1921–1928

Thirty-First President of the United States: 1929–1933

Chairman, Commission on Organization of the Executive Branch of the Government: 1947–1949 and 1953–1955

Died: October 20, 1964, New York City, New York

Additional resources available for this president at www.amomentintime.com.

HERBERT HOOVER:
ENGINEER AND HUMANITARIAN

Few presidents have been as professionally or intellectually as prepared for the White House as Herbert Clark Hoover. Born to a middle-class Iowa Quaker family, young Bertie developed those small-town moral values of religion, generosity, thrift, self-reliance, and rugged individualism that he carried throughout his professional life. He was one of the first students at Leland Stanford's new university in Palo Alto, California. There he met and courted his future wife, the talented Lou Henry, who shared his passion for geology.

Graduation during the Panic of 1893 meant employment was hard to come by, but his geological and engineering skills took him into gold and mineral mining in the U.S., Australia, and China. By the start of World War I, he was a very wealthy man, but not one insensitive to society's needs.

Consistent with the service inclination of the Quakers, Hoover believed that from those who have much, much is expected. He became perhaps the world's most noted humanitarian, directing wartime food distribution in Belgium, America, Eastern Europe, and the Soviet Union. He joined the U.S. delegation to the Versailles Peace Conference and then returned home to accept appointment as Presidents Warren Harding and Calvin Coolidge's Secretary of Commerce. When President Coolidge bowed out of the 1928 election, the Republicans turned to Herbert Clark Hoover.

HERBERT HOOVER:
ELECTION OF 1928

Under Secretary of Commerce Hoover, there emerged an unprecedented alliance between business and government. He had a record of success in both, and he worked hard to foster a voluntary relationship with commercial enterprises to help them succeed in the white-hot economy of the mid to late 1920s. The problem with Hoover was that he had no experience with electoral politics. He was an accomplished public servant, but he had never stood for office or understood the need for political sensitivities in the formulation of public policy. Hoover also benefitted from the absence of appealing alternatives.

So with some trepidation among party leaders and absent any real opposition, Hoover sailed to a July nomination at the Republican National Convention in Kansas City. At a huge rally at Stanford Stadium, he promised to continue the conservative policies of the Warren Harding and Calvin Coolidge administrations. His campaign against Democrat Alfred Emanuel Smith, the first Catholic nominated by a major party, was a spirited one—though Hoover was not a particularly inspiring speaker.

The Republican benefitted from, though he did not contribute to, a vicious anti-Catholic campaign in some religious communities. His party engaged in an unartfully disguised appeal to white supremacists in the South and carried normally Democratic states in that region: Florida, Texas, Virginia, North Carolina, and Tennessee. Hoover won the election with 58 percent of the popular vote and an overwhelming 444 votes in the Electoral College.

HERBERT HOOVER: STOCK MARKET CRASH AND GREAT DEPRESSION

Seven months after the president took the oath of office, the economic miracle that was the 1920s came to a resounding halt. On September 3, 1929, the Dow Jones Industrial Average reached its peak, riding a wave of speculation by many small investors who had borrowed on their savings in the false hope that the market always went up. The London Stock Market collapsed on September 20, which caused tremors in equity markets worldwide. This price contraction continued with only occasional reversals until July 8, 1932, when the market reached its lowest point in the twentieth century.

The decline of the stock market heralded the beginning of the twelve-year-long Great Depression. President Hoover was faced with what Theodore Roosevelt called the "great moment." He failed miserably.

Contrary to popular belief, President Hoover was not idle in the face of the deteriorating situation. However, the things Hoover tried were always hobbled by his fear that if the state intervened too much, it might stifle freedom and asphyxiate individual initiative. He tried to reassure an increasingly skeptical public of the nation's fundamental soundness. Yet, it was becoming painfully obvious that Herbert Hoover was out of his depth as unemployment rocketed from its low in 1929 (3 percent) to an astronomical 25 percent in 1932.

HERBERT HOOVER:
ECONOMIC EFFORTS, FOREIGN
POLICY, SMOOT-HAWLEY

As it became apparent that this downturn was far more serious than those that had proceeded it, President Hoover began to turn his talents to find a solution. He persuaded Congress to pass a tax cut to put more money in circulation. He expanded the Federal Land Banks and the Federal Farm Board to provide support for homeowners and farmers. He expanded government spending on public works, more than all previous presidents put together.

Then he made it worse: Congress passed and Hoover reluctantly signed the draconian Smoot-Hawley Tariff (1930). This prompted retaliatory duties by other countries, making it difficult for trade to help attenuate the deepening contraction. Smoot-Hawley is considered by economists to be one of the key causes of a long, deep depression.

Hoover revived a wartime financial measure and renamed it the Reconstruction Finance Corporation, which lent money to banks, railroads, insurance companies, and struggling businesses. Hoover called for businesses to retain workers and keep wages stable; he also encouraged people to be generous with those in need and many responded, but it was just not enough. One historian wrote that "it was like using a peashooter to stop a rhinoceros."

HERBERT HOOVER:
SINKING POPULARITY AND
ELECTION OF 1932

Despite everything he tried, the Depression deepened and people began to openly blame him for the nation's misfortune. Many of the impoverished were soon found to be living in makeshift shantytowns—which were famously called "Hoovervilles"—but the president refused to consider direct relief. When veterans descended on Washington in June 1932, demanding advance payment of the wartime bonus they had been promised in 1924, there were clashes with the Washington police in which two were killed. President Hoover set Army Chief of Staff General Douglas MacArthur on them and against Hoover's orders he attacked the camp and scattered the veterans.

Through it all, surrounded by a nation where people were cutting back on essentials and with destitution on the rise, each night—even when they dined alone—Herbert and Lou Hoover dressed in black tie and evening clothes and formally consumed seven-course meals.

Before it even began, the election of 1932 was over. Eggs, rotten fruit, and insults were hurled at his campaign train. The Democratic ticket of Franklin Roosevelt and John Nance Garner buried Herbert Hoover under a 58 percent popular majority—nearly twenty points under his 1928 total. In the Electoral College, Roosevelt's victory was even more decisive: 472 to 59.

HERBERT HOOVER: POST-PRESIDENCY AND LEGACY

Bitter at his loss, Herbert and Lou Hoover moved to New York and then to their home in Palo Alto. Not one to remain idle, Hoover helped form humanitarian groups to aid nations under Nazi control, but after Pearl Harbor, he was not called to help in the wartime effort because of his long-running political feud with President Franklin D. Roosevelt.

As candidate and president, he fostered the retreat of Republican support for the black community and compounded this racially explosive policy by turning the government against Hispanics as well. Falsely thinking them responsible in part for the economic downturn, he began deporting hundreds of thousands of innocent Mexicans, including many birthright American citizens.

For decades the Democratic Party made Herbert Hoover the villain in the tragedy that was the Great Depression, and in many ways his policies and persona invited this scorn. The limited scope of his vision, the hardness of his convictions (against government action), and his inability to convey empathic compassion toward a suffering nation meant that the same people who voted overwhelmingly for him in 1928 would turn against him. Hoover was incapable of addressing the nation's needs beyond the values he learned as a child-thrift, self-reliance, small government, and neighborliness. The world had left him behind.

32

FRANKLIN D. ROOSEVELT

FRANKLIN D. ROOSEVELT:
LIFE PAGE

Born: January 30, 1882, Hyde Park, New York

Education: Groton School

       Harvard University, BA

       Columbia University Law School

Married: Eleanor Roosevelt, 1905

Member, New York Senate: 1911–1913

Assistant Secretary of the Navy: 1913–1920

Governor of New York: 1929–1932

Thirty-Second President of the United States: 1933–1945

Died: April 12, 1945, Warm Springs, Georgia

Additional resources available for this president at www.amomentintime.com.

FRANKLIN D. ROOSEVELT:
EARLY LIFE AND MARRIAGE

Franklin Roosevelt was the scion of three wealthy aristocratic families (Roosevelt, Aspinwall, and Delano) who migrated early to New Amsterdam and Massachusetts and became affluent landowners by prospering in railroads, shipping, and coal investments. Graduating in 1903 from Groton School in Massachusetts, Roosevelt attended Columbia University Law School (no degree), passed the New York State Bar, and took a position with a prominent Wall Street law firm.

In the meantime, he met, courted, and married Eleanor Roosevelt, a distant cousin, in 1905. Eleanor, shy and already insecure, avoided the social and political scene in which Franklin excelled.

Eleanor's insecurities were intensified when it became clear that Franklin was a serial adulterer, something that was not acknowledged outside their tight circle of family intimates until after Eleanor's death in the 1960s. Early in their marriage, Eleanor found love letters from her former social secretary, Lucy Mercer, and confronted Roosevelt. She made him promise never to see Lucy again, but Franlin did not keep his promise. Their son Elliot claimed that Franklin also had a long affair with his private secretary, Marguerite "Missy" Lehand.

Eleanor never forgave him his infidelity, but they did hammer out brilliant separate lives and careers—one of the most significant political collaborations in U.S. history. Gradually esteem, deference, and mutual respect returned for the couple. Love never did.

FRANKLIN D. ROOSEVELT:
EARLY POLITICAL CAREER

Buried at the low end of a Wall Street law firm, Franklin Roosevelt found himself extremely bored. His inheritance meant that he did not need to work, but he did need an outlet for his restless energy and ebullient personality. He found it in politics. By 1910, he had won a seat in the state Senate.

In Albany, Roosevelt made a reputation as a progressive and was overwhelmingly re-elected in 1912. As Chair of the Agriculture Committee, he advanced legislation supportive of farmers and labor and burnished his progressive image by strengthening social programs benefiting women and children. In the momentous election of 1912, he supported New Jersey Governor Woodrow Wilson, and this led to Roosevelt's appointment as Assistant Secretary of the Navy.

After the declaration of war, Roosevelt tried to volunteer for fleet service, but Wilson insisted he remain at the Navy Department. To help manage the huge expansion of the Navy and then its demobilization after the Armistice.

With Wilson incapacitated by his stroke and his administration winding down, Roosevelt looked to his own political future. He let it be known that he was open to nomination by the Democratic Party for vice president in the 1920 election. The contest ended in a Republican sweep, but Roosevelt campaigned vigorously and made political allies for future use.

FRANKLIN D. ROOSEVELT:
POLIOMYELITIS

In August 1921, while vacationing at the family home on Campobello Island, Roosevelt began demonstrating symptoms of paralysis of the torso, face, and the digestive track. At the time, he was diagnosed with poliomyelitis; but in the years since, researchers have suggested that his symptoms are analogous to Guillain-Barré syndrome. This is an autoimmune disease that attacks the nervous system, often causing paralysis. Whatever the cause and despite all efforts, Franklin Roosevelt was soon completely paralyzed from his waist down and remained so for the balance of his life. When he returned to politics, he managed an extraordinary exercise in political prestidigitation. The press and fellow politicians—probably because they were in awe of what he was trying to accomplish—engaged in a gentlemen's agreement not to photograph him or in any way call attention to his disability. His energetic presentations and jovial manner distracted people from what should have been obvious, and his popularity soared.

His mother wanted him to retire from public life, but Eleanor and his political advisor, Louis McHenry Howe, insisted Roosevelt continue his rehabilitation but also keep his party connections well-tended. Al Smith convinced Roosevelt to run for New York governor in 1928, mostly to bolster Smith's own chances of carrying the state against Republican Herbert Hoover. Roosevelt reluctantly agreed and, after a spirited campaign in what was clearly to be a Republican year, he prevailed in a narrow victory (though Smith lost both nationally and even in New York).

FRANKLIN D. ROOSEVELT:
GOVERNOR OF NEW YORK–
PRESIDENTIAL APPRENTICESHIP

Because it was a Republican year, his 1928 election as governor was a closely held thing—he won but only by about 1 percent. Having proven his ability, his re-election in 1930 was a wipeout. In both terms, he demonstrated his inclination toward progressive politics. Roosevelt's first proposal was for cheaper power generation by means of government hydroelectric dams. This was just one of several projects designed to help farmers, many of whom took out loans to buy farming equipment to meet wartime demand and then found themselves over-extended with the collapse of said demand after the Armistice.

Roosevelt advocated a form of social security for older New Yorkers and unemployment insurance. In his second term,[1] he pushed through a program of government subsidies—the Temporary Emergency Relief Administration—for workers laid off after the collapse of the stock market in October 1929. In both his terms he correctly acted as though the economic crisis was far more serious than the sanguine predictions of President Herbert Hoover. This determination attracted national attention and slowly built support for his 1932 run for president.

Unlike the Hoover administration's seemingly feeble efforts to right the economic ship, Roosevelt took on the problems with an enthusiasm and zest that was infectious.

FRANKLIN D. ROOSEVELT: GREAT DEPRESSION AND ELECTION OF 1932

Franklin Roosevelt entered the 1932 election season in a strong position. The Great Depression had the nation's economy by the neck. Since 1929, the stock market was down by 83 percent, the national income was down by half, 25 percent of the workforce was unemployed, and crop prices were so low that farmers were burning their corn for warmth—that is, if they had not lost their land to foreclosure. The Hoover administration's attempts at arresting the decline were largely ineffectual. Private charities and public welfare programs were either exhausted or taxed way beyond their ability to help.

Roosevelt won the Democratic presidential nomination, and as the campaign continued, the contrast between the two presidential candidates could not have been more stark. Matched against the dour, much maligned President Herbert Hoover was the witty, charming, optimistic, electric personality of Franklin Roosevelt. Here was a man whom nature had dealt a severe physical blow, but who had risen, crutches and all, to summon a suffering nation to regain its hope and reclaim its future.

Roosevelt won the election of 1932 in a landslide. The election is considered by historians to be a classic realignment election,[2] joining 1800, 1828, 1860, and possibly 1896 as years in which American electoral politics was transformed from the period that proceeded it by circumstances or presidents. What President-elect Franklin Roosevelt would do with this mandate remained to be seen.

FRANKLIN D. ROOSEVELT: THE FIRST HUNDRED DAYS AND REPEAL OF PROHIBITION

In his inaugural address, Roosevelt built on his "New Deal" speech to the Democratic Convention by assuring Americans that their only real fear was "fear itself." Over the next several months, his resonant reassuring voice—often delivered over radio during his famed "fireside chats"—and his optimistic activism served to lift the spirits of the American people.

In the days leading up to the inauguration, the banking system approached collapse. On his second day in office, Roosevelt declared a bank holiday and called Congress into session. During the interim before the banks' re-opening, Congress passed the Emergency Banking Act based on a Hoover recovery administration plan. Roosevelt waved his optimistic political wand over the Act, and when the banks re-opened the panic seemed to evaporate.

Then came the famous hundred-day flood of federal legislation designed to flesh out Roosevelt's philosophy. He brought Prohibition to an end and proposed the Federal Emergency Relief Administration (FERA), which sent money to help sustain state governments; the Public Works Administration (PWA), which began construction on vital infrastructure projects (dams, roads, bridges, schools); the Civilian Conservation Corps (CCC), which employed 250,000 people to work on rural projects, such as the Blue Ridge Parkway. He strengthened the Reconstruction Finance Corporation to provided funding for railroads and industry.

FRANKLIN D. ROOSEVELT: NEW DEAL LEGISLATION

In the most productive period of legislative activity in U.S. history to that point, Franklin Roosevelt marshalled the forces of his administration and the congressional majority in an awe-inspiring, reassuring series of laws designed to lift America from the depths of despair and out of the economic contraction. The first hundred days were followed by a continued flow of laws that took the federal enterprise far deeper than ever before into state and local affairs and into the lives of citizens.

Did the New Deal help end the Great Depression? Some of the New Deal laws set up regulatory systems that only indirectly affected economic activity, but the Public Works Administration (PWA), the Civilian Conservation Corps (CCC), the National Industrial Recovery Act (NIRA), the Agricultural Adjustment Act (AAA), and the Bonus Act (which gave direct cash assistance to veterans), pumped the economy with the modern equivalent of billions of dollars and had an extremely stimulative effect. Unemployment fell precipitously in the first years of Roosevelt's presidency, rose slightly in 1938, and then fell dramatically in the war years. During his terms in office, the economy added over eighteen million jobs. Some have suggested that Roosevelt's programs were ineffective, that if he had done "little or nothing," the economy would have recovered anyway; but since Roosevelt, American institutions have almost never done "little or nothing" in the face of severe economic contraction.

FRANKLIN D. ROOSEVELT: SOCIAL SECURITY AND THE SECOND NEW DEAL

Typically mid-term elections go against the president and his party—but not in 1934. Voters that year increased the number of Democrats in Congress, an astounding affirmation of Roosevelt, his program, and his party. The president immediately began to implement his vision of a social insurance regime. Social Security would become one of the most cherished programs to emerge from the Second New Deal, commanding into the twenty-first century the loyalty of a vast majority of Americans.

Roosevelt funded Social Security's support for old people, the unemployed, the disabled, and dependent children through a payroll tax, which secured from its recipients an intense intergenerational loyalty. They paid in and expected to collect. He correctly predicted, "With those taxes . . . no damn politician can ever scrap my Social Security program."

Much of the Second New Deal legislation was intended to help parts of the Roosevelt electoral coalition. This was intentional, as the president was facing re-election in 1936. He called for increased taxes on large fortunes and signed the Revenue Act of 1935. The income from the law was relatively meager, but politically it satisfied a strong inclination among potential voters in the 1936 election.

FRANKLIN D. ROOSEVELT: RE-ELECTION AND SECOND TERM LEGISLATION-I

As Roosevelt offered himself for re-election in 1936, more than eight million workers were still unemployed, but the economy had improved and the president enjoyed extraordinary popularity. In fact, blacks voted Democratic for the first time in 1936. Roosevelt buried the Republican candidate, Governor Alf Landon of Kansas, and carried with him a huge Democratic majority in Congress, three fourths control over both houses.

Throughout his first term, Franklin Roosevelt demonstrated an amazing level of perfect political pitch. In his second term, his political acuity gave serious signs of decay. Having such an enormous majority in Congress created problems for the president in that his election also brought to Washington many conservative Democrats, some of whom were skeptical of more New Deal–type reform. He was able to pass some legislation; the Fair Labor Standards Act, which governed the relationship between employees and employers, was the last major New Deal law.

In 1937, there was a brief recession, in part caused by Roosevelt-initiated cutbacks in New Deal programs and other government spending. Industrial production, the stock market, and employment fell precipitously. Chastened, Roosevelt turned the spigot on again with a large spending package for the WPA, which began to hire hundreds of thousands of workers. Gradually the economy righted itself.

FRANKLIN D. ROOSEVELT:
RE-ELECTION AND SECOND TERM
LEGISLATION-II

Contrary to popular conception of Roosevelt as a doctrinaire liberal committed to continuous deficit spending, he was actually a much more conservative steward of the economy. In 1932, he ran on a platform advocating a balanced budget and returned to those principals in 1937–38 when he slammed on the spending brakes and then watched the economy tank. The problem was the U.S., indeed the world, economy was still suffering from reduced demand for goods and services. It was clearly not the time to cut government spending in order to balance the budget. Franklin Roosevelt's embrace of the Keynesian idea of countercyclical spending[3] was less ideological than it was pragmatic. The ever-practical Roosevelt was always willing to experiment if it kept the economic ship afloat. Seeing recovery imperiled by his effort to balance the budget, he reversed course and the economy soon righted itself.

FRANKLIN D. ROOSEVELT:
COURT-PACKING PLAN

In a political life that was marked by extraordinary perception, Franklin Roosevelt made his greatest error in 1937. He attempted to correct the Supreme Court's anti–New Deal orientation by packing the court with additional justices of his own choosing.

For a variety of reasons, in the early Roosevelt years, the Court began to strike down state and federal laws deemed to be injurious to businesses' economic liberty or private contracts. In 1935 and 1936, the Court eviscerated Roosevelt's two prime vehicles of state intervention in the economy, the National Industrial Recovery Act (NIRA) and the Agricultural Adjustment Act (AAA), and was considering challenging the Social Security Act and Wagner Act.

Determined to reign in the Court before it destroyed his entire program, Roosevelt introduced the Judicial Procedures Reform Bill (1937), which proposed to add a member to the Court when any justice reached the age of seventy. The move was a transparent effort to "pack the Court" to Roosevelt's advantage. It was a measure much too clever by half, and the bill almost immediately ran into a coalition of liberals and conservatives who opposed this packing of the Court on the grounds of the separation of powers. The Democratic leadership in Congress quietly let the proposal die. Despite his defeat, the president would soon have a Court more accommodating to his legislation. By 1941, seven of the nine justices on the Supreme Court had been appointed by Franklin Roosevelt. The Court began to allow his legislation to become law.[4]

FRANKLIN D. ROOSEVELT: FOREIGN POLICY BEFORE WORLD WAR II

Given the nature of the national crisis when he took office, it is not surprising that most of President Roosevelt's energy and attention would be focused on domestic priorities. Nevertheless, the need to mend fences in the Western Hemisphere and the growing international crises in Europe, Africa, and Asia were not far from his mind.

In Latin America, Roosevelt reshaped U.S. policy and initiated the Good Neighbor Policy. While the U.S. clearly needed its image burnished in the region, he wanted to strengthen the defense posture of the hemisphere, but also to open markets for U.S. goods in the region. Perhaps most importantly, the U.S. became a signatory of the Montevideo Convention, giving up the right to militarily interfere in the life of countries in Latin America.

While serving as Assistant Secretary of the Navy during World War I, Roosevelt absorbed Woodrow Wilson's internationalist spirit. Unfortunately, foreign policy in the 1930s was dominated by isolationism. Sentiment in the U.S shifted when Germany began to eat up Czechoslovakia after the Munich Agreement (1938) and when attacks on Jewish people became more overt. Slowly Roosevelt began assembling a coalition of Southern Democrats and Republican businessmen to support his efforts to prepare for war. When a group of interventionist congressmen proposed the first peacetime draft, Roosevelt supported the effort and signed the Selective Training and Service Act (1940). By mid-1941, more than a million Americans were under arms.

FRANKLIN D. ROOSEVELT:
RE-ELECTION AND RUN-UP TO WAR

Like his actions in so many other arenas, Franklin Roosevelt broke tradition as he approached the election of 1940. The president became convinced that he alone had the experience and expertise to lead the country through perilous times; Roosevelt won his third term by 55 percent in the popular vote and a shut-out in the Electoral College.

Roosevelt's third and fourth terms were consumed with foreign policy and fighting World War II. Before and after the election of 1940, Roosevelt slowly ramped up his efforts to aid the beleaguered British, who stood alone in Europe against Adolf Hitler. Roosevelt and Prime Minister Winston Churchill met in secret in August 1941 to draft the Atlantic Charter, outlining wartime strategy and international goals after the defeat of their enemies. Roosevelt turned aside Churchill's plea that the U.S. declare war against the Axis powers by explaining that Congress would most certainly turn down his request—though U.S. sentiment was changing in a pro-war direction.

When a German submarine attacked the destroyer USS *Greer* in September, Roosevelt commissioned the U.S. Navy to conduct convoy escort service across the Atlantic and granted it permission to "shoot on sight" should any German submarine threaten Navy ships or their charges. This, plus the material aid Roosevelt was sending to Britain and China, was a virtual, if not actual, declaration of war against Germany and Japan. His opponents attacked the president as a jingoist bent on taking America to war, but this did little to put a brake on Roosevelt's determination.

FRANKLIN D. ROOSEVELT:
DAY OF INFAMY—PEARL HARBOR

At 7:55 a.m. on December 7, 1941, air and naval forces of the Empire of Japan attacked U.S. airfields and the naval station at Pearl Harbor in Hawaii. A significant portion of the Pacific battleship fleet was damaged or destroyed and over 2,400 servicemen and civilians were killed.

U.S. relations with the Japanese had been worsening for some time. Roosevelt's support of the Chinese following Japan's invasion of Manchuria, and particularly after the Japanese conquest of the northern part of French Indochina, convinced Japan to cast its lot with Germany and Italy in the Tripartite Pact. In July 1941, the United States imposed an embargo on Japanese oil imports. This cut off nearly all of the Japanese oil supply.

Japan and the U.S. began diplomatic efforts to end the embargo, and when these talks broke down, the Japanese government authorized the strike on Pearl Harbor—launching simultaneous assaults on Hong Kong, Thailand, the Philippines, and other objectives.

The next day, Roosevelt addressed Congress. "Yesterday, December 7, 1941—a day which will live in infamy—the United States of America was suddenly and deliberately attacked by . . . the Empire of Japan." With near unanimity, Congress voted to declare war. Three days later, Adolf Hitler followed Japan and declared war against the U.S.

In a single stroke, Japan had resolved the angry political dispute in America. Thanks to Japan's sneak attack, the nation was united.

FRANKLIN D. ROOSEVELT: ALLIED STRATEGY—NORTH AFRICA AND ITALY

A mericans were fervent in their determination to retaliate against
Japan because of its attack on Pearl Harbor, but Roosevelt and
Prime Minister Winston Churchill agreed that the major focus of war
strategy would be in Europe, then Japan. Less than a month had passed
since the assault on Hawaii when the U.S., Britain, China, the Soviet
Union, and twenty-two other countries affirmed the declaration by
United Nations in which the signatories—the Allies—pledged to defeat
the Axis—Germany, Italy, and Japan.

To develop joint strategy, building on the Atlantic Charter, the
Allied leaders began a series of bilateral and multilateral conferences,
beginning with Churchill's long visit to the White House in December
1941. Roosevelt and Churchill met twelve times during the war.

From the beginning, Joseph Stalin insisted that a second, western
invasion be initiated to relieve the pressure on his troops. Therefore,
Roosevelt directed that the first U.S. action be in North Africa. To
crush the Italians and Germans, the Americans—working from the
west—would create a pincer movement with the British, who had been
fighting in eastern North Africa since the beginning of the war.

Operation Torch, led by General Dwight D. Eisenhower, landed
Americans in North Africa in late 1942; the following May, over
250,000 Axis troops surrendered after the combined assault of the Allies. The next target for attack would be Italy. Because of fierce German
and Italian resistance, the complete capture of Italy took until 1945.

FRANKLIN D. ROOSEVELT: ALLIED STRATEGY—EUROPE THEN JAPAN

Roosevelt first encountered Joseph Stalin when he and Churchill met with the Soviet ruler at the Tehran Conference in November 1943. They met again, with the war in Europe approaching its end, in February 1945 at Yalta. Roosevelt wanted Stalin's help in the invasion of Japan and promised Stalin control of Asian territory, such as Sakhalin Island.

Roosevelt's actions at Yalta have been criticized as being much too accommodating to Stalin concerning the future of the countries Russia had captured from the Nazis, but the reality was that Stalin had already captured those countries, and the other Allies had very little they could do short of continuing the war against the Soviet Union to affect change in Eastern Europe. Almost everyone wanted the war to end. Germany surrendered to the Allies in May 1945, a month after Franklin Roosevelt's death.

In the Pacific, the U.S. scored an impressive series of victories. The largely ineffectual, but morale-boosting, Doolittle Raid on Tokyo was followed by the holding action at the Coral Sea. Then came the amazing destruction of much of the Japanese navy at Midway in late spring 1942. After that, the U.S. engaged in a "island hopping"[5] strategy to cut off their enemy's logistics chain and reduce Allied casualties.

With the majority of his energies devoted to the European theater, Franklin Roosevelt left tactical military and naval operations in the Pacific to his subordinates, but he did reserve overall strategic decisions for himself.

FRANKLIN D. ROOSEVELT: ON THE HOME FRONT

Wartime needs and the military build-up drove the unemployment rate to nearly 1 percent, and Roosevelt achieved the full employment goal he had sought all during the Great Depression. The demands of industry from 1942 to 1945 created an acute labor shortage. Farmers and country-dwellers moved to the cities, and the Great Migration of African Americans out of the South accelerated. Many migrants moved to the West Coast to get jobs in defense industries.

During the war, Congress and President Roosevelt had a running conflict over revenue. Roosevelt kept proposing very high taxes on wealthy Americans and Congress kept turning him down, but they did agree on the Revenue Act of 1942. This enlarged the tax base, set very high taxes for the rich, and established withholding taxes on workers' income, which stabilized the federal revenue stream and guaranteed the government revenues on a year-round basis.

In his 1944 State of the Union address, Roosevelt asserted that Americans should be able to rely on an economic bill of rights—including a useful job, a decent home, a good education, and adequate medical care. Roosevelt's most significant long-term accomplishment in his third term was the G.I. Bill, which provided returning soldiers with health care, post-secondary education benefits, unemployment insurance, job counseling, and loans for businesses and homes. The legislation passed both Houses unanimously and has continued to transform educational opportunities for servicemen into the twenty first century.

FRANKLIN D. ROOSEVELT: MANHATTAN PROJECT

One of the most significant wartime decisions made by Franklin Roosevelt was made long before the U.S. entered World War II. In late summer 1939, the president received a letter from Leo Szilard and Albert Einstein outlining recent discoveries in the field of nuclear physics. Atomic scientists had learned of the remarkable properties of nuclear fission and concluded that it could be used to create a weapon of enormous destructive power. Szilard and Einstein were very concerned that German nuclear research was reaping positive results. The letter awakened in Roosevelt the fear that Germany could acquire this technology and use it in the war. He gave permission to begin nuclear research and funded it.

After U.S. entry into the war, Roosevelt placed General Leslie Richard Groves in charge of what became known as the Manhattan Project. Groves began construction of a huge interlocking network of installations devoted to research, fabrication, and delivery of nuclear weapons. On July 16, 1945, at the New Mexico test sight, history's first nuclear bomb was detonated—near perfect success. A similar bomb, "Fat Man," was dropped on Nagasaki, Japan, to devastating effect on August 9, 1945. Three days prior, the fission bomb "Little Boy" obliterated Hiroshima, Japan.

The decision to use the bombs was made by Franklin Roosevelt's successor, President Harry Truman, but the decision to pursue nuclear research was one of Franklin Roosevelt's lasting legacies.

FRANKLIN D. ROOSEVELT:
ELECTION 1944, DECLINING
HEALTH, AND DEATH

As far back as before the war, Roosevelt's health had begun to deteriorate. He suffered from various diagnosed ailments, including coronary artery disease causing angina and high blood pressure, and congestive heart failure. Soon it became obvious to acquaintances and even to Roosevelt himself that his health was in precipitous decline.

Nevertheless, he ran for a fourth term, but not before shedding Henry Wallace from the ticket and adding Missouri Senator Harry S. Truman as vice president. The Roosevelt–Truman ticket won in a walk away.

In late March, he departed for his home at Warm Springs, Georgia, to rest and prepare for the founding conference of the United Nations. His guests included his daughter Anna and Lucy Mercer Rutherford, whose affair with Roosevelt thirty years before had nearly destroyed his marriage. On April 12, 1945, he was relaxing while having his portrait painted at the commission of Mrs. Rutherford. Suddenly he said, "I have a terrible headache." He fell forward into unconsciousness and was carried to his bed. At 3:35 p.m., he died of a massive cerebral hemorrhage at the age of sixty three.

FRANKLIN D. ROOSEVELT:
LEGACY—RACE RELATIONS
AND THE HOLOCAUST

The legacy of Franklin Roosevelt is so extensive that it is necessary to look at it from a variety of angles. If, according to Otto von Bismarck, politics is the art of the possible, then Roosevelt was a gifted artist. His normal practice of politics was pitch perfect.

Because of Roosevelt, Chinese, Filipino, and African Americans flocked to join the New Deal coalition. On the other hand, he formed a Black Cabinet to advise him on racial matters and formed the Fair Employment Practices Committee to enhance opportunities for blacks to get jobs with government contractors.

The experience of Japanese Americans were not as sanguine. Early in the war he signed an Executive Order creating internment (concentration) camps in the American interior for hundreds of thousands of immigrant—as well as loyal, native-born—Japanese. This was perhaps the lowest ebb of Roosevelt's moral legacy.

Also of questionable statue was his treatment of Jewish people fleeing the Nazi Holocaust in Europe. Bound by the racist strictures of the Immigration Act (1924), he was not able to respond to the desperate circumstances of the Jews seeking to escape the Nazi "Final Solution." He let in a few, but nothing approaching the need of the Jews under persecution.

FRANKLIN D. ROOSEVELT: LEGACY–NUCLEAR DEVELOPMENT, ECONOMIC REVITALIZATION, AND RESTORATION OF HOPE

Historians consistently rank Franklin Roosevelt with George Washington and Abraham Lincoln as the three greatest presidents. The challenges he faced—depression and war—were extraordinary, and his leadership during his long period in office was exemplary.

Roosevelt's perceptive recognition of the dangers and opportunities of nuclear power after the Sizlard–Einstein letter provided the Allies with the means of bringing Japan to its knees without the invasion and the anticipated effusion of blood on both sides. His decision also opened the possibilities of the peaceful use of nuclear energy.

Roosevelt's legacy was also extended through the vast expansion of federal employment and involvement in state and local infrastructure. This growth reached into people's lives—particularly through Social Security and, during the 1930s, direct employment of citizens in programs such as the Public Works Administration (PWA) and the Civilian Conservation Corps (CCC). He established the definition of American liberalism, which has extended into the twenty first century.

Additionally, Roosevelt drove the United States into the international arena, where it assumed the leadership role in worldwide institutions. Except for brief upsurges in isolationist spirit, Americans have accepted the Rooseveltian approach to foreign relations and its military component. Finally, Franklin Roosevelt changed the way Americans viewed the presidency. He entered the White House when the country was being crushed by the worst economy malady it had ever faced. As historian Jean Edward Smith vividly described it, "He lifted himself from a wheelchair to lift the nation from its knees."

33

HARRY S. TRUMAN

HARRY S. TRUMAN: LIFE PAGE

Born: May 8, 1884, Lamar, Missouri

Education: Spalding's Commercial College

       Kansas City Law School (University of Missouri Kansas City School of Law)

Married: Bess Wallace, 1919

Military Service: Missouri National Guard, 1905–1911

                  United States Army, 1917–1919

                  United States Army Reserve, 1920–1953

Vocation: Retail Clothier

       Politician

Judge, Jackson County, Eastern District of Missouri: 1923–1925

Presiding Judge, Jackson County, Missouri: 1927–1935

United States Senator: 1935–1945

Thirty-Fourth Vice President of the United States: 1945

Thirty-Third President of the United States: 1945–1953

Died: December 26, 1972, Kansas City, Missouri

Additional resources available for this president at www.amomentintime.com.

HARRY S. TRUMAN: MACHINE POLITICIAN AND VICE PRESIDENT

Born in the heartland of the nation, Truman reflected the values of his Missouri heritage as he struggled to establish himself as a man of note. Alone among twentieth-century presidents, save William McKinley, he did not receive a college degree. He tried to find a pathway to success in a variety of fields—banking, retail clothing, mining, farming—but perhaps his most instructive experience was in the military. Too old for the World War I draft, he volunteered and led his tough, working-class artillery unit in heavy fighting in France.

One of his wartime friends and a fellow veteran was the brother of Tom Pendergast, the Democratic political "boss" of Kansas City and Jackson—Truman's home county. Pendergast groomed the young man for political office. Truman was elected first as district judge and then spent nearly a decade as presiding judge of Jackson County. He was then elected to the U.S. Senate in 1934.

In Washington, Truman proved himself a hard-working, loyal supporter of President Franklin D. Roosevelt and the New Deal. When Roosevelt ran for a fourth term in 1944, Truman reluctantly accepted the vice-presidential nomination. The Roosevelt–Truman ticket coasted to victory. Then on April 12, 1945, Truman was called to the White House and First Lady Eleanor Roosevelt told him of the president's death. To his query if he could help, she said, "Is there anything we can do for you? You are the one in trouble now."

HARRY S. TRUMAN:
ATOMIC BOMB DECISION

When word came of Franklin D. Roosevelt's death on April 12, 1945, Truman was suddenly laden with the extraordinary burden of leading a great nation engaged in a giant global conflict. The two had only met twice since the inauguration, and the president shared very little wartime or domestic political details with his vice president. Truman had not been informed about the extremely expensive Manhattan Project and the powerful weapon it was developing. Finally, on April 25, Secretary of War Henry Stimson briefed Truman and informed him that the new president would have to decide whether to use the atomic bomb against Japan.

He was assured that the uranium bomb, "Little Boy," would work, but the plutonium bomb, "Fat Man," needed to be tested.

While Truman was meeting with Joseph Stalin and Winston Churchill at the Potsdam Conference, he was informed that the Trinity test on July 16 had been successful. Truman considered the tenacity of the Japanese defense of the outer islands, particularly Okinawa, and the prospects of 250,000 to 500,000 Allied casualties, and many more Japanese, should an invasion of the Japanese home islands prove necessary. He authorized the use of the two bombs in existence. On August 6 and then on August 9, Hiroshima and Nagasaki were destroyed with eventual casualty estimates ranging as high as 226,000. Japan sued for peace and surrendered on September 2, 1945.

HARRY S. TRUMAN:
COLD WAR, THE MARSHALL PLAN,
BERLIN AIRLIFT

Soon after Victory in Europe (VE) Day, it became clear that Joseph Stalin and the Soviet Union would not simply retire behind Russia's pre-war boundaries. Russia extended its control over East Germany, Czechoslovakia, Rumania, Bulgaria, and the Baltic States. This provoked the Cold War—four decades of hostility between the Soviets and the western allies. Truman's determination to block further Soviet expansion was described by Ambassador George Kennan in 1949 as a policy of "containment."

Two important milestones marked the Cold War during Truman's first term. To a destitute Western Europe, the U.S. provided $10 billion in loans and grants to help. It was a brilliant success resuscitating Europe, but by increasing trade helped the U.S. negotiate the transition from war to peaceful pursuits.

The next milestone was in the city of Berlin. To put pressure on the city, in late June 1948 the Soviets closed off land access to the Allied sectors. The city was going to starve. President Truman and the Allies decided to supply the city by air. Over the next eleven months, thousands of flights with over a million tons of food and other essentials saved West Berlin. Finally on May 11, 1949, the Soviets relented and opened road access.

HARRY S. TRUMAN: NATO AND RECOGNITION OF ISRAEL

To confront and resist Soviet aggression in Europe, the Allies formed the North Atlantic Treaty Organization (NATO), a military and economic alliance of the U.S., Canada, and non-Soviet democracies in Europe. In addition to the obvious coordinated military preparations, NATO sent a strong signal to the Soviet Union and its allies that the Western alliance was prepared to protect democratic institutions and national boundaries in Europe.

As a long-time supporter of the Jewish community, Truman was particularly interested in securing a homeland for survivors of the Holocaust (in fact, as Senator Truman, he called for it in a 1943 speech). There was some reluctance among his advisors at both the State Department and the Defense Department when President Truman was considering whether to recognize the putative Jewish homeland. U.S. leaders did not wish to offend Arab sensibilities or risk the loss of Saudi Arabian petroleum reserves that might be needed in a time of war.

Truman struggled with the decision, but when the new State of Israel declared its existence on May 14, 1948, the president extended diplomatic recognition within minutes and oriented U.S. policy to become one of Israel's most consequential allies. He later wrote, "Hitler had been murdering Jews right and left. . . . The Jews needed some place where they could go. . . . The American government couldn't stand idly by while the victims [of] Hitler's madness are not allowed to build new lives."

HARRY S. TRUMAN: DESEGREGATING THE ARMED SERVICES

The Democratic Party coalition was fascinating. Racially biased southerners were allied with Northern urban African Americans. Despairing of hope for economic, social, and political progress in the South, many blacks had moved North and began to put pressure on the national party to begin redressing discrimination and racial suppression in U.S. society—North and South.

Facing bleak election prospects in 1848 Truman moved to shore up his prospects with urban black voters whose support he would need in carrrying Northern states. Within days of the 1948 Democratic National Convention, President Truman signed two momentous Executive Orders. Number 9981 racially integrated the armed services of the United States. Number 9980 fully integrated federal departments. Truman did this out of political necessity and a conviction that all citizens should have equal treatment before the law. But he was personally somewhat ambivalent about the idea of social equality for blacks in an overwhelmingly white society, a notion he shared with most white people of his era. Nevertheless, his courageous action during a campaign in which his party's divisions were on full display directed the military establishment—one of the most conservative institutions in America—to take the lead in ending discrimination.

HARRY S. TRUMAN:
ELECTION OF 1948

Almost no one thought Harry Truman had a chance to win the election on his own in 1948. The GOP fielded a strong team, Governors of New York and California, Thomas Dewey and Earl Warren. The Republicans controlled Congress and the Democrats were divided. Socialists ran former VP Henry Wallace and after the Democrats passed a strong civil rights in their platform, Deep South delegates bolted and ran Governor Strom Thurmond of S.C. on the Dixiecrat ticket. The president, however, saw possibilities and early on declared his intentions to run.

Truman's fiery acceptance speech at the Democratic National Convention set the tone for the campaign to come. At the climax of the speech, he called Congress back to Washington for a special session. At that time he presented strong progressive proposals and dared the Republicans to reject them—which, of course, they did. Truman then turned this to his advantage by making the theme of his campaign rejection of the do-nothing Republican Congress.

The president and first lady climbed aboard the *Ferdinand Magellan* and took his case to the American people in a 21,928-mile odyssey, giving hundreds of speeches to millions of people who gathered track-side to hear the beleaguered president joyfully fight for his political life. On Election Day, in one of the most stunning upsets in U.S. presidential history, Truman won. The president prevailed in a close popular contest and triumphed in the Electoral College.

HARRY S. TRUMAN: MCCARTHYISM-I

In 1949, after years of diplomatic support and billions of dollars of aid, the Nationalist Chinese government of Generalissimo Chiang Kai-shek succumbed to the communist revolution forces under Mao-Zedong. There was little the U.S. could do to prevent this unravelling of the despotic regime of Chiang short of direct military intervention—something the American public would not countenance. Nevertheless, in the context of the Cold War it seemed that the Western alliance had "lost" China.

For the first time in a century there was a credible ideological challenge to the ideals set forth in the U.S. *Declaration of Independence* and Constitution. The Western liberal consensus was under attack and it seemed set back on its heels by Communism. While this challenge from evangelical Marxism would ultimately fail, the West underwent a crisis of confidence. Soviet advances in Europe and Asia threatened the very existence of democratic institutions and states.

Cracks began to appear in U.S. society, tossed up by the insecurities aroused by communist advances. The First Red Scare following World War I had faded, but the fearful sentiments aroused at that time lingered in U.S. society. Truman contributed to a growing national hysteria with an Executive Order in March 1947, requiring all civil-service employees to be screened for "loyalty." He later considered his move to be a terrible mistake because it helped unleash a torrent of unwarranted political passion.

HARRY S. TRUMAN:
MCCARTHYISM-II

Fears that communists had infiltrated key governmental, jour-
nalistic, academic, and social institutions began to dominate
the national conversation. This was the perfect background for
the campaign of a little-known freshman senator, Joseph Raymond
McCarthy (R–Wisconsin). In February 1950, he spoke to the
Republican Women's Club of Wheeling, West Virginia, alleging
that the state department was harboring 205 employees with
communist sympathies. His accusations were most certainly not
true, but he soon attracted a following among Republicans and
many Southern Democrats. The McCarthy era had begun.

Congressional hearings ripped at the national fabric as people
in many fields were falsely accused of communist sympathies.
The Hollywood Blacklist ended the careers of many show
business figures as they were misleadingly accused of outright
Marxist sympathies. Political reputations and the careers of many
politicians, and even future presidents—such as Richard Nixon
and Ronald Reagan—were built on their anti-communist exploits
during the McCarthy era.

By the mid-1950s, McCarthy had been discredited and his
indictments proven to be wildly exaggerated, if not downright
untrue. His name however is permanently associated with the term
McCarthyism, the unsubstantiated, inaccurate, or false accusations
of treason, sedition, subversion, or any other political activity the
accuser deems worthy of assertion.

HARRY S. TRUMAN: KOREAN WAR AND FIRING MACARTHUR-I

Soon after the successful conclusion of the Berlin Airlift, word came that the Soviet Union had tested its first nuclear weapon. Later it was determined that nuclear espionage against the U.S. nuclear program had made possible this achievement. With the communist takeover of China, Truman and his advisors were unusually concerned when, on June 25, 1950, word came that North Korea (PRK) had attacked South Korea (ROC).

Truman asked the United Nations to defend ROC, and the U.N. authorized a police action led by General Douglas MacArthur.

U.S. troops poured into the southeastern quadrant of Korea and stabilized the situation around Pusan, halting the PRK advance. MacArthur then executed one of the most spectacular reversals in U.S. military history. He led a risky amphibious landing, which completely surprised the enemy and nearly cut them off from retreat. He then ordered U.N. forces to wheel around and head north toward the Chinese border on the Yalu River.

China then intervened with a huge invasion and pushed the Allied armies back into South Korean territory. The U.N. forces counterattacked, pushed the Chinese and their PRK allies back up to the thirty eighth parallel, and then war entered a long, bloody stalemate—at essentially the position the two sides held before the war began.

HARRY S. TRUMAN: KOREAN WAR AND FIRING MACARTHUR-II

By the early months of 1951, the Korean War had descended into a grinding, gory stalemate at the thirty-eighth parallel. This basically restored the *status quo ante* to where it had been before the North Korean invasion. By this time, U.S. public support for the war was on the decline.

Supreme Allied Commander Douglas MacArthur was frustrated. His war strategy was in tatters and he began to disobey the express instructions of his Commander in Chief as expressed by the Joint Chiefs of Staff. He sent word to congressional Republicans that the U.S. was not in the war to win. He further began communicating with foreign governments indicating his support of policies President Truman did not sanction. President Truman concluded MacArthur had become disobedient and insubordinate. He had to go. On April 11, 1951, Truman fired MacArthur.[1]

The public reaction was swift and bitter. The firing of the general was a short-term political disaster for Truman, one of the most unpopular presidential actions in U.S. history. Truman, however, never doubted the rightness of his action, and gradually the public joined historians and commentators in coming to agree with Truman's protection of civilian control of the military.

HARRY S. TRUMAN: LEGACY

When Harry Truman boarded the train for his return to Missouri, the railroad station was packed with enthusiastic well-wishers. After nearly two decades in Washington, it was time to go home. Though the station partisans were exuberant, they might have been the last few Americans who held the former president in affection.

Consider his legacy. He concluded World War II with a courageous decision to use the first nuclear bombs, perhaps sparing Japan and the Allies millions of casualties. He nursed the U.S. economy and U.S. society through the stressful transformation from wartime emergency to peaceful pursuits. He prevented the political enemies of the New Deal from dismantling the social safety net that Franklin D. Roosevelt had put into place. At the same time, he introduced improvements to the enterprise of social engagement (health care, education, employment insurance, welfare) that would be realized in future progressive administrations.

He and his lieutenants built the alliance that prevented further Soviet gains in Europe and shaped the policy of containment that eventually brought an end to Soviet expansion. He desegregated the American armed forces and federal bureaucracy and accomplished an extraordinary political triumph in 1948, advocating the strongest civil rights political party platform since the nineteenth century. He blocked the North Koreans and Chinese from absorbing South Korea into the Marxist alliance. Finally, he sacrificed his popularity and a second full term by upholding—once and for all—civilian control of the military. Historians consistently rank Truman among the near-great American presidents. Soon Americans who rejected him came to respect this extraordinary man of ordinarry pedigree.

34

DWIGHT D. EISENHOWER

DWIGHT D. EISENHOWER:
LIFE PAGE

Born: October 14, 1890, Denison, Texas

Education: United States Military Academy, BS

Vocation: Military Officer

Married: Mamie Doud, 1916

Military Service: Various Posts, 1916–1952

Supreme Commander, Allied Expeditionary Force (SHAEF): 1943–1945

Military Governor of U.S. Occupation Zone in Germany: 1945

Sixteenth Chief of Staff, United States Army: 1945–1948

Thirteenth President of Columbia University: 1948–1953

First Supreme Allied Commander in Europe (NATO): 1951–1952

Thirty-Fourth President of the United States: 1953–1961

Died: March 28, 1969, Bethesda, Maryland

Additional resources available for this president at www.amomentintime.com.

DWIGHT D. EISENHOWER:
SUPREME ALLIED COMMANDER

Born in Texas and raised in Kansas, Dwight Eisenhower grew up in a family where education was important, but he came to understand privation when his father's business failed. Because of his family's financial situation, he sought admission to a service academy, first Annapolis, but, due to his age, applied and was accepted at West Point.

Eisenhower graduated in 1916 and was on active duty in San Antonio when he met and married Mamie Doud. Ironically, in view of the heights he would reach in the military, Ike never led men in combat. His expertise ran to training, organization, and co-ordination—which made him invaluable in the years between and during the two world wars. By the opening of World War II, he had risen to the rank of Brigadier General; after that his rise was meteoric, as President Franklin D. Roosevelt and Pentagon leaders recognized his skills and, at wartime, demanded his organizational expertise.

Ike's ability to muster the support and cooperation of strong personalities such as Charles de Gaulle, Winston Churchill, George Patton, and Bernard Montgomery insured the effective planning and execution of the Normandy invasion and, eventually, the defeat of Germany.

DWIGHT D. EISENHOWER: MODERN REPUBLICAN-I

In 1948, Ike became president of Columbia University and began his transition to civilian life. It was not a perfect match on either side, as he soon began to clash with the faculty—not necessarily because of policy disagreements, but rather because many saw him as an absentee president who was furthering his own political interests by traveling and fundraising. His supporters among the Columbia trustees saw him as a likely candidate for president at some point and wanted to keep him in the public eye.

At the beginning of the Korean War, President Harry S. Truman asked Eisenhower to take a leave of absence and become the Supreme Allied Commander Europe. During his time in Paris, he received regular delegations of Republicans urging him to run for president. In October 1951, he reached a conclusion and signaled his openness to a convention draft in a letter to Senator James Duff (R–Pennsylvania), announcing that he was a "liberal Republican." After the draft secured his victory in the New Hampshire Primary in March 1952, Eisenhower returned to the States to begin campaigning. He won nomination at the Republican Convention, narrowly defeating the champion of the conservative Old Guard, Senator Robert A. Taft (R–Ohio).

Eisenhower was widely popular and, using the simple slogan, "I Like Ike," soared to a landslide victory. He won with a convincing 56.2 percent, to 44.3 percent, in the popular vote and an overwhelming margin, 442 to 89, in the Electoral College.

DWIGHT D. EISENHOWER: MODERN REPUBLICAN-II

During the campaign of 1952, Eisenhower was clear that there would be no attempt to undo the significant social and economic changes that were made during the Great Depression. After his inauguration, he and his Cabinet appointees preserved Social Security, high progressive tax rates, cooperation with organized labor, and the aggressive foreign policy initiated by former President Harry S. Truman. The lingering influence of the conservative Old Guard was diminished even more when the first Eisenhower budget emerged looking suspiciously like the last Truman budget.

The only real influence that the old-line conservative Republicans had in the administration was through Vice President Richard M. Nixon. However, he was not consulted on substantive matters, had almost no influence over policy, and was at first disliked by the president (though that changed over the years).

When the Democrats regained control of Congress in 1955, the president worked with the congressional majority, led in the Senate by majority leader and future president, Lyndon B. Johnson. Eisenhower's advocacy of progressive conservatism frustrated many of those with right-wing opinions in the Republican party, but his advocacy of a middle way rehabilitated the party. Many Americans associated Republicanism with the calcified reaction of the Hoover administration during the Great Depression and the hard opposition of the Old Guard to the New Deal.

DWIGHT D. EISENHOWER: FOREIGN POLICY AND THE U-2 INCIDENT

In many ways the Eisenhower years were consumed with international challenges. In 1953, Ike passed word to China through back channels that the U.S. was considering the use of nuclear weapons to break the impasse in Korea. An armistice was signed on July 27, 1953.

Eisenhower and his secretary of state, John Foster Dulles, demonstrated cautious support for emerging democracies. Therefore, they articulated the so-called "Eisenhower Doctrine" (1956) through which the U.S. would provide financial aid, military assistance, and even armed intervention to assist newly emerging friendly states in the development of democratic institutions and prevention of communist advances.

Throughout the Eisenhower administration, the U.S. stood firm against Soviet aggression in Europe. Fundamental to this strategy was insight into the current status of Soviet arms, therefore the U.S. embarked on an aggressive espionage campaign. In May 1960, a U-2 spy plane was shot down over Russian airspace by a Soviet missile. At first Ike and Dulles denied the facts, but when the Soviets revealed they had the pilot, and then at trial forced him to confess the true mission of the U-2, the U.S. had been caught in a lie. Eisenhower refused to apologize, which undermined his attempts to improve relations with the Soviets.

DWIGHT D. EISENHOWER: SPACE RACE AND INTERSTATE HIGHWAY SYSTEM

Under President Eisenhower, the United States committed itself to two new massive ventures that transformed earth-bound transportation and celestial exploration. He proposed the construction of an Interstate Highway System through the Federal Aid Highway Act (1956). It was a struggle to get it funded at first, but Ike successfully argued that it was a military necessity. Congress voted $25 billion to kickstart this project, which at that time was the largest single domestic program in the nation's history.

By the early months of 1957, President Eisenhower was aware that the Soviets had the ability to put a small object in orbit. When *Sputnik* flew later that year, an aroused public demanded a revision of Ike's rather diffident support for U.S. space efforts. He responded by consolidating the American space program under NASA (National Aeronautics and Space Administration) and vastly ramped up spending on space exploration, higher technology education, and scientific research. The administration began developing spy satellite technology to detect enemy ballistic missile installations and threatened launches. Finally, Eisenhower commenced construction of a tripartite nuclear offensive configuration, which included B-52 bombers, land-based intercontinental ballistic missiles, and submarine launched nuclear missiles. His goal was to make the U.S. capabilities so overwhelming that it would act as a deterrent.

DWIGHT D. EISENHOWER:
MCCARTHYISM

The anti-communist campaign of Senator Joseph McCarthy posed a serious problem for President Eisenhower. On one hand, the senator's crusade of unfounded accusations were abhorrent to a growing number of Americans and Ike himself.

President Eisenhower's problem was that McCarthy was very popular among the conservative Old Guard and the Republican rank and file. Ike needed the votes and enthusiasm of this part of the party base for election and governing. Therefore, he never publicly denounced McCarthy. He did work behind the scenes to undermine the senator, but he could never make a moral claim to leadership that led to McCarthy's downfall and the removal of this scurrilous injury to the body politic. In 1954, McCarthy was censured/condemned for, among other things, "bring[ing] the Senate into dishonor and disrepute."

After the Senate action, McCarthy went into political and personal decline. As a symbol of a difficult time in American life, he was ignored by his colleagues, lampooned in the cultural media, and condemned by a world that passed him by. He descended into severe alcoholism from which he could not escape. There is some evidence that he also had become addicted to morphine. Joseph McCarthy died of "hepatitis, acute, cause unknown" on May 2, 1957. He was accorded a state funeral.

APN Photography / Shutterstock.com

DWIGHT D. EISENHOWER: CIVIL RIGHTS

In 1954, a unanimous Supreme Court led by Chief Justice Earl Warren decided for the plaintiff in *Brown vs. Board of Education of Topeka*. The ruling mandated the end of segregated schools. He eventually made it clear that he would enforce court rulings and did so in 1957 when the governor of Arkansas, Orvil Faubus, sided with demonstrators seeking to prevent the integration of Little Rock Central High School. Eisenhower federalized the Arkansas National Guard and enforced the Court's ruling.

Ike was much more emphatic on the issue of integrating the federal government and armed forces. He pursued the goal of complete integration with vigor, writing, "There must be no second-class citizens in this country."

Eisenhower acquiesced in his administration's discrimination against homosexuals. The president issued Executive Order 10450, aimed at ridding the government of lesbian and gay civil servants. More than five thousand federal employees were fired during the Eisenhower years because they were suspected of being gay. Such restrictions gradually began to be lifted in the 1970s.

Eisenhower did advance two civil rights measures (1957, 1960) and secured their passage—though opposition from Southern Democrats significantly weakened the bills. They represented the first substantial civil rights legislation since 1875.

DWIGHT D. EISENHOWER: HEALTH CRISIS AND ELECTION OF 1956

From his years at West Point, Eisenhower was a heavy smoker. This may have complicated his health while he was president. During a golf vacation in Denver in September 1955, Ike suffered a massive heart attack. It was initially misdiagnosed as indigestion, but his doctors finally announced his true condition and committed him to a six-week hospital recovery. Vice President Richard M. Nixon and the presidential staff kept Eisenhower informed and the press up-to-date on Eisenhower's progress. Doctors recommended he run for a second term to aid in regaining his health.

One of the consequences of his heart attack was an aneurysm in the left ventricle of the heart. This in turn led to a small stroke in November 1957. He was also a victim of Crohn's disease—inflammation of the small intestine—which required surgery in June 1956. During the years after 1955 until his death, he suffered seven heart attacks, demonstrated evidence of cholecystitis and inflammation of the gall bladder, and had glandular removal surgery.

Ike was re-elected in a 1956 reprise contest with Adlai Stevenson. He beat the Democrat with an even larger margin than in 1952—57.4 percent to 42 percent, and 457 to 73 in the Electoral College. After losing to Ike in 1952, the ever-witty Stevenson quoted Abraham Lincoln on the experience, "It hurts too much to laugh, but I'm too old to cry." It was a sentiment he could not have expressed more eloquently, having twice lost to a national hero.

DWIGHT D. EISENHOWER: LEGACY

Dwight Eisenhower came to the White House with a firmly established legacy as the commander of the victorious forces who won the European conflict. His time in the White House focused more on national goals rather than those closely identified with the Republican party. However, he did help rehabilitate the reputation of the Republican party, which had suffered since the depths of the Great Depression.

Eisenhower offered up a confirmation and slight expansion of the New Deal safety net embodied in Social Security and pursued a continuation of the Truman challenge to Soviet aggression and communist expansion. His initial reluctance after *Brown vs. Board of Education of Topeka* did not keep him from enforcing the law when conservatives in the South violently resisted the mandate to integrate public schools. The administration's harassment and firing of thousands of otherwise fully qualified gay and lesbian civil servants seems repulsive in retrospect. On the other hand, he aggressively continued and completed the integration of the armed services and sponsored the first national civil rights legislation since the Reconstruction. Additionally, he laid the groundwork for expanded economic prosperity and pushed America forward in the race to the moon.

The last president born in the nineteenth century, Dwight Eisenhower was a transitional chief executive, inclined toward conservatism but confirming America's move away from the traditional approach to society and government. Eisenhower's warning in his farewell address of the looming threat to liberty of a "military-industrial complex" reminded the nation of its need to be vigilant in protecting and advancing the fruits of freedom.

JOHN F. KENNEDY

JOHN F. KENNEDY: LIFE PAGE

Born: May 29, 1917, Brookline, Massachusetts

Education: Princeton University

Harvard University (BA)

       Stanford University

Vocation: Journalist and Public Servant

Married: Jacqueline Lee Bouvier, 1953

Military Service: Lieutenant, United States Navy

                 Motor Torpedo Squadron 2

Member United States House of Representatives: 1947–1953

United States Senator: 1953–1960

Thirty-Fifth President of the United States 1961–1963

Assassinated: November 22, 1963

Additional resources available for this president at www.amomentintime.com.

JOHN F. KENNEDY: PT-109 AND
SENATORIAL SERVICE

John Fitzgerald "Jack" Kennedy, later referred to as JFK, was born into wealth and privilege, attended private preparatory schools, and graduated from Harvard University. Kennedy joined the U.S. Naval Reserve after college and served as commander of several PT boats in the South Pacific. In August 1943, his boat, *PT-109*, was cut in half by a Japanese destroyer. Over the next several days, Kennedy led the remaining crew in a search for security, food, and water. They were rescued several days later. He was later decorated for his courage under fire.

His father, Joe Kennedy, wanted one of his sons to be president of the United States. When Jack's oldest sibling, Joe Jr., was killed on a secret bombing mission over the English Channel, it fell to Jack to pick up the family torch and seek political office. He won election first to the House of Representatives and then the U.S. Senate.

As a senator, he was known as an affable but not particularly hard-working legislator. One reason for this was that he had several operations on his spine and was at times near death. He was in the hospital and thus was spared having to vote on censure for Senator Joseph McCarthy, a family friend who had dated Jack's sister Patricia.

At the 1956 Democratic Convention, Kennedy fell just short in the vote for vice-presidential nominee. He made a gracious concession speech and was spared the association with the Democrat's failed second bid for the White House. After the election, Kennedy began positioning himself for a run at the 1960 presidential nomination.

JOHN F. KENNEDY:
HOUSTON MINISTERS AND
CHURCH-STATE RELATIONS

If he was to be a serious presidential candidate, Kennedy had to address the issue of his faith. The last Catholic nominated by a major party for president, Al Smith, was crushed by Herbert Hoover in 1928—in part because of his religion. Kennedy addressed the issue with a two-part strategy: a challenge against prejudice and humor.

After a spirited contest, he narrowly won nomination on the first ballot at the Los Angeles Democratic National Convention. His opponents questioned his lack of experience, but his eloquence and charm overcame this opposition. He was also politically clever. Against the advice of most of his advisors, he offered the vice-presidential slot to one of his rivals: Majority Leader Senator Lyndon Baines Johnson (D--Texas), a Southerner and a Protestant.

Kennedy fought a come-from-behind campaign against Vice President Richard M. Nixon, who was ahead in the polls in early fall 1960. In mid-September, Kennedy spoke to the Greater Houston Ministerial Association and hit the issue of separation of church and state hard. He questioned whether Catholics, fully one-quarter of the population, should be counted as second-class citizens. "I am not the Catholic candidate for president. I am the Democratic Party candidate for president who happens to be a Catholic."

By turning the issue into one of freedom rather than one of church versus state, he almost guaranteed that Catholics would rally to his candidacy.[1]

JOHN F. KENNEDY:
TV DEBATES AND ELECTION OF 1960

Having secured the nomination of his party, Jack Kennedy took on Vice President Richard M. Nixon in the general election. It was a close contest almost from the beginning, with Nixon touting his experience and defending Eisenhower's presidential stewardship. Kennedy countered with the need for a new generation of leadership. He also claimed that the Republicans had permitted the Soviets to gain an advantage in offensive missile technology and open a "missile gap." This last was most certainly not true but conformed to the public concern following *Sputnik* and other Russian firsts in space exploration.

Nixon and Kennedy met in a series of televised debates focusing on various issues facing the country. The first debate may have decided the election. Nixon had committed to campaign in all fifty states instead of concentrating on key "battleground states." While campaigning in North Carolina, he injured his knee and lost two valuable weeks being treated for infection in the hospital. When he arrived in Chicago on September 26, his clothes were ill-fitting because he had lost weight; he refused to wear make-up to cover his "five-o'clock shadow;" and he perspired profusely, appearing unprepared and haggard. In contrast, Kennedy was tanned and fit, spoke eloquently, and demonstrated his full control of the medium of television.

In November, Kennedy beat Nixon by one of the closest elections in memory—49.7 percent to 49.5 percent—or a little over 112,000 votes nationwide. In the Electoral College, Kennedy prevailed 303 to 219.

JOHN F. KENNEDY: CAMELOT

Perhaps no president in the twentieth century so captured the imagination of the American public as did John Kennedy and his wife, Jacqueline Bouvier Kennedy. He was the youngest president elected to the White House[2] and stood in marked contrast to the apparent age and lethargy of his predecessor. The Kennedys were young, athletic, masters of the new medium of television, and—like so many of their generation—were contributing to the baby boom. Scenes such as John Jr. crawling through the opening in the Oval Office's Resolute desk helped Kennedy bond to the emerging post-war leadership class.

The Kennedys were treated almost as rock stars, with magazine photo spreads and a pop-culture following that allowed them to dictate fashion sense. Jackie helped restore the White House with new art and furniture, and together they hosted artists, literary greats, and intellectuals at glittering dinners and musical events in the executive mansion.

After JFK's assassination, Mrs. Kennedy shared in an interview that Jack had a passion for the Broadway musical *Camelot*, particularly the concluding scene during which a discouraged King Arthur is conducting a siege of the castle in which his wife and her lover are trapped. Arthur encounters the future Sir Thomas Mallory and sends him back to England to carry on the traditions of the Round Table: "Don't let it be forgot, that once there was a spot, for one brief, shining moment that was known as Camelot." She concluded, "There'll be great presidents again . . . but there will never be another Camelot."

The memory of a president cut down on the cusp of greatness, has animated public affection and opinion long after his passing.

LAUNCH STANDS

17 MISSILE ERECTORS

JOHN F. KENNEDY: BAY OF PIGS AND CUBAN MISSILE CRISIS

During the Eisenhower administration, Fidel Castro had over-thrown Cuban dictator Fulgencio Batista and quickly began to reveal his communist sympathies and affinity for the Soviets. Eisenhower had set into motion a Central Intelligence Agency (CIA)–led attempt at overthrowing Castro. Kennedy continued the planning and agreed to the execution of the attack, during which a rag-tag group of 1,400 Cuban exiles landed at the Bay of Pigs on the southwestern coast of Cuba. Kennedy refused to allow direct U.S. land or air support for the rebels, and they were quickly overcome by Castro's forces.

Despite this humiliating defeat of the U.S. backed rebels, Castro was concerned that the U.S. would eventually succeed. He convinced his Soviet allies to install offensive nuclear missiles in Cuba as a preventive measure. The ever-volatile Russian premier, Nikita Khrushchev, accommodated Castro, and the world was set for the Cuban Missile Crisis.

In October 1962, CIA spy planes detected the installation of those offensive Soviet missiles in Cuba. After a tense exchange of letters, Kennedy and Khrushchev agreed on a compromise. The U.S. would agree not to invade Cuba and the Soviets would remove and not base nuclear missiles in Cuba. Secretly, the U.S. agreed to pull obsolete Jupiter nuclear missiles from Turkey and Italy.

The crisis ended but was the closest the world has come to nuclear war. Kennedy's firmness caused his approval ratings to soar. Because many in the Soviet Politburo felt they had received a set-back, political support for Khrushchev diminished, and he was soon removed from his positions of leadership.

JOHN F. KENNEDY:
CIVIL RIGHTS

One of the most pressing issues facing the nation during the Kennedy presidency was civil rights. A fundamentally cautious politician, Jack Kennedy expressed his support for integration and civil rights during the campaign. Nevertheless, he understood the importance of Southern white voters to sustaining the Democratic majority in Congress and even to securing his own re election.

He enforced federal court rulings that integrated the University of Mississippi and the University of Alabama, even when the governors of those states attempted to block that integration. He watched as black activists protesting discrimination in Birmingham, Alabama, were battered with billy clubs, set upon by dogs, and hit with high-pressure fire hoses. He heard the stories of freedom riders who rode through the South trying to integrate lunch counters and accommodations.

Finally, he acted.

On the evening of June 11, 1963, President Kennedy spoke to the country in a nationally televised address in a *Report to the American People on Civil Rights*. Kennedy said it was time that we "treat our fellow Americans as we want to be treated." He outlined the most far-reaching civil rights legislative program in U.S. history.

JOHN F. KENNEDY: VIETNAM

From the beginning of his time in the White House, JFK was confronted with the vexing question of Vietnam. He had continued the anti-communist struggle of his two predecessors and had sustained U.S. support for the southern part of Vietnam after the 1955 partition, but the situation in South Vietnam was becoming more perilous for America's friends.

Despite the presence of U.S. advisors, the South Vietnamese Army was failing in its attempts to withstand the communist insurgency; Kennedy really did not know what to do. In October 1963, Kennedy signaled to Vietnamese army officers that if they overthrew but did not kill the ineffective and unpopular President Ngo Dinh Diem, they would have U.S. backing. When they conducted the coup and then brutally murdered Diem and his sadistic brother, Kennedy was stunned.

Soon, however, Kennedy was expressing major skepticism. He had already signed a directive pulling one thousand advisors out of South Vietnam by the end of 1963, and all of them by 1965.

In contrast to Kennedy's growing uncertainty, the ever-confident National Security Director McGeorge Bundy prepared an Action Memorandum on steps the U.S. could take, including increased economic and military aid, to fight communism in South Vietnam. He intended to present it to Kennedy when the president returned from his November fence-mending political trip to Texas.

JOHN F. KENNEDY: ASSASSINATION

In order to win re-election in 1964, Jack Kennedy would need to carry Texas. Complicating that were divisions within the Democratic party in the Lone Star State. Liberals led by Senator Ralph Yarborough and conservatives led by Governor John Connelly were at odds over civil rights and other issues. The president traveled to Texas a year before the election to help smooth over this intra-party squabble. Between 150,000 and 200,000 Texans viewed the motorcade on its route from the airport to the Dallas Trade Mart where Kennedy was scheduled to make a speech to city business and political leaders. When they reached Dealey Plaza, just five minutes from their destination, Lee Harvey Oswald—a Marine veteran, an employee of the Dallas School Book Depository, and an admirer of Cuban strong-man, Fidel Castro—fired three shots from a window high in the depository, assassinating Kennedy and injuring Governor Connelly.

After a moving and enthralling funeral in Washington, D.C., the slain president was laid to rest in Arlington National Cemetery, joined in later years by his wife, their two deceased children, and his two brothers. Almost immediately, newly sworn-in President Lyndon B. Johnson appointed a commission headed by Chief Justice Earl Warren to examine the assassination. After months of deliberation, it concluded that Oswald, acting alone, murdered the president. Many Americans have long harbored doubts about the Warren Commission's conclusions and have trafficked in multiple conspiracy theories, none of which have ever reached the level of plausibility.

JOHN F. KENNEDY: LEGACY

For a president with only a brief tenure in office, John F. Kennedy has retained a remarkably consistent hold on the national imagination since his assassination in 1963. One historian explains that JFK didn't so much as "lift" the office of president as much as "cripple" the presidents that succeeded him, so difficult it was to live in the shadow of his legend.

His election as a practicing Catholic went a long way to ending religious prejudice and expanding the nation's ethnic and sectarian diversity. Nevertheless, a historical case can be made that Kennedy was more successful in death than in life. He signed no significant piece of legislation, but finally, just prior to Dallas, he did propose an expansive and inspiring liberal program. Having passed it would have fulfilled the ultimate legislative aspirations of both Theodore and Franklin D. Roosevelt, as well as Truman. It was left to the political genius of his successor to make significant advances in civil rights, health care, voting rights, and social transformation.

The myths of Camelot remain—the glittering, athletic couple; the handsome children cavorting through the White House; the vigorous defense of western liberties and American values; the elegant use of presidential humor. These memories are combined with the clear, articulate expression of the aspirations of the rising post-war leadership class in Kennedy's inaugural address, "Let every nation know, whether it wishes us well or ill, that we shall pay any price, bear any burden, meet any hardship, support any friend, oppose any foe, in order to assure the survival and the success of liberty."

36

LYNDON B. JOHNSON

LYNDON B. JOHNSON: LIFE PAGE

Born: August 27, 1908, Stonewall, Texas

Education: Texas State University (BA)
Georgetown University

Military Service: United States Navy, 1940–1964
Silver Star

Married: Lady Bird Taylor, 1934

Member, U.S. House of Representatives: 1937–1949

U.S. Senator: 1949–1961

Senate Majority Leader: 1955–1961

Thirty-Seventh Vice President of the United States: 1961–1963

Thirty-Sixth President of the United States:1963–1969

Died: January 22, 1973, Stonewall, Texas

Additional resources available for this president at www.amomentintime.com.

LYNDON B. JOHNSON: CONGRESSIONAL CAREER

Lyndon Johnson descended from two of the most prominent Texan families, but he grew up on the edge of poverty and never forgot it. He took a break from college and taught Mexican-American children in a segregated school south of San Antonio. The experience made a lasting impression on Johnson. As he managed his ambitious march to prominence, he never forgot those children and other disadvantaged minorities; he was determined to be their champion.

He began his long political climb as a congressional aide. Then as a Roosevelt loyalist, he ran the Texas National Youth Administration, helping young people get education and jobs. He ran for Congress in 1937 and returned to Washington to continue his political climb.

In 1948, Johnson defeated popular Governor Coke Stevenson in a primary contest so close—87 votes out of a million statewide—and so fraught with rumored corruption that Johnson's reputation was stained, and he was forever afflicted with the nickname "Landslide Lyndon." It might have been close, but that was enough for Johnson. In the Senate, he was particularly adept at pushing legislation forward and developed an intimidating style of leadership known as "The Treatment." Journalists Robert Novak and Rowland Evans said it included "supplication, accusation, cajolery, exuberance, scorn, tears, complaint, the hint of threat. . . . He moved in close, his face a scant millimeter from his target . . . an almost hypnotic experience and rendered the target stunned and helpless."

LYNDON B. JOHNSON: VICE-PRESIDENT AND SUCCESSION

Part of political fallout from the *Brown vs. Board of Education of Topeka* decision on integrating schools and the civil rights movement in general was the gradual dissolution of the Democratic "Solid South." He believed that he needed a Southerner on the ticket to arrest the decline of Southern support.

Almost alone among his inner circle, Kennedy believed he needed to include his arch-rival for the nomination, Senator Lyndon Baines Johnson (D–Texas). Overcoming resistance from even his brother Robert, Kennedy offered and, shockingly, Johnson accepted the vice-presidential nomination. The Democrats went on to win an extraordinarily close election against Vice President Richard M. Nixon. Johnson's presence on the ticket probably made their victory possible.

Johnson hated the job. Having surrendered his position as Senate majority leader, where he had real power, he ended up in a sinecure that was mostly pomp, circumstance, and puffery. Kennedy actually sympathized with Johnson and tried to give him jobs to keep his mind occupied. The vice president was included in the Cabinet and National Security Council meetings. He was given general supervision over U.S. space exploration initiatives. Lyndon was also helpful in congressional relations, though the legislative accomplishments of the Kennedy years were meager.

LYNDON B. JOHNSON:
KENNEDY LEGISLATIVE AGENDA

After Kennedy's assassination, President Johnson seized Kennedy's legislative agenda and made it his own. He put forward a large tax cut to further stimulate the economy, a civil rights bill, and an anti-poverty program that morphed into his signature War on Poverty.

After the tax cut passed, Johnson was ready to begin the real heavy lifting. President Johnson was not going to settle for an attenuated civil rights effort. The bill banned discrimination in public accommodations and public facilities, empowered the attorney general to enforce desegregation in public schools, increased the power of the Commission on Civil Rights, forbade discrimination in federally funded projects, and enhanced equal opportunity in employment preventing discrimination on the basis of race, color, religion, sex, or national origin.

Under a viable threat of a discharge petition, the House Rules Committee—which had bottled up the bill for weeks—finally released it to the House floor where it passed in its final form, 289 to 126. In the Senate, Southerners conducted a weeks-long filibuster, but in the end the bill's sponsors mustered enough votes to cut off debate; the bill passed 73 to 27. President Johnson signed the Civil Rights Act of 1964 into law on July 2, 1964.

LYNDON B. JOHNSON:
ELECTION OF 1964

Any fears Lyndon Johnson had that he might lose the election in 1964 were quickly disabused by the Republicans. In the four years following the defeat of Richard M. Nixon, right-wing conservatives had mastered the party electoral enterprise and secured the nomination of Senator Barry Goldwater of Arizona. He was an articulate and determined right-wing reactionary and allowed himself to be painted as an extremist. In his acceptance speech at the San Francisco Republican National Convention, Goldwater's crucial paraphrase of Marcus Tullius Cicero sealed his fate: "I would remind you that extremism in the defense of liberty is no vice. And let me remind you also that moderation in the pursuit of justice is no virtue."

In a masterful exploitation of the voter's fears of the Arizona conservative's careless rhetoric about military solutions to Cold War antagonism, Johnson ran perhaps the most effective negative ad of this, or any, campaign. "The Daisy Field" portrayed a young girl picking apart a flower followed by a nuclear explosion and a call to voters to support President Johnson.

On November 3, they did. In the largest popular vote to date in U.S. history, Johnson and his running mate, Senator Hubert Humphrey, were elected in a landslide. The popular vote was 61.05 percent to 38.5 percent. In the Electoral College, Johnson swept Goldwater aside 486 to 52.

LYNDON B. JOHNSON:
JOHNSON LEGISLATIVE AGENDA

In the wake of the John F. Kennedy tragedy and the Republican self-destruction, President Johnson had a political opportunity no president had enjoyed since Franklin D. Roosevelt's landslide election in 1936. In addition to the Johnson–Humphrey wipe-out, the Democratic majority was increased to two-thirds in both houses of Congress.

There followed the most extraordinary tsunami of social, regulatory, and civil rights legislation in living memory. It was driven by a master politician with dazzling skills of organization and persuasion. In addition to the three major initiatives of President Kennedy—a tax cut, civil rights, and anti-poverty legislation—Lyndon Johnson sent forward and brilliantly maneuvered a large number of bills through a receptive Congress.[1]

There is no comparable period of legislative creativity in presidential history—with the possible exception of Roosevelt's first and second terms. Though some of these initiatives have drawn criticism, many still remain a vital part of the social safety net and have won the support of voters and law makers alike.

LYNDON B. JOHNSON: CIVIL RIGHTS

From the time of his college teaching experience in a school segregated on the basis of race, he harbored a desire to lift the burdens of racial discrimination from the shoulders of minorities.

Using sympathies aroused by the assassination of President John F. Kennedy, Johnson orchestrated the epic Civil Rights Act (1964) through Congress. Johnson then began to tackle the vexing problem of voter suppression. In the Voting Rights Act (1965), the president opened the door to millions of African Americans to be able to exercise their civic privileges, empower the attorney general to enforce voting rights protections, and restricted certain Southern states from making changes to their voting laws without "preclearance" from the Department of Justice. He also began attacking and prosecuting the Ku Klux Klan—a first for a president since Ulysses S. Grant.

Using the national revulsion at the assassination of Dr. Martin Luther King Jr., President Johnson proposed a third Civil Rights Act (1968)—which sought equal opportunity and outlawed discrimination in housing based on race, creed, or national origin. He appointed Thurgood Marshall, a prominent civil rights litigator, as the first African American on the Supreme Court. Johnson's appointments further solidified his reputation as a champion of civil rights, minority preferment, and black progress.

| 1900 | 1925 | 1950 | 1975 | 2000 | PRESENT |

LYNDON B. JOHNSON: VIETNAM

Lyndon Johnson did not want a land war in Asia. He understood that a U.S. military engagement in South Vietnam would sap national energy and resources for his Great Society program in a war that might not be winnable. Additionally, Johnson believed that failing in Vietnam would tempt the Soviets and China into further aggressive military pursuits.

Like John F. Kennedy, Johnson feared that failure to pursue a winning strategy in Vietnam would arouse a right-wing reaction that would damage the dominance of the Democratic party far into the future. Ironically, Johnson's fears were the reverse of reality. Wider engagement in the war brought a left-wing reaction that destroyed his presidency.

Using the excuse of an imaginary attack by North Vietnamese patrol boats on U.S. destroyers in the Tonkin Gulf in 1964, Johnson secured congressional approval for an open-ended commitment to expanded U.S. military engagement in Vietnam. He initiated an American bombing campaign that dropped more ordinance on Vietnam than all Allied bombing in World War Two combined, largely to no avail. Johnson committed upwards of 525,000 troops (by 1967) and a vast support structure to the Vietnam War, which ended in U.S. defeat and the loss of millions of Vietnamese and 58,000 American lives.

LYNDON B. JOHNSON: ANTI-WAR
UPHEAVAL AND DOMESTIC UNREST

President Johnson's main goals after his triumphant election in 1964 were domestic—civil rights, health care, education, anti-poverty programs, and regulatory reform. Therefore, he chose the disastrous course of attempting to distract the people with his build-up of U.S. forces in Vietnam. His failure to effectively engage the American people in a national debate on the value of the war—and the need for sacrificing the blood of their children and hard-earned treasure—led to growing domestic opposition, undermined support for the troops in the field, and even weakened support for Johnson's domestic agenda.

It became increasingly obvious that Vietnam was a losing proposition. Continuing its prosecution daily added to the death count on both sides with no appreciable progress toward peace. Anti-war demonstrators were present nearly everywhere, and the ever-suspicious Johnson ordered the FBI to monitor participants and leaders of the anti-war movement; the president inaccurately suspected that they were driven by communist sympathies and acting as agents of the Soviets.

On January 30, 1968, support for President Johnson's Vietnam War policy and his presidency collapsed.

LYNDON B. JOHNSON: TET
OFFENSIVE AND DECLINING TO RUN

Years of falsely optimistic reports on progress in Vietnam came to a careening halt on January 30, 1968. North Vietnam and its Viet Cong allies launched the infamous Tet Offensive. They attacked U.S. bases and the U.S. Embassy in Saigon, as well as the five largest South Vietnamese cities and many strategic installations. In retaliation, the U.S. and South Vietnamese armies virtually wiped out the Viet Cong as a viable political or military force, and North Vietnam lost a significant portion of its offensive military capability.

Nevertheless, the Tet irrevocably turned public opinion against the war. The American people were no longer willing to send their sons into the Vietnam meat-grinder. On March 31, in a speech to the nation, Johnson announced his willingness to halt the bombing in North Vietnam and openness to peace talks. Then he announced, "I shall not seek, and I will not accept, the nomination of my party for another term as your president."

As the parties grew close to a settlement that would end the bombing, Republican candidate Richard M. Nixon sent a back-channel message to the Saigon regime promising better terms if they delayed their agreement until after the election. Steps toward peace, which might have helped Vice President Hubert Humphrey win the election, were thus undercut and Nixon won.

LYNDON B. JOHNSON: LEGACY

More than most presidents, Lyndon Johnson was a force of nature. Perhaps the most successful "presidential legislator" in U.S history, he managed to get through Congress a glittering array of legislative accomplishments unequalled by the vast majority of the occupants of the White House throughout U.S. history. He believed in the efficacy of state engagement in problem solving. He was motivated not by some secular social creed, but in the spiritual imperative of the Christian faith he learned in his youth. Therefore, his saw his solutions to long-term-term vexing U.S. social and legal problems as a moral crusade.

If President Johnson is a bell-weather of the dazzling potential of presidential power in the hands of a master political logician, he is also a clear signal that such power has its limitations. His inability to imagine a solution to the problem of Vietnam short of full-scale war; his determination, ignoring all the warning bells going off in his head, to take the nation into what became an unwinnable land war in Asia; and his unwillingness to find a way to extract the U.S. from its commitments in time to prevent the inevitable American collapse in Vietnam has forever stained his presidency. Historian Robert Dallek calls him "an exceptional chief, a flawed giant."

For students of the presidency, Johnson will always remain a fascinating mixture of success and failure, of dreams evolved and dreams abated, of dynamic ability in many things, paired with occasionally tragic miscalculation—a man with divine ambition irrevocably married to human frailty.

37

RICHARD M. NIXON

RICHARD M. NIXON: LIFE PAGE

Born: January 9, 1913, Yorba Linda, California

Education: Whittier College, BA

                  Duke University, JD

Married: Thelma "Pat" Ryan, 1940

Military: United States Navy Reserve, 1942–1966

          Commander

Member, U.S. House of Representatives: 1947–1950

U.S. Senator: 1950–1953

Thirty-Sixth Vice President of the United States: 1953–1961

Thirty-Seventh President of the United States: 1969–1974

Died: April 22, 1994, New York City, New York

Additional resources available for this president at www.amomentintime.com.

RICHARD M. NIXON: CONGRESS AND VICE PRESIDENT

Richard, or Dick, Nixon grew up during the Great Depression in a family that struggled financially but was strengthened by its Quaker faith. After marriage to Thelma "Pat" Ryan—a popular Whittier, California, high school teacher—and Navy service in the South Pacific, he decisively won election to a conservative southern California congressional district.

When Dwight D. Eisenhower was seeking a vice-presidential running mate in 1952, he needed to firm up his support with the Republican right-wing "Old Guard." Nixon fit the bill. When accusations emerged of a corrupt Nixon slush fund provided the candidate by his California donors, Eisenhower considered dumping Nixon from the ticket. Nixon saved himself with the famous "Checkers" television broadcast denying the charges. Eisenhower and Nixon went on to a landslide victory.

President Eisenhower invited Nixon to sit in on Cabinet and National Security Council meetings and sent him on international travel, but he insured that Nixon had little real influence on the making of policy. Nixon held Eisenhower in almost paternal reverence and dutifully followed the remit the president laid out for him—though privately he chaffed under his debased role in the administration. President Eisenhower retained Nixon on the ticket in the 1956 re-election campaign and the two won convincingly.

RICHARD M. NIXON: LOSS TO KENNEDY—1960

As the campaign of 1960 reached its climax, Vice President Nixon retained a small but significant lead over Senator John F. Kennedy. Nixon was seeking to extend the mandate of an administration that was hobbling to its anemic dénouement. He sought to contrast his dutiful, experienced stability to the energetic fresh opportunities promised in the Massachusetts senator's call for "getting the country moving again." Kennedy proposed to awaken America from its 1950s lethargy and wielded his most effective weaponry in the newly significant medium of television.

When they met at the first televised debate in Chicago, radio listeners gave the debate to Nixon, but the telegenic Kennedy clearly bested Nixon in the visual medium. The vice president, who was recovering from a knee injury, appeared haggard, had lost weight—which showed in his loosely fitted suit—and did not use make-up to hide his "five o'clock shadow." Kennedy slowly moved into the lead in late polling. Four debates were quite enough for Nixon; it was not the field upon which he could excel. He never again subjected himself to a presidential debate.

The outcome was one of the closest in American history. Less than 115,000 votes (.02 percent) separated the two candidates in the popular vote. There was a tight spread in the Electoral College as well. While he did not contest the election, Nixon was bitter about the outcome.

RICHARD M. NIXON: DEFEAT IN CALIFORNIA — 1962

Disappointed in the presidential election outcome, Dick and Pat Nixon returned to California. He practiced law and wrote his bestselling book, *Six Crises*. Unable to resist the call of politics, he only weakly resisted first attempts to draft him to run for governor of California in 1962.

His opponent, incumbent Governor Pat Brown, was a savvy political operator in his own right and exploited the disturbingly accurate notion that Nixon was just using this campaign to keep himself viable for future national efforts. It was a lively campaign, but one that knocked the luster off a former vice president who had stooped low to grab a place-holding political job.

Nixon lost to Brown by five percentage points. The next morning, an embarrassed and bitter Richard Nixon held a press conference. Blaming a biased press corps for its supposed preference for Brown, he concluded, "You won't have Nixon to kick around anymore because, gentlemen, this is my last press conference." Of course it was no such thing. Politics for Dick Nixon was mother's milk. It was irresistible to him and drew him slowly and surely like the mythical Icarus upward to his tragic fate.

RICHARD M. NIXON: COMEBACK
AND ELECTION–1968-I

After the loss in the governor's race in 1962, the Nixons moved to New York, where he became the senior partner in a major law firm. There he began to meet the men who would help him orchestrate his return to national politics—among them John Mitchell, who would become Nixon's attorney general.

The Nixon family supported his desire to run for president a second time and, with him, believed that a Democratic party ripped apart by Vietnam gave the Republicans a fighting chance in 1968. Nixon's insight was confirmed as the nation stumbled forward through the chaotic events of that year. The Tet Offensive, Lyndon B. Johnson's decision not to run, and the assassinations of Senator Robert F. Kennedy and Dr. Martin Luther King Jr. all heightened the nation's anxiety, creating an opening for Nixon's appeal to stability. In 1968, an exhausted nation turned to Richard Nixon.

The final result was strongly influenced by Nixon's secret back-channel encouragement to the South Vietnamese government to stonewall the Vietnam peace process. He promised them a better deal if they would help him defeat his Democratic rival, Vice President Hubert H. Humphrey. The South Vietnamese's stubborn resistance at the peace talks probably tipped the election to Nixon. He won 43.4 percent to 42.7 percent over Humphrey, with Wallace trailing the two at 13.2 percent. In the Electoral College, Nixon prevailed 301 to 141 to 46, respectively.

RICHARD M. NIXON: COMEBACK AND ELECTION – 1968 · II

In 1968, Nixon's chances were immeasurably enhanced by his alliance with Senator Strom Thurmond (R–South Carolina) and their adoption of a "Southern Strategy." Through this candidate, Nixon lured white Southerners skeptical about African American progress into the GOP with promises of appointing "strict constructionist judges" and soft-pedaling the enforcement of civil rights laws. As allegedly predicted by President Lyndon B. Johnson after signing the 1964 civil rights bill, Nixon's initiative expedited the decades-long migration of Southern white voters into the Republican party.

Such an effort meant a wrenching change in the Republican *raison d'tre*. The party was created in the 1850s to halt the spread of slavery to U.S. territories. Under Abraham Lincoln, Republicans prosecuted the Civil War, preserved the Union, and constitutionally ended slavery in the U.S. forever.

In reality, the Nixon/Thurmond conspiracy was just the latest episode in a belatedly acknowledged but long-term Southern strategy: a continuation by Republican presidents to reach out to Southern voters skeptical of African American progress—an effort that stretched back to the administration of Theodore Roosevelt. These attempts meant the party was abandoning its legacy of support for black civil rights.

RICHARD M. NIXON: VIETNAM—
BOMBING AND NEGOTIATIONS

As he took office, President Nixon concluded that victory was impossible and that the U.S. needed to extract itself from the southeast-Asian conflict. Nixon, like Lyndon B. Johnson before him, believed that bombing and heightened military pressure was essential to getting North Vietnam to take a reasonable position at the negotiating table.

As the talks continued, North Vietnam still held to the position that a U.S. withdrawal was their top priority. After consultations with the South Vietnamese, in 1969 Nixon initiated a phased withdrawal of U.S. troops. It was managed under a policy he euphemistically called "Vietnamization," a gradual process of turning the war over to South Vietnam. This was a merely a lightly veiled cover strategy for the U.S. departure from Vietnam.

Fighting in Vietnam, which had continued virtually unabated since 1945, came to an end with the Paris Peace Accords of 1973. A cease fire permitted the withdrawal of the American troops that still remained in Vietnam. Ominously, there was no requirement that over 150,000 North Vietnamese troops also withdraw; when U.S. combat operations ended, the ceasefire ended as well, and in 1975, the North finally succeeded in subjugating all of Vietnam.[1]

RICHARD M. NIXON: ANTI-WAR MOVEMENT

President Nixon promised in the 1968 campaign that he had a plan to end the war in Vietnam, but in reality he had no such thing. Despite his protestations that he was bringing the war to an end, the killing continued, the bombing continued, the dying continued. He was particularly angered when confronted with a young generation of critics who took to the streets to protest the war.

In April 1970, Nixon announced the Cambodian "incursion," a bombing and land invasion of Cambodia, the western neighbor of Vietnam. Americans who thought the war was winding down were shocked at this action, though few knew U.S. planes had been bombing Cambodia and Laos for more than a year. This action tossed up the largest and most outraged anti-war protests in American history. In May, six students were killed during peaceful demonstrations at Kent State University in Ohio and Jackson State University in Mississippi. Nixon proved himself incapable of relating to a younger generation that opposed his policies.

By the time the U.S. had lost the war and pulled out of Vietnam, upwards of 58,000 U.S. troops had paid the ultimate price. Their sacrifice was particularly poignant because they died in service to a failed policy that stretched back through five administrations under Presidents Harry S. Truman, Dwight D. Eisenhower, John F. Kennedy, Lyndon B. Johnson, and Nixon.

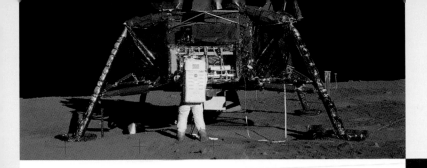

RICHARD M. NIXON: DOMESTIC POLICY AND MOON LANDING

President Nixon's forte was foreign policy, but he was engaged in a surprisingly liberal series of policy initiatives. He permitted the creation of the Environmental Protection Agency (EPA) and the Occupational Safety and Health Administration (OSHA), expanded food stamps, and allowed the Labor Department to move in the direction of affirmative action regulation.

At the same time, Nixon kept his connections with conservatives well-oiled—particularly with the Southern variety—by slowing down implementation of the Voting Rights Act and school busing. He honored his promise to appoint "strict constructionist" Supreme Court justices who would please Southern voters. Unfortunately, his first two nominees—federal judges Clement F. Haynesworth Jr. and G. Harold Carswell—were rejected by a Democratic Senate. These actions—combined with his continuation of the Republican Southern Strategy, with its racist overtones that began under President Theodore Roosevelt—helped transform American politics for generations to come.

Nixon basked in the national pride provoked by the first manned landing on the moon in July 1969, but he reduced funding for NASA's plans for a permanent moon base and a manned trip to Mars. Nixon's fears of cost overruns forced the space program to make serious choices about its future, which would include the Skylab space station and construction of the first space shuttle.

RICHARD M. NIXON: OPENING TO CHINA AND THE SOVIET UNION

President Nixon saw that his legacy would be measured by his foreign policy. He teamed with his intelligent and ambitious national security advisor and then secretary of state, Professor Henry Kissinger, to create new and bold initiatives that helped make significant changes in international relations.

Having moved the competing parties in Vietnam to peace discussions, Nixon and Kissinger began to explore relations with both China and the Soviet Union. Kissinger began secretly visiting China to lay the groundwork for a Nixon visit. Simultaneous announcements by China and the U.S. paved the way for the visit in February 1972. President Nixon met with Chairman Mao Tse-tung and Premier Zhou Enlai, visited the Great Wall, and recognized Taiwan as a part of China. The meeting allowed Nixon to put pressure on the Soviet Union at a time when Chinese–Soviet relations were at absolute rock bottom. Later in 1972, the president visited Moscow and had meetings with Kremlin leaders, which yielded real results. The leaders initialed SALT I, the first nuclear arms limitation agreement, and an anti-ballistic missile treaty.

Nixon and Kissinger believed that improved relations with both China and the Soviet Union was good in itself, but it also might put pressure on North Vietnam to become more forthcoming at the negotiating table. It was clear to the North Vietnamese that Nixon wanted out of Vietnam at any cost and was ready to abandon the forlorn Saigon regime anyway.

RICHARD M. NIXON:
RE-ELECTION 1972

The 1972 Nixon campaign was a brilliant success. It was well-funded by legitimate contributions and millions of dollars in secret contributions. The polls showed him ahead during much of the campaign season. It seemed that Nixon's excessive fears that drove him to extreme measures (see chapters on Watergate) were unfounded.

The Democrats nominated Senator George McGovern of South Dakota, whose impeccable reputation as a candidate with firm liberal and anti-war credentials threatened even some Democratic Party leaders. Nixon confined his campaign speeches to large gatherings of enthusiastic supporters. McGovern expressed support for abortion rights, and some of his advocates were suspected of favoring a softening of U.S. drug policy. When McGovern dumped his running mate, Missouri Senator Thomas Eagleton—who had undergone electroshock psychiatric treatment for depression—any hopes of re-taking Nixon were dashed.

In November, the ticket of Richard Nixon and Spiro Agnew romped to one of the greatest electoral triumphs in U.S. history. In contrast to the tortured result of 1968, Nixon won an over-whelming outcome in both the popular vote, 60.7 percent to 37.5 percent, and in the Electoral College, 520 to 17.

RICHARD M. NIXON:
RESIGNATION OF VICE PRESIDENT SPIRO T. AGNEW

Vice President Spiro Theodore Agnew was a little-known Maryland governor when Richard Nixon tapped him as his running mate in 1968. His Southern connections and articulate delivery as the Nixon attack dog soon proved invaluable.

After their victory, Nixon teamed Agnew with speechwriter Pat Buchanan and sent him off on a crusade against the president's enemies, particularly the press. In the mid-term elections of 1970, his alliterative attacks on liberal opponents as "nattering nabobs of negativism" solidified his national reputation and support among conservatives.

Yet, Spiro T. Agnew was corrupt to the core. By 1973, a team of Justice Department investigators had determined that Agnew accepted bribes and kickbacks for favorable treatment in construction projects while county executive and governor. The payoffs continued—even in the White House. On October 10, 1973, Agnew appeared in federal court in Baltimore and pleaded no contest to a single felony charge of income tax evasion in 1967. He then submitted his resignation to Secretary of State Henry Kissinger, was fined $10,000, and served three years of unsupervised probation. Nixon then nominated House Minority Leader Gerald Ford to replace Agnew as vice president.

RICHARD M. NIXON: WATERGATE-I

When the 1972 campaign season began to ramp up, the Nixon re-election effort was driven by a chief executive whose fears and paranoia were focused on domestic enemies of his Vietnam policy. In 1971, an impulsive young presidential aide, Tom Charles Huston, developed an extreme plan of attack against Nixon's opponents.

One part of the "Huston Plan" that survived was the formation of a group of clandestine operatives, "The Plumbers," who carried out "black bag" jobs.

In June 1972, the Plumbers, led by James "Jim" Walter McCord Jr., were caught attempting to plant electronic bugs at the headquarters of the Democratic National Committee in the Watergate Complex in Washington. McCord later turned state's witness and implicated numerous members of President Nixon's staff and the Committee to Re-Elect the President (CREEP). Initially, President Nixon's strategy was to downplay the break-in as a "third-rate burglary" and attack the press investigations as inaccurate and jaundiced. In an attempt to deflect scrutiny, the president cleaned out the White House of those associated with the break-in on April 30, 1973. Nixon nominated Elliot Richardson as the new attorney general, who appointed former Solicitor General Archibald Cox as Watergate special counsel.

RICHARD M. NIXON: WATERGATE-II

In mid-May 1973, Attorney General Elliot Richardson appointed a special counsel to investigate what Nixon's press secretary, Ron Ziegler, called a "third rate burglary" of the Watergate headquarters. At the same time, Congress got involved with the appointment of the special Senate Watergate Committee in mid-May 1973.

While Special Counsel Archibald Cox engaged in quiet inquiries, the Senate committee's deliberations were shepherded before a live television audience and presented a dazzling stream of high-level witnesses; testifying were close associates of the president, including Domestic Advisor John Ehrlichman, Chief of Staff Harry Robbins, H.R "Bob" Haldeman, and White House Counsel John Dean.

Their testimonies hinted at Nixon's role in shaping the attack on his political enemies, but except for Dean, they fell short of implicating the president in wrong doing. Dean warned the president that a "cancer was growing on the presidency," and testified his suspicions that the president had helped in the cover-up.

The Senate hearings went on into the summer of 1973, but they were gradually beginning to lose steam. That all changed with the testimony of the Federal Aviation Administration (FAA) administrator and former White House aide, Alexander Butterfield. He revealed the existence of a secret taping system in the oval officeand in other White House meeting rooms. From that point on the Watergate inquiry were engaged in prying loose those tapes from the hands of the president.

RICHARD M. NIXON: WATERGATE-III

It is now clear that Nixon knew there was incriminating and unflattering dialogue on those tapes. He resisted their release with all legal means necessary. When Special Counsel Archibald Cox tried to subpoena those tapes, Nixon fired him in the so-called "Saturday Night Massacre" on October 20, 1973. During this drama, both Attorney General Elliot Richardson and Deputy Attorney General Ruckelshaus resigned on principle rather than fire Cox themselves. Finally, Solicitor General and Acting Attorney General Robert Bork fired Cox, but so swift and thunderous was the public clamor, that Nixon was forced to appoint a new special counsel, Leon Jaworski, who continued the investigation where Cox left off.

Finally, on July 24, 1974, the Supreme Court unanimously ruled that Nixon had to give up all the tapes completely—and he had to do so immediately. One tape, the infamous "Smoking Gun" tape, revealed that while Nixon had not ordered the break-in, he had quickly learned of the circumstances surrounding it and had participated in attempts to cover-up White House involvement.

At that point, Republican leaders sadly went to Nixon and warned him that impeachment and removal from office were assured. After a nationally televised address filled with pathos and self-justification, on August 9, 1974, Richard Nixon became the first president to leave office by resignation.

RICHARD M. NIXON: RESIGNATION

Having exhausted all his legal and political options, Richard Nixon realized he had no choice but to resign. Like some Greek tragedy, he believed all the forces that had conspired against him year after year—throughout his entire career—were at last combining to drive him from office. In a series of hubristic acts equal to that of a modern-day *Oedipus*, Nixon had handed over the cudgels of circumstance and power to his opponents, who then beat the life out of his presidency. A year later, he admitted to interviewer David Frost that he had let the country down.

The day after his national address signaling withdrawal from office, he spoke to his staff and admirers gathered in the East Room of the White House. He talked of his deprived childhood and his early exclusion from the world of affluence and social esteem—feelings he shared most acutely with the first lady. They hungered to "belong" and now once again were being shown the door, banished from the heights of power. Their circumstance was due as much to the shell of resentment and bitterness which they built around themselves as it was to any imagined enterprise of their enemies.

The Nixons boarded *Marine One*. It took them to the blue Air Force plane that would bear them to their western exile. Somewhere above the heartland, as if by some constitutional alchemy, the plane became no longer *Air Force One*. It was just an ordinary Boeing 707 on an ordinary day carrying an ordinary politician to his home in disgrace.

1750   1775   1800   1825   1850   1875

RICHARD M. NIXON: LEGACY

Richard Nixon, even in his humiliation, was one of the most successful politicians in American history.

A month after Nixon resigned, President Gerald R. Ford issued a full and complete pardon of Richard Nixon for any crimes that he may have committed as president. Forty-eight of his associates were indicted and convicted of actions associated with the break-in, the cover-up, or other nefarious administration projects. He alone among the conspirators remained free, unprosecuted save by the judgement of history.

On the plus side, his brilliant foreign policy initiatives advanced the United States' power and helped restore national prestige after America extracted itself from the Vietnam morass. On African-American civil rights, Nixon honored his promise to Southern voters that he would abridge the ambitious goals of his two predecessors. His continuation and refinement of the Republican Southern strategy, with all its racial overtones, transformed the national political landscape into the dawn of the twenty-first century. Finally, he midwifed the tragic and disruptive alliance of politics and dark corporate money that has tarnished the world of public policy to this day.

Like his predecessor, Richard Nixon was a flawed giant. Yet, he was almost as engaging in his dark times of struggle, years of disgrace, and wandering in the political wilderness as he was at the heights of power and prestige. He died of a massive stroke on April 22, 1994.

38

GERALD R. FORD

GERALD R. FORD: LIFE PAGE

Born: July 14, 1913, Omaha, Nebraska as Leslie Lynch King Jr.

Education: University of Michigan (BA)

Yale Law School (JD)

Military Service, United States Navy: 1942–1946

Married: Betty Bloomer, 1948

Member, U.S. House of Representatives: 1949–1973

Minority Leader, U.S. House of Representatives: 1965–1973

Fortieth Vice President of the United States: 1973–1974

Thirty-Eighth President of the United States: 1974–1977

Died: December 26, 2006, Ranch Mirage, California

Additional resources available for this president at www.amomentintime.com.

GERALD R. FORD: HOUSE SERVICE AND VICE PRESIDENT

Gerald Ford had a successful academic and athletic career at the University of Michigan and then attended Yale Law School. After graduation, he briefly practiced law, but after Pearl Harbor he enlisted in the U.S. Navy, where he served in the Pacific and rose to the rank of lieutenant commander prior to his discharge.

In Congress, he slowly accumulated seniority and served in leadership positions. He was held in esteem by his colleagues, though his largely failed attempt to block President Lyndon B. Johnson's legislative tsunami earned the president's ire, who said, "Jerry Ford is so dumb that he can't fart and chew gum at the same time."

As Richard Nixon's Watergate problems mounted, the scandalous resignation of Vice President Spiro Agnew provided an opening for Ford. Democratic House Speaker Carl Albert made it clear that only Jerry Ford was acceptable to the opposition. For the first time, the United States had a vice president who had not faced the voters. Shortly after Congress voted to make him vice president, Ford took the oath of office. This process was made possible through the mechanism established in the Twenty-Fifth Amendment.

On August 1, 1974, he was informed that investigators had found the "smoking gun," the confirmation that President Nixon had engaged in criminal malfeasance. Days later, Ford heard that a resignation was imminent. On August 9, he was sworn in as the thirty-eighth president of the United States.

GERALD R. FORD: SUCCESSION AND
PARDON FOR NIXON

After the national trauma of Vietnam and Watergate, the leadership of the profoundly decent Gerald Ford was beyond refreshing, at least at first. The words from his short inaugural address—"our long national nightmare is over"—resonated with a public that was weary of scandal and conflict. He genuinely seemed to desire a national healing. He cultivated the press, invited former occupants of President Richard M. Nixon's "enemy list" to the White House, and demonstrated an everyman demeanor to a nation used to distant, inaccessible chief executives. In turn, he received spectacularly positive press coverage.

Unfortunately for Ford, his honeymoon with America lasted just a single month. On September 8, 1974, Ford issued a full and unconditional pardon for any crimes Nixon may have committed as president. The first reaction was national disgust and wide-spread conviction that some "corrupt bargain" had guided the new president—specifically that he had promised a pardon in exchange for Nixon's resignation so that Ford could ascend to the presidency. This suspicion was almost certainly not true. Ford's pardon was most probably issued for two reasons: 1) sympathy for the Nixon family and for his longtime friend and 2) a desire to remove the issue of Nixon's guilt or innocence forever from the national agenda.

Whatever his reasons, the pardon placed an acute shadow over Ford's term in office and was seen by many Americans as "profoundly unwise, divisive, and unjust." It undoubtedly cost him his chance to win an elected term to the White House.

GERALD R. FORD:
ELECTION OF 1976

By the mid-1970s, right-wing conservatives were a boisterous—if not completely dominant—part of the Republican coalition. Hoping to head-off opposition to his election, President Ford announced his intention to run in November 1975. Right-wing Republican increasingly began to throw their support to former Governor Ronald Reagan of California in his challenge to the president for the Republican nomination.

Neither arrived at the convention in Kansas City with enough delegates, but in the end Ford won. His fight with Reagan so weakened Ford that he couldn't win the general election against former Governor Jimmy Carter of Georgia.

The Reagan challenge was not Ford's only problem. He faced an uphill battle throughout the campaign. He had to shoulder the burden of the Watergate memory and the Nixon pardon, an economy still struggling against the twin evils of unemployment and inflation, and a series of gaffs in the televised debates. He muffed one answer on Soviet domination of Eastern Europe, mistakenly saying it didn't exist. He really meant that Soviet occupation would never diminish the hopes for liberty and the spirit of freedom among the occupied states, but by that time it was too late.

In the end, Carter prevailed over President Ford, but only in a very close election.

GERALD R. FORD: LEGACY

Considering the challenges he faced, it is remarkable that President Ford was able to accomplish anything in his short term of office. His greatest accomplishment was in restoring integrity to the office of president. After more than a dozen years of assassination, war, disappointment, and scandal, the White House was at last inhabited by a decent man with strong character and an inspiring leadership style. Despite his reputation for personal rectitude, Ford's pardon of Nixon was considered to be ill timed and of poor judgement. It probably ensured that Ford would lose his quest for election to the White House in 1976.

Ford survived two assassination attempts in September 1975. The first in Sacramento, California, by Lynette "Squeaky" Fromme, a follower of Charles Manson; and the second in San Francisco, California, by Sara Jane Moore. Both assassins were tried and received life sentences but were paroled in 2009 and 2007, respectively.

His swift reaction to Kampuchea's (Cambodia) attack on the Sea-Land Container ship SS *Mayaguez* and North Korea's attack on U.S. and South Korea served notice that the loss in Vietnam meant that the American eagle still had sharp claws and was not an inconsequential player in the international arena.

After his loss to Jimmy Carter, Ford and his wife eventually settled in Ranch Mirage, California, and Vail, Colorado. He led an active life until his death on December 26, 2006. He was ninety-three years old.

39

JIMMY CARTER

JIMMY CARTER: LIFE PAGE

Born: October 1, 1924, Plains, Georgia

Education: Georgia Institute of Technology

                United States Naval Academy (BS)

Married: Rosalynn Smith, 1946

Military Service: U.S. Navy, 1943–1953

                U.S. Naval Reserve, 1953–1961

Member, Georgia State Senate: 1963–1967

Seventy-Sixth Governor of Georgia: 1871–1975

Thirty-Ninth President of the United States: 1977–1981

Volunteer with Habitat for Humanity

Recipient of the Nobel Peace Prize: 2002

Additional resources available for this president at www.amomentintime.com.

JIMMY CARTER:
SOUTHERN MODERATE

The story of Jimmy Carter seems as if crafted from the nineteenth century. He grew up on a peanut farm in southwest Georgia, graduated from Annapolis, became a submariner, and served from World War II through the Korean Conflict. Over the next decade, Carter and his wife, Rosalyn, mastered the intricacies of agribusiness and turned their prosperity into the foundation of a political career.

When a state Senate seat opened up in 1962, he parlayed his experience as a local school board chairman to enter the contest. Carter's problem was that he was inclined to be supportive of black civil rights, integration, and liberal social issues, but this meant downplaying his true preferences.

He ran twice. Carter won in 1970 using near-racist language in a bitter primary campaign against former Governor Carl Sanders. After winning, in a head-snapping inaugural address, Carter reversed course and set the tone for his four years as governor, "no poor, rural, weak, or black person should ever have to bear the additional burden of being deprived of the opportunity for an education, a job, or simple justice." Suddenly, Carter became the symbol of the progressive New South—complete with a cover story in *Time Magazine*.

JIMMY CARTER:
ELECTION OF 1976

With an uncanny sense of the conflicting impulses afoot in the southern American electorate, Carter set about shaping his image to match the mood of the voters. Building on his growing reputation as representative of New South politics, he positioned his state reputation to further his national ambitions. He appointed many blacks to state jobs and judgeships and he tried to anticipate issues that would enflame racial animus to avoid political unrest.

When Governor Carter announced his candidacy for president in early 1976, he had 2 percent name recognition, but he had allies in the national news media who rather openly promoted his candidacy. With overwhelmingly positive press coverage and a thirty-seven-state speaking tour before any of the well-known candidates had even declared, his outsider campaign registered with voters in Iowa and New Hampshire. He won on the first ballot at the Democratic Convention in 1976 and, to cement his relationship with the progressive wing of the party, chose Hubert Humphrey–acolyte Walter Mondale as his running mate.

Carter started off way ahead of Ford, but the race tightened. But then, the president's stumble over Soviet domination of Eastern Europe in the second debate froze his resurgence and Carter won in November. It was a close outcome, 50.1 percent to 48 percent in the popular vote, 297 to 240 votes in the Electoral College.

JIMMY CARTER: FOREIGN POLICY
AND CAMP DAVID ACCORDS

Within the Carter administration, two impulses on foreign policy struggled for supremacy. Secretary of State Cyrus Vance advocated an openness to detent with the Soviet Union, while National Security Advisor Zbigniew Brzezinski urged the president to a more militant international posture.

The Soviets began to push the edges of post–Vietnam War U.S. resolve in the world arena through increased defense spending and by using Cuban troops in Africa. Carter tilted his policies toward Brzezinski, advocating a return to the traditional Cold War–policy of containment, higher military expenditures, and soft-pedalling the international human rights initiative that he announced in his inaugural address.

Nevertheless, in June 1979, Carter and the ailing Soviet leadership traveled to Vienna and initialed the START II treaty, which projected a rough nuclear parity between the two superpowers.

One of Carter's most outstanding achievements was to help broker a break-through in the Middle East. In September 1978, he invited Israeli Prime Minister Menachem Begin and Egyptian President Anwar Sadat to the presidential retreat at Camp David. In thirteen days of intense back-and-forth negotiation, Carter brought the two leaders together in a peace accord—a peace treaty that ended three decades of armed conflict.

JIMMY CARTER: PANAMA CANAL TRANSFER TREATY

The United States completed construction of the Panama Canal in 1914. Provisions of the Hay-Bunau-Varilla (H-B-V) Treaty (1903) with Panama gave the U.S. control over the canal and the canal zone in perpetuity. Over the years, the Republic of Panama grew restive under the terms of the treaty and its lack of ability to profit from the commerce that traversed its territory.

Panama wanted the U.S. to surrender the canal. In 1972, however, during the Nixon administration, serious efforts to reach comity began to bear fruit. When Jimmy Carter came to office, he was determined to resolve this on-going international conflict. Negotiations led by Ambassador Ellsworth F. Bunker and Sol Myron Linowitz led to two treaties that were eventually ratified by the U.S. Senate.

The first treaty allowed the U.S. to continue its protective stewardship of the canal should any power threaten the neutral use of the canal by all nations. The second treaty guaranteed that ownership of the canal and canal zone would revert to Panama on December 31, 1999.

The signing of the treaties provoked a searing debate in the United States. Conservatives, including future President Ronald Reagan, accused the president of willful surrender of a valuable American military and economic asset.

JIMMY CARTER: IRAN HOSTAGE CRISIS AND AFGHANISTAN

In October 1977, a coalition of leftist and Islamists in Iran began a campaign of peaceful protests against the regime of Shah Mohammad Reza Pahlavi. Under Carter, the normal American position of lock-step support for the Shah's reign had begun to weaken due to human rights abuses by the royal regime and because of his support for the Organization of the Petroleum Producing Countries' (OPEC) oil increases during the 1970s. The political pressure against the Shah increased, and by early 1979 he had departed on his last exile.

Later in 1979, the new Iranian republic—under the Supreme Leader Ayatollah Ruhollah Khomeini—permitted an allied student organization of Islamic militants to take over the U.S. Embassy and hold fifty-two American hostages for 444 days. To get them released, the president imposed severe economic sanctions against Iran, and in April 1980, he ordered an ultimately failed rescue attempt resulting in the loss of eight American fighters.

In 1978, Communists seized power in Afghanistan. When brutal tactics by two successive presidents worsened the situation, on December 24, 1979, the Soviet Union invaded and installed Soviet loyalist Babrak Karmal as president. Originally Carter was surprised by the invasion, but he quickly moved to inflict retribution on the Soviets, fearing a threat to the Persian oil supply and the stability of both Iran and Pakistan. The firm stand Carter initiated in 1980 hastened the 1989 withdrawal of the Soviets from Afghanistan.

JIMMY CARTER: ELECTION OF 1980

Any hope that President Carter could achieve re-election was dashed with the failure of Operation Eagle Claw. This aborted rescue operation of the fifty-two American hostages held by Islamic militants at the U.S. Embassy in Teheran was a good try but suffered from failed equipment and poor unit cohesion among the rescuers. Of course, President Carter rightly accepted the blame that was universally attributed to his leadership. He went to political war with a divided Democratic party unenthusiastic about his leadership.

He faced a no-longer divided Republican party and a spirited and well-funded challenge from actor-turned-politician, former Governor Ronald Reagan of California. With his mastery of humor and soaring command of the rhetorical high-ground, Reagan could not have been a more vivid contrast to the dour Carter. Carter's correct perception of reality was that the U.S. was facing a new era of restraint, but Americans used to hearing their destiny involved prosperity, expansion, and worldwide influence found his opponent and that message more alluring. After the first and only debate, Reagan experienced a surge, and in November, he yielded a massive landslide in both popular votes (51 percent to 41 percent) and the Electoral College (489 to 49). In a bittersweet aftermath to Reagan's inauguration, as the new president finished his twenty-minute speech, Iran released the fifty-two hostages it had held for 444 days. President Carter was on-hand as presidential emissary to receive them when they landed in Germany.

JIMMY CARTER: LEGACY

Few presidents have presented themselves to the voters after facing the kind of challenges faced by Jimmy Carter. After enduring the loss of the war in Vietnam, the American people still believed that the U.S. should project its power and values in the international arena. This was a conundrum that would defeat most leaders, but President Carter labored on through it.

He was slow in developing the personal and political skills that made Washington work, often expecting Congress to come to the presidential heel. As a result, his legislative accomplishments were meager. He failed to enact a much-needed comprehensive energy program and wide-ranging national health-care system that was much desired by his party. His failure is most acute given that during his entire term the Democrats controlled Congress.

After his crushing loss to Ronald Reagan, Carter returned to Plains, Georgia, set his financial house in order, and embarked on one of the most successful post-presidential careers in U.S. history, comparable only to John Quincy Adams, Martin Van Buren, Theodore Roosevelt, and Herbert Hoover. He established the Carter Center, which worked to enhance human rights, assuage misery, and improve the lives of people in eighty countries or more.

As he has outlived his detractors—from pigmy partisan pundits to political opponents—Jimmy Carter has demonstrated the strength of character and basic human decency that attracted voters to his long-shot presidential bid in 1976. That he was unable to overcome the challenges that he faced perhaps says more about the enormity of those challenges than the presidential stewardship of this profoundly virtuous public servant.

40

RONALD REAGAN

RONALD REAGAN: LIFE PAGE

Born: February 6, 1911, Tampico, Illinois

Education: Eureka College (BA)

Vocation: Actor and Motivational Speaker

Politician: 1937–1965

Military Service: United States Army and U.S. Army Air Forces: 1937–1945

Married: Jane Wyman, 1940; divorced 1949
        Nancy Davis, 1952

President, Screen Actors Guild: 1947–1949; 1959–1960

Thirty-Third Governor of California: 1967–1975

Fortieth President of the United States: 1981–1989

Died: June 5, 2004, Los Angeles, California

Additional resources available for this president at www.amomentintime.com.

RONALD REAGAN:
ENTERTAINMENT CAREER

In Hal Wallis's film *Kings Row* (1942), Drake, the distressed hero played by a young Ronald Reagan—noticing that his legs had been amputated—cried out "where's the rest of me?" Reagan used that famous line as the title for his 1965 autobiography. It was an appropriate title for a life in transition. Reagan was at the still point of a life-change, moving decisively out of entertainment into public policy and politics.

After college graduation and a brief turn in sports broadcasting, Reagan received a film contract after a screen test in 1937. At Warner Brothers, he began a career performing in a long serious of "B" movies that were, for the most part, imminently forgettable.

On active duty during World War II, he performed in morale boosting and military training films as a part of First Motion Picture Unit of the Army Air Forces. He was married to actress Jane Wyman in 1938, and after their divorce in 1949, he married Nancy Davis. They enjoyed a long "close, authentic, and intimate" relationship until his death in 2004. She became one of his most trusted advisors in his political ascent.

Reagan did two turns as President of the Screen Actors Guild, thereby getting experience in a highly visible political position while representing the acting community as a union official.

In the 1950s, seeing the film business changing and his career in eclipse, Reagan shifted over to television as a contract actor, hired by General Electric to host the *General Electric Theater*. The company also featured him as a motivational speaker to its 200,000 employees, and his speeches reflected the philosophical metamorphosis, from Democrat to Republican, from liberal to conservative, that transitioned Ronald Reagan from acting to politics.

RONALD REAGAN:
GOVERNOR OF CALIFORNIA-I

Even when Ronald Reagan was a Democrat, prior to 1962, he was involved in politics. He was an intense fan of Franklin D. Roosevelt, campaigned in 1948 with Harry S. Truman, and supported Helen Gahagan Douglas in the bitter 1950 senatorial campaign against Richard M. Nixon.

However, through the influence of his new wife, her ultra-conservative family, and right-wing General Electric (GE) executives, Reagan began to shift from his New Deal roots to an increasingly conservative philosophy. This—and his superb rhetorical skills—increased his appeal to the growing right wing of the Republican party. In 1964, he was perhaps the most effective surrogate for Barry Goldwater in the senator's doomed presidential bid. "The Speech," televised on Goldwater's behalf, took an honored place in the mythical pantheon of American conservative oratory. In it, Reagan distilled all the sermonic themes of his GE speeches into a clarion call for a conservative renaissance. "We must choose not between a left or right, but I suggest . . . only an up or down. Up to . . . the maximum of individual freedom consistent with order—or down to the ant heap of totalitarianism." And of course, he preached, the Democrats have definitely chosen the latter.

So effective was his advocacy that Reagan emerged from the disaster that was 1964 as one of the few Republicans whose reputation and national visibility remained unsullied. Seeking a plausible candidate for governor in 1966, two Californians formed "Friends of Ronald Reagan" to advance his candidacy. Not yet fully able to disengage from his former life, Reagan responded to press queries as to what kind of governor he would be with, "I don't know; I've never played a governor."

RONALD REAGAN:
GOVERNOR OF CALIFORNIA-II

Having abandoned the liberal convictions of his youth, Reagan established his conservative bona fides with the power players on the far-right wing of the California Republican party. They needed an ideologically acceptable, photogenic candidate with a glib and winning delivery to take on two-term Governor Pat Brown. Influenced by his conservative wife, her ultra-right-wing family, and General Electric executives who provided his livelihood for more than a decade, Reagan evidenced all the characteristics of a true conservative believer. Needy candidate and needy supporters gradually embraced each other.

In late 1965, Reagan announced his candidacy for governor. He won the Republican nomination in the spring and went on to sweep the November election against Brown (57.5 percent to 43.2 percent). The themes of the Reagan campaign would become familiar to those who followed his career as president. He called for sending the "welfare bums back to work" and, both in the campaign and as governor, went head to head with various protest movements. In 1969, Governor Reagan first sent state troopers and then the National Guard to quell student-led protests at the so-called "People's Park" in Berkley. His dispatch of state authorities led to the death of one student, the blinding of an on-looker, and injury to over a hundred law enforcement personnel.

Governor Reagan was re-elected in 1970. During his two terms, he signed bills permitting therapeutic abortion, repealing California's open carry gun law, and establishing no-fault divorce. Later, he said he regretted signing all three of these initiatives. Governor Reagan declined to run for a third term. As early as 1968, he had begun to set his sights on a higher goal.

RONALD REAGAN:
ELECTIONS OF 1968 AND 1976

Soon after his installation as Governor of California, Reagan and his closest advisors began planning for a run for president. He ran three times in 1968, 1976, and 1980. His last was successful, but each of the previous aborted attempts ingratiated him to the growing conservative base of the Republican party and increased his national visibility.

Governor Reagan pursued the nomination in 1968 as part of a "stop Nixon" effort led by Governor Nelson Rockefeller of New York. This effort was frustrated when the former vice president arrived with a tiny but decisive twenty-five vote margin, giving him the nomination. Reagan came in third.

During Nixon's presidency, and as the president was strangled by the Watergate scandal, Reagan quietly continued building his national support network. After he completed his second term as governor, he set his sights on challenging President Gerald R. Ford for the 1976 nomination. Both candidates won a share of primary delegates but neither arrived at the Kansas City Convention with the nomination secured. Ford prevailed by just over one hundred delegate votes to win the party's nod—but then went on to lose the election to Jimmy Carter.

Reagan kept himself in the national spotlight with a series of radio commentaries and speeches on behalf of Citizens for the Republic, a political action committee that worked to raise the putative candidate's public awareness and funds to fuel his coming 1980 presidential campaign.

RONALD REAGAN:
ELECTION OF 1980

The Reagan campaign was a well-funded and well-led juggernaut that ran over the beleaguered President Jimmy Carter, achieving along the way a landslide in the Electoral College. The campaign reflected the candidate's signature issues: lower taxes, smaller government, and increased spending on the military. Reagan expressed his support for states' rights in the first speech he made after his nomination—at the Neshoba County Fair near Philadelphia, Mississippi. This was a clear signal to white Southerners that Reagan was sympathetic to their vision of an ordered society. It was also a marker of the Republicans' intent to challenge Jimmy Carter and the Democrats on their home turf, in the heart of the Solid South.[1]

Playing on Reagan's decades of visibility, sunny personality, and executive experience as a two-term California governor, the campaign recognized that if they could get Reagan on the same stage as the president, his visible confidence and easy demeanor would compare favorably with the dour Carter. In Cleveland, Reagan carried the day and cemented his lead in the polls with his reaction to Carter's assertion that he opposed Medicare. With four little words—"There you go again"—Reagan seemed to lecture a sitting president. He incorrectly deflected Carter's critique, dealt with his alleged problem of inexperience, and appeared presidential. He carried the debate and the election. Reagan's popular margin was diminutive (50.7 percent to 41.0 percent), but the Electoral College was substantial (489 to 49).

RONALD REAGAN: ASSASSINATION ATTEMPT-I

Though his 1980 electoral vote total was high, Ronald Reagan's popular vote was rather modest. His victory was as much a repudiation of his opponent than it was a vote for Reagan. It was certainly no mandate for his ideas, his policies, or even himself. That all began to change in the early afternoon of March 30, 1981. Reagan was returning to his limousine after making a speech to representatives of the AFL-CIO union organization at the Washington Hilton Hotel when he was shot. John Hinkley Jr., an emotionally disturbed neurotic, fired six rounds from a Röhm RG-14 .22 LR blue steel revolver, which he legally purchased at a gun shop in his home town of Dallas, Texas.

One shot hit Presidential Press Secretary James Brady in the head, causing severe brain damage. Two others struck police officer Thomas Delahanty and Secret Service Agent Tim McCarthy. Reagan was protected from a direct shot by McCarthy, who placed himself in front of the president, but endured a shot that glanced off the armored side of his limousine and connected with the president's left underarm, grazed a rib, and lodged in his lung less than an inch from his heart. Then the left presidential lung collapsed.

RONALD REAGAN:
ASSASSINATION ATTEMPT-II

His condition was deemed critical, "close to death." Attending physicians operated on President Reagan, removing the bullet, and his condition stabilized.

The concern of the nation was palpable. What they heard was soothing and inspiring. The wounded president took pains to assure the nation that he was alive and in full possession of his faculties. And he did it with humor—the best kind of political palliative.

When the first lady first arrived at the emergency room, he ripped off Jack Dempsey's remark to his wife after being beaten by Gene Tunney: "Honey, I forgot to duck." When he was being prepped for surgery, he removed his mask and said, "I hope you are all Republicans," whereupon the lead surgeon, a liberal Democrat, said, "Today, Mr. President, we are all Republicans."

Up to that time there had been much public skepticism about Reagan's ideas. As he recovered from the assassination attempt, his popularity soared. His calmness under fire, his warm, sunny personality, and his personal courage won over some of his toughest critics and broke the logjam in Congress. This secured for him the political capital to enact many of his signature proposals.

Reagan was the first president to have survived an assassination attempt.[2]

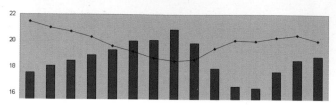

40-G1

RONALD REAGAN: REAGANOMICS-I

The domestic program advocated by Ronald Reagan in the early days of his administration has been called the "economics of joy." It was designed to reduce the inflation rate when he came into office (which was at 12.5 percent), cut marginal tax rates on all Americans, bring down unemployment from President Jimmy Carter's high rate of 7.5 percent, introduce vast new military expenditures, and at the same time slice federal spending and the national debt—all of this without inducing an iota of political pain.

He pursued *laissez-faire*, free-market policies that were designed to accomplish his incredibly optimistic and often contradictory policy goals because they were based on the "supply side" theories of conservative economist Arthur Laffer. This notion posited that if you reduced tax rates enough you would expand the tax base by bringing more taxpayers into the system, igniting an explosion of economic growth, and raising government revenue so as to achieve all of Reagan's ambitions.

In order to do this, Reagan had to abandon traditional Republican orthodoxy about balanced budgets and smaller government. He first began with a huge cut in marginal tax rates, followed by large tax increases in each year of his presidency. The net effect of all this fiscal churning was negligible. The government took in more, cut social programs, and then spent wildly on the military build-up, agricultural price supports, and Medicare and Medicaid. The national debt grew enormously. Inflation declined, but that was mostly due to the severe decline in oil prices and the restrictive monetary policies of the Federal Reserve.

RONALD REAGAN: REAGANOMICS-II

After two years of recession that ended in December 1982, the economy began to grow, and it continued to grow each year of the 1980s. This was not necessarily because of Reagan's policies, but rather it followed a similar pattern of recoveries through U.S. history—aided, of course, by the oil price collapse. In 1982, unemployment spiked to the highest level since the Great Depression, but it reverted to an average of 7.5 percent over the course of his presidency. The president's program of tax cuts for his wealthy supporters has been proven to be of questionable value, or, in the words of his successor, George Bush, in the 1980 campaign, "voodoo economics."

Even after the stock market crash of 1987 revealed the sham that was "Reaganomics," "Teflon" Ronald Reagan was able to avoid a retributive voter reaction to his questionable economic record. This was, in part, due to the normal recovery and steady financial improvement after 1982 and, in part, to voter's stark memories of the terrible economy under his three predecessors.

Far more devastating to the less-fortunate in America were Reagan's brutal cuts to social programs—reducing funds for food stamps, the Environmental Protection Agency (EPA), and education programs; purging the Social Security disability rolls; freezing the minimum wage; cutting assistance to state and local governments; removing funding for public housing and rent subsidies; wiping out anti-poverty programs; and trying to cut the Medicaid budget—to make way for tax cuts for the wealthy and massive increases in military spending.

RONALD REAGAN:
ELECTION OF 1984

By 1984, a majority of the American people were feeling quite good about the nation's prospects. They could answer in the affirmative the Reagan question from 1980, "Are you better off than you were four years ago?" Unemployment had peaked and was coming down. Inflation was being reduced by the hard-nosed monetary policies of the Federal Reserve and the marginal reduction in oil prices. National optimism was heightened by the stunning victories of American athletes at the Summer Olympic Games in Los Angeles—which Reagan opened.[3]

The Democrats nominated former Vice President Walter Mondale, who led in most polls particularly due to fears about President Reagan's advancing age and his poor performance in the first debate. In the first debate, Reagan seemed confused and unfocused, but the president rebounded in the second debate, using humor to deflect the growing concern about his ability. He said, "I am not going to make age an issue in this campaign. I am not going to exploit, for political purposes, my opponent's youth and inexperience." Even Mondale laughed at that.

The election then reversed course on a dime and Reagan won an astounding victory: 49 states, 58 percent to 40.6 percent in the popular vote, and 525 out of 538 electoral votes.

RONALD REAGAN: MILITARY BUILD-UP AND REAGAN DOCTRINE

Foreign policy in the Reagan years was dominated by the president's life-long obsession with communism. He believed the system was destined for the ash heap of history, but he felt the architecture of Marxism needed a push down the hill toward that heap. Under the so-called Reagan Doctrine, the U.S. provided financial aid, covert training, and arms support to anti-communist resistance movements around the world—in Africa, Asia, and Latin America.

Reagan began a multi-year increase in military spending designed to confront the tottering Soviet regime. The Soviets were already spending at a level they could not sustain, and, as later described by Secretary of Defense Caspar Weinberger, the plan was to increase military spending in the U.S. to a level that any attempt to increase its already high military budget would injure the Soviet economy—which was already under terrible stress.

At the same time, Reagan wanted to reduce the threat of nuclear weapons. He faced an unstable and sclerotic Soviet leadership until, in 1985, he found a bargaining partner in the pragmatic, technocratic reformer, Mikhail Gorbachev. Over several meetings, they hammered out a new approach to arms control embodied in the INF Treaty, which began the process of actually destroying nuclear weapons. This was made possible by authentication that Reagan described in the words of an old Russian epigram, "*doverey, no provery*—trust but verify."

Mark Reinstein / Shutterstock.com

RONALD REAGAN:
WAR ON DRUGS

In 1971, President Richard Nixon declared a War on Drugs (WOD). The Nixon administration recognized it was opposed by two large and vulnerable communities: anti-war activists and blacks. As described by John Ehrlichman, Nixon's disgraced former domestic policy czar, "we couldn't openly declare war against war protestors or blacks, but by getting the public to associate hippies with marijuana and Blacks with heroin and then criminalizing both heavily, we could . . . arrest their leaders, raid their homes, break up their meetings" and, of course, marginalize their communities and their activities.

President Reagan increased funding for the WOD and established mandatory penalties for even minor drug offenses. Reagan's immediate successors continued and amplified the WOD. Unfortunately for Reagan's legacy, the WOD has been an abysmal failure. Drug use has grown over the decades. Perhaps the most serious consequence of the WOD in American society is the stark racial disparity in drug sentencing and incarceration. Black and hispanic boys, young men, and fathers have been packed off to serve long jail sentences for the essentially non-violent crime of possession. Much as Prohibition had done in the 1920s, the WOD failed because it eliminated legal sources for the drugs. It turned drug marketing over to shadowy criminal enterprises (cartels). These then, by violent means, established the illegal distribution network and met America's growing drug demand.

1,000,000+
500,000-1,000,000
100,000-500,000
50,000-100,000
10,000-50,000
-10,000

RONALD REAGAN:
RESPONSE TO AIDS

The Reagan presidency began as the first signs of a strange new pandemic began to victimize members of the homosexual community and intravenous drug users. The administration demonstrated almost no concern for years as the disease spread and began claiming lives.

As the epidemic began to reach epic proportions in the mid-1980s, the Center for Disease Control (CDC) began to beg for greater funding for its work on HIV/AIDS. However, until the late 1980s, requests for more funds were routinely rejected by the White House. Finally, in 1985, President Reagan first mentioned the word "AIDS" in public, and in 1986 he devoted an entire prepared speech to the subject. By that time, 20,849 people had died of the scourge. His commitment to supporting research and treatment began to grow after that speech and there were large funding increases. During his administration, almost $6 billion were devoted to the HIV/AIDS crisis.

President Reagan's hesitation may have been due to in part to the low esteem with which homosexuals were held in Republican circles, particularly among conservative evangelicals. For many of these believers, homosexuality was an anathema. Some of them actually believed HIV/AIDS was a well-deserved punishment from God for homosexuals because of their so-called "unbiblical" lifestyle and sexual proclivities.

Mark Reinstein / Shutterstock.com

RONALD REAGAN: IRAN-CONTRA-I

Ronald Reagan's life-long passion for the destruction of communism cascaded throughout his administration. The intensity of his commitment to this cause affected foreign policy and also the clandestine operations of the intelligence community. Reagan's crusade soon collided with international reality and congressional oversight of foreign policy.

The administration nursed growing hostility to the revolutionary Nicaraguan government led by the left-wing Sandinista party of President Daniel Ortega. The Reaganites favored the Contra rebels, who were conducting a guerilla war against Ortega from bases in Honduras. Congress was determined to block active U.S. support for the Contras and, therefore, passed the Boland Amendment. Named for Representative Edward Boland (D–Massachusetts), it was actually three amendments to defense appropriations bills over multiple years that forbade the intelligence community from providing any covert or direct lethal aid to the Contras to help overthrow the Sandinistas. It was a prohibition, but it provided no penalties for officials who violated the law.

In Middle-Eastern affairs, the U.S. was continuing its campaign against the revolutionary government of Iran by calling on nations worldwide not to sell arms, military hardware, or spare parts to Teheran. At the same time that the U.S was carrying on this public promotion, the Reagan administration was selling arms and spare parts to Iran, ostensibly to curry favor and strengthen a so-called "moderate" faction within the Iranian military.

From its beginning in 1981, the secret flow of U.S. arms and military spare parts to Iran had been hidden to congressional and international scrutiny by using the Israelis to facilitate the exchange.

In the mid-1980s, seven Americans were detained and held as hostage by the Lebanese-based Hezbollah, a terrorist group closely allied with the Iranian Revolutionary Guard. President Reagan wanted those hostages freed, but he hesitated at first to use arms sales to do it. In December 1985, Reagan was made aware of Iran's willingness to press Hezbollah for the release of the hostages in exchange for increased arms sales—particularly TOW anti-tank missiles. Reagan authorized the swap and then, unfortunately, left the implementation of the trade to his trusted aides on the National Security Council (NSC). Soon there was loose, secret cash floating out there, heading back to the U.S and ripe for exploitation.

The conspiracy deepened in 1985 when NSC military aide Lieutenant Colonel Oliver North proposed diverting funds from the Iranian arms sales to the administration's pet Contra project. As could be expected, such a complex and bone-headed arrangement was bound to fail and be exposed. In late 1986, a leak appeared in the Lebanese magazine *Ash-Shiraa*. The strategy was further revealed when a plane filled with arms destined for the Contras crashed in Nicaragua with survivors who admitted the cargo was sent by the CIA.

RONALD REAGAN:
IRAN-CONTRA-III

In two nationally televised speeches on the subject, President Reagan first denied (November 13, 1986) and then admitted (March 4, 1987) that Iran arms sales were used for hostage exchange. From November 20 through 25, 1986, National Security Council (NSC) officials—including Oliver North and National Security Advisor Admiral John Poindexter—began "burning their papers." On November 25, Poindexter resigned and Reagan fired Oliver North.

Subsequent investigations were conducted by the Tower Commission appointed by Reagan, a Justice Department special counsel chosen to determine if crimes had been committed, and in nationally televised congressional hearings. While all acknowledged that the diversion of Iran arms sales were an illegal breach of the Boland Amendment, none of the investigations discovered evidence that Reagan personally authorized or even had known about the scheme to divert funds to the Contras. Congress had a final word on Reagan: "If the president did not know what his national security advisers were doing, he should have."

Reagan's popularity precipitously dropped in the aftermath of the scandal, and for the first time in his administration, the so-called "Teflon President" faced severe and sustained criticism.

RONALD REAGAN: LEGACY-I

Ronald Wilson Reagan lived into his nineties, though in his last years he was afflicted by the curse of Alzheimer's disease. In his twilight years, in that period when he could reflect, he could not have been anything but satisfied with his life accomplishments. He had a moderately successful acting career, served his nation in war, and was well-married to two strong women—one of whom was his deeply devoted life partner.

Reagan's transition into politics reflected all the techniques he learned as an actor. His mastery of the rhetorical arts was unequalled in the twentieth century, save perhaps by the Roosevelts and John F. Kennedy. His use of humor to deflect criticism and ingratiate himself to voters and fellow politicians was superb. Working with a talented group of speech writers like Peggy Noonan, the president's words guided the nation.

Ronald Reagan, by his example and through his policies, led America to abandon long-held notions of thrift and self-denial. During the eighties, family spending levels—often financed through loans on consumer goods, automobiles, and ever-increasingly expensive home purchases—rose precipitously.

One of the ironic outcomes of his largely failed but inventive economic stewardship was that it probably undermined the prospects for President George Bush's re-election in 1992. So enormous were the Reagan deficits that his successor was forced to renege on his campaign promise of "No New Taxes."

Mark Reinstein / Shutterstock.com

RONALD REAGAN: LEGACY-II

By 1989, the Soviet-dominated communist system in Europe was in collapse. Reagan partisans, and then those of President George W. Bush, have claimed far more than is their due in the decline of Marxism. Nevertheless, if calling them the "winners of the Cold War" is naïve and unhistorical, then it must be said on their behalf that Reagan and Bush were brilliantly alert to the possibilities within Soviet weaknesses and helped facilitate the ruin of a system already headed for President Reagan's "ash heap of history."

His presidency was not without its disappointments. Reagan finally acknowledged his early failure to recognize, sympathize, and act to ameliorate those suffering with Human Immunodeficiency Virus Infection/Acquired Immune Deficiency Syndrome (HIV/AIDS), but he slowly rectified his position. By the end of his term, he had initiated the early stages of the funding miracle that has curbed the trajectory of the epidemic and laid the groundwork for a possible future cure of this curse.

His detached management style finally came home to haunt him in the Iran–Contra scandal. His subordinates went too far in implementing the president's clearly stated desires to rid Nicaragua of its left-wing government and broke the law doing it. As a result of his failure of leadership and their failure to honor his trust, Reagan suffered a serious blow to his popularity and the perception of his competence.

1750   1775   1800   1825   1850   1875

Yet, his legacy remains on the positive side. If his terms in office did not exactly bring "Morning in America," as his 1984 campaign slogan claimed, it could be fairly said that after years of mid-morning storms, America under Reagan had emerged into the bright light of a noonday sun.

41

GEORGE H. W. BUSH

GEORGE H. W. BUSH: LIFE PAGE

Born: June 12, 1924, Milton, Massachusetts

Military Service, U.S. Navy: 1942–1945

Education: Yale University (BA)

Married: Barbara Pierce, 1945

Member, U.S House of Representatives: 1967–1971

Tenth Ambassador to the United Nations: 1971–1973

Chair, Republican National Committee: 1973–1974

Second Chief of the U.S. Liaison Office to the People's Republic of China: 1974–1975

Eleventh Director of Central Intelligence: 1976–1977

Forty-Third Vice President of the United States: 1981–1989

Forty-First President of the United States: 1989–1993

Died: November 30, 2018

Additional resources available for this president at www.amomentintime.com.

GEORGE H. W. BUSH: OIL PATCH EXECUTIVE, CONGRESS

Son of a United States senator, George Herbert Walker Bush was born into a prominent New England family. During distinguished service in the Pacific theater in World War II, he married the remarkable Barbara Pierce, and after his discharge, they moved to New Haven, where he attended Yale University. After graduation, he moved to west Texas, where his years of involvement in the oil industry made him a millionaire by the 1960s.

In 1959, Bush moved his family to Houston and got involved in Harris County Republican politics and helped ease the way for conservative Democrats to transition into the Republican coalition. Bush ran twice, unsuccessfully, for the U.S. Senate (1964 and 1970), but he served two terms in the U.S. House representing the 7th Texas Congressional district. In Washington, he compiled a record as a moderately conservative legislator. He supported the Civil Rights Act of 1968, though it was not popular in his district, and was a supporter of a woman's right to determine her own means of birth control. And as a member of the powerful Ways and Means Committee, he backed the effort to reshape the U.S. military into an all-volunteer service.

In 1970, President Richard M. Nixon enticed Bush out of the House to run for the Senate seat being vacated by Ralph Yarborough. Nixon came to Texas to campaign for Bush, but Democrat Lloyd Bentsen prevailed in the general election. This left Bush out of electoral politics for the foreseeable future.

GEORGE H. W. BUSH: UNITED NATIONS (U.N.), REPUBLICAN NATIONAL COMMITTEE (RNC), CHINA, CENTRAL INTELLIGENCE AGENCY (CIA), AND VICE PRESIDENT

After his failed 1970 Senate effort, Bush commenced a voyage of presidential appointments to high-profile positions. At the U.N., he unsuccessfully resisted the expulsion of the Republic of China and transfer of the China chair to the Peking regime. As Chair of the RNC, he helped the party navigate the treacherous shoals of Watergate, finally calling on his mentor, the president, to resign when Nixon's guilt became undeniable.

In China, Bush acted as though he was an ambassador—although he could not be the official envoy. His work in Peking helped smooth and improve Sino–American relations. As head of the CIA, he helped the agency through a period of assault by congressional investigators. Bush helped lift the agency's flagging morale. In 1999, CIA headquarters at Langley, Virginia, was named the George Bush Center for Intelligence in his honor.

At the Republican convention, Reagan chose Bush as his running-mate, and the two went on to a convincing win in the general election. Consistent with his loyal service as an appointed official in the Richard M. Nixon and Gerald R. Ford administrations, Bush attended Ronald Reagan as a faithful partner in their eight year term.

GEORGE H. W. BUSH:
ELECTION OF 1988

In many ways, the election of 1988 represents a parable of the life and political career of George Herbert Walker Bush.

Vice President Bush began his run almost as soon as the echo faded on his vice-presidential inauguration oath in 1985, but he struggled to define himself to the voters. Was he a New England aristocrat, Yale educated and white-glove bureaucrat, or a hard-scrabble businessman from the Texas oil-patch? He thrashed about trying to emulate his mentors Presidents Richard M. Nixon and Ronald Reagan, but he lacked the intellectual underpinning of the first and the smooth, media-shaped eloquence of the latter. His own reputation for sound judgement was challenged by his choice of the clearly unqualified running mate, Senator Dan Quayle of Indiana.

Despite his patrician veneer, much of the vitriolic 1988 campaign—one of the filthiest in the modern era—originated in the conviction that his class, family, and generation brooked no challenge and deserved to rule. To win, he embraced and implemented the tactics of one of the dark masters of modern campaign sleaze, his campaign manager, Lee Atwater.[1]

Bush and Quayle scored a comfortable but unpretentious popular win (53.4 percent to 45.6 percent), though his Electoral College margin was much more convincing. The president-elect became the first sitting vice president to enter the White House since Martin Van Buren in 1836.

GEORGE H. W. BUSH:
DOMESTIC POLICY

Almost from the beginning of his single term, President Bush struggled with the issue of President Ronald Reagan's enormous budgetary debt and on-going annual deficits, which by 1990 had grown to more than $220 billion a year. Republicans were demanding severe cuts in government spending, along with a zero increase in federal levies. Bush's dilemma was heightened because of his 1988 pledge at the Republican Convention, "Read my lips. No new taxes."

In the end, he had to yield to the demands of the congressional majority, raising marginal tax rates with no corresponding spending cuts. He never recovered his popularity with Republican lawmakers or voters and came to regret this bargain. He signed the revolutionary Clean Air Act and the sweeping Americans with Disabilities Act.

Perhaps his most singular domestic achievement was to mid-wife a national emphasis of voluntarism, an initiative he called a "thousand points of light." As the inspiration for the Points of Light Foundation, President Bush could claim to have stimulated an important surge in voluntary efforts nationwide. He saw this as the "soul of America [by which] ordinary people reach beyond themselves to touch the lives of those in need, bringing hope and opportunity, care, and friendship."

Joseph Sohm / Shutterstock.com

GEORGE H. W. BUSH: GULF WAR

In 1990, Iraq invaded and overwhelmed the Kuwaiti armed forces. It established a puppet government. Believing that this action undermined regional stability, President Bush condemned the invasion and immediately began recruiting an international coalition to throw back the Iraqis. By January 1991, there were sufficient coalition forces in the region and they began a four-week assault on Iraqi defenses—complete with eye-popping videos of a new generation of smart weapons and guided bombs. On February 24, U.S.-led coalition ground troops attacked, one force going directly against Iraqi forces in Kuwait and a second wheeling west to cut of Iraqi forces engaged in a desperate attempt to retreat north toward Bagdad. It was a rout and delivered a devastating blow to Iraqi prestige and honor.

Sensinghe had neither congressional nor international support for a full invasion and occupation of Iraq, President Bush halted U.S.-led forces and did not seek the overthrow of Iraqi dictator, Saddam Hussein. Neo-conservatives, among them future Vice President Richard Cheney and future Secretary of Defense Donald Rumsfeld, saw his reluctance to engage in a full invasion to be weak and indecisive.

Bush's domestic approval rating exploded upwards to stratospheric levels, reached nearly 79 percent. For a brief moment of euphoria, the Gulf War helped shape the national focus on American accomplishment. Unfortunately for President Bush, this moment of exhilaration was short lived.

Mark Reinstein / Shutterstock.com

GEORGE H. W. BUSH: LEGACY

One historian deemed the Bush years as the "guardianship" presidency, casting up the image of comfortable and contented national stewardship that was lacking—as Bush so awkwardly put it—"the vision thing." People admired the forty-first president but were never willing to commit to the love affair between leader and people—similar to Theodore and Franklin D. Roosevelt, and Ronald Reagan—that marks a truly majestic presidency.

The end of the Cold War removed a unifying factor from American political discourse. Surprisingly, anger was summoned forth with ease against feminists, gays, immigrants, minorities, pro-abortion advocates, and others who did not fit into "normal" America. This social and religious mêlée began to stir passions and shift opinions in the Republican party.

Perhaps one of the first victims of this transformation was George Herbert Walker Bush, one who could claim at least partial credit for the defeat of the nation's Cold War enemy and absolute credit for America's heartening comeback victory in the Gulf. Yet, even that stunning triumph could not convince a growing number of Republican far-right wingers that Bush was worthy of continued service. This left Bush far short in the election of 1992.[2] One of the profound parts of the legacy of George H. W. Bush was that he took the humiliation of his 1992 loss to Bill Clinton and Ross Perot with a large measure of grace and noble resignation. Even in defeat, he led the nation he loved.

42

BILL CLINTON

BILL CLINTON: LIFE PAGE

Born: August 19, 1946, Hope, Arkansas as William Jefferson Blythe III

Education: Georgetown University (BS)

      Yale Law School (JD)

      University College, Oxford University, Oxford, United Kingdom

Married: Hillary Rodham, 1975

Fiftieth Attorney General of Arkansas: 1977–1979

Fortieth and Forty-Second Governor of Arkansas: 1979–1981, 1993–1992

Forty-Second President of the United States: 1993–2001

Additional resources available for this president at www.amomentintime.com.

BILL CLINTON: NEW DEMOCRAT

The migration of Southern white voters and working-class Democrats into the Republican coalition gave rise to conservative government under Ronald Reagan. In turn, Democrats began to shift their policy positions to reflect the changing electorate and a series of presidential losses in 1980, 1984, and 1988.

One of the leaders of this reassessment was Arkansas Governor William Jefferson "Bill" Clinton. Assuming the autograph "New Democrat," he was one of the founders of the Democratic Leadership Council. They advocated welfare reform, smaller government, and market-based solutions to the nation's problems.

Clinton rose above his troubled childhood and through hard work, academic achievement, and sheer intellectual horsepower graduated from Georgetown University and Yale Law School with a turn as a Rhodes Scholar at Oxford. He met the talented Hillary Rodham at Yale, and together they formed one of history's most successful personal, professional, and political relationships—one that has lasted well into the twenty-first century. Elected five times governor and heading the National Governors Association for one year, Clinton was receiving increasing scrutiny as a possible contender for the White House as a centrist, a New Democrat from the New South. Clinton was selected to deliver the nominating speech for Governor Michael Dukakis at the 1988 Democratic Convention. The speech was long and turgid, but it was a mark of his growing prominence in the party.

BILL CLINTON:
ELECTION OF 1992

If the scripted Ronald Reagan was capable of soaring rhetorical heights, Bill Clinton reached his audience and kept his popularity through the ability to demonstrate empathy for their circumstances. After initially polling low, he came within a hair of winning the New Hampshire primary. During the run-up to the vote, Gennifer Flowers's accusation of an affair with Clinton emerged from the Arkansas political caldron. The Clintons' awkward appearance on *60 Minutes* denying the charges and the subsequent turn-around in the polling probably saved Clinton's campaign. Clinton was nominated on the first ballot at the convention and chose Senator Al Gore of Tennessee as running mate.

George H. W. Bush was leading a party divided over cultural issues and many were resentful of his reneging on the "Read my lips. No new taxes" pledge in 1988.

Polls showed that Ross Perot had a negligible effect on the final outcome, as he drew equally from Bush and Clinton. Perot cut into the popularity of both both Bush and Clinton, denying to the President his re-election and denying to Clinton a popular majority. The vote yielded a Clinton victory (43 percent to 37.4 percent with Perot at 18.9 percent). Clinton triumphed in the Electoral College 370 to 168.

BILL CLINTON: REPUBLICAN VICTORY IN 1994 MIDTERM ELECTIONS

President Clinton was thwarted in his attempt to revamp the nation's healthcare system. Though initially it received strong public support, it faced strong concerted opposition from a coalition of the American Medical Association, conservative Republicans, and the health insurance industry. The administration's highly visible effort was headed by First Lady Hillary Clinton and suffered from a lack of coordination within the White House and cooperation in Congress.

The Clintons were also plagued with investigations of their finances and various "scandals." Lingering resentments growing out of the "Don't Ask, Don't Tell" debate (gays in the military), as well as union opposition from within the Democratic coalition to the 1994 passage of the North American Free Trade Agreement (NAFTA), diminished party enthusiasm in the run-up to the mid-terms of 1994. Clinton's signing of the Brady Bill, and later signing of a ten-year ban on assault weapon sales, were used by the National Rifle Association (NRA) to turn out the vote for Republicans.

The mid-terms became a rout, a prelude to the so-called Republican Revolution of the mid-1990s. The GOP took both houses of Congress with an eight-seat gain in the Senate and a fifty-four-seat turn-around in the House. This was the first time Republicans had controlled both houses of Congress in four decades.

BILL CLINTON: DOMESTIC POLICY-I

Reflecting the president's New Democrat emphases, the administration shaped its domestic agenda based on the composition of Congress—through which it had to maneuver its priorities. During the time Congress was under Democratic control, Clinton had more options to adhere to the traditional party program. Faced with enormous Reagan/Bush deficits, President Clinton advanced the Omnibus Budget Reconciliation Act (1993)—which raised taxes on those with high incomes and reduced those with low incomes—but had to wait until 1997 to address the circumstances of middle-class taxpayers. By that time, unemployment was down, the stock market was quite high, and the U.S. budget was balanced and generating a surplus for the first time since 1969.

In addition to the Brady Bill (1993), President Clinton raised the Earned Income Credit to help low-income workers. The Democratic Congress passed and Clinton signed the Omnibus Crime Bill (1994), which not only put a ten-year ban on assault weapons sales and went after the drug distribution network, but was also used to incarcerate large numbers of Hispanic and African-American men for possession of small amounts of controlled substances. Critics continue to hold Clinton and congressional Democrats responsible for the unintended consequence of the unbalanced detention rate which devastated these minority communities.

BILL CLINTON: DOMESTIC POLICY-II

President Clinton also quietly signed into law the Defense of Marriage Act (DOMA) in 1996. The act was designed to preserve "traditional" marriage and also to deflect contemporary criticism of Clinton that he was pandering to the gay community. That said, Clinton's actions throughout his entire two terms opened up opportunities for members of the LBGTQ community to more fully participate in American life. Specifically, by Executive Order he made it possible for openly gay citizens to gain and hold federal employment. He also championed increased funding for HIV/AIDS research and treatment and came within a single vote of the Senate passing the Employment Non-Discrimination Act.

Since the Great Depression, the Glass–Steagall (GS) provisions of the U.S. Banking Act (1933) had declared legal war against "affiliation," the practice of commercial banks to engage in the trading of investment-grade securities. This was designed to protect depositors from risky investment practices by the banks who were stewards of people's savings. Gradually over the years, Congress and the Federal Reserve had loosened the GS provisions; in 1999, Congress passed and the president signed the Gramm–Leach–Bliley Act (G-L-B), which repealed the GS affiliation provisions. There remains a healthy debate among scholars as to whether this repeal hastened the collapse of the economy in the Great Recession of 2008–2009.

BILL CLINTON: IMPEACHMENT AND ACQUITTAL

Almost from the beginning of his term, President Clinton and First Lady Hillary Rodham Clinton were challenged by public suspicions about their ethical behavior. Most of the accusations proved to be illusory, but two legal proceedings ended up converging and nearly bringing down his presidency.

In 1994, Paula Jones sued President Clinton, alleging that after rejecting his sexual advances, she lost opportunities for promotion in Arkansas state government. Clinton eventually settled with Ms. Jones (for $850,000), but not until after he had made denials of sexual misconduct under oath in pre-trial depositions. Jones's new aggressive defense team (recruited from conservative legal circles) inquired about Clinton's relationship with a twenty-two-year-old White House intern, Monica Lewinsky. He answered evasively and negatively. Then, as the story exploded in the media, he initially and publicly denied that he had sexual relations "with that woman. Ms. Lewinsky."

The investigation eventually yielded charges against the president of perjury as well as obstruction of justice. The House impeached him on those two articles, though the vote was not overwhelming. Since a two-thirds vote for conviction is required in the Senate, the president was easily acquitted. Public opinion moved strongly in favor of the president based on the widespread conviction that he was being impeached and then tried on a matter that was basically a personal matter.

BILL CLINTON: LEGACY-I

President Bill Clinton had some notable achievements in both domestic and foreign policy. He helped broker the peace in Northern Ireland and furthered discussions between Israel and the Palestinian Authority, though this last did not yield an agreement due to some understandable intransigence on the Palestinian side.

As a result of the first World Trade Center bombing (1993), the 1998 attacks on U.S. embassies in East Africa, and the USS *Cole* (2000), Clinton began to pursue the Al-Qaeda network led by Osama bin Laden. The leader was not captured, but the president delivered hard-hitting cruise missile strikes against suspected terrorist targets. Clinton handed over to the incoming George W. Bush administration strong evidence of Al-Qaeda's intent to pursue targets in the United States.

Clinton's record on lesbian, gay, bisexual, transgender, and questioning (LBGTQ) issues was mixed. His "Don't Ask, Don't Tell" compromise was an improvement over past policy and his increase in HIV/AIDS funding and opening of federal employment for gay civil servants helped that community. His signing of the Defense of Marriage Act (DOMA) was negative in the extreme, a reality he recognized in 2013 when calling for its repeal.

He still defends his signature on the Omnibus Crime Bill (1994), but serious criticism has been leveled at him due to the unintended consequence of unbalanced sentencing. This incarcerated, for long terms, a disproportionate number of Latin and African-American men for little more than possession of small amounts of drugs.

BILL CLINTON: LEGACY-II

Clinton's 1996 re-election over Senator Robert Dole did not yield a popular majority due to the presence of Ross Perot in the vote, but it did lay the foundation for further progress on the domestic side. He hoped to build on his record, which included the Family and Medical Leave Act (1993), the Brady Bill (1993), and an increase in the Earned Income Credit. His large tax increase on high income taxpayers, combined with slight reductions in military and civilian expenditures, yielded the first budget deficits since the late 1960s. The resulting budget surplus gave the president and Congress an opportunity in 1997 to cut middle-class taxes, provide college tax credits, and secure a reduction in the growth of Medicare spending. When he lost control of Congress in 1994, Clinton's shrewd use of the political device known as "triangulation" allowed him to accomplish more than would be expected otherwise.

The Clinton legacy of achievement has to be seen in light of his impeachment, only the second such action against a sitting president in the life of the republic. His intellect, political skills, and clear accomplishments must be compared to what he might have achieved were it not for his destructive self-indulgence. So noxious was his personal reputation in some circles that his putative successor hesitated to too-closely attach himself to Clinton and his scandalous record. This probably cost Vice President Al Gore the presidency in the election of 2000, one of the closest in U.S. history.

43

GEORGE W. BUSH

GEORGE W. BUSH: LIFE PAGE

Born: July 6, 1946, New Haven, Connecticut

Education: Yale University (BA)

                Harvard University (MBA)

Married: Laura Welch, 1977

Forty-Sixth Governor of Texas: 1995–2000

Forty-Third President of the United States: 2001–2009

Additional resources available for this president at www.amomentintime.com.

GEORGE W. BUSH: PREPARATION

The future President George W. Bush grew up in Midland and Houston, Texas. He attended Phillips Academy Andover and Yale University. During the Vietnam War, Bush served in both the Texas Air National Guard and the Alabama Air National Guard. After completing his service, he attended Harvard Business School where he received his MBA in 1975—the only president to receive that degree.

Building on his family name and connections, Bush established an oil exploration business in 1977. He continued in the petroleum industry until 1989, when he sold his oil stock for a profit and used it to purchase stock in the Texas Rangers baseball team. Bush led the team as managing partner for five years. His promotional and political skills contributed to the spectacular growth of the franchise. When he sold his share in 1998, his early investment of about $800,000 yielded a $15,000,000 windfall.

George W. Bush's marriage to Laura Welch was successful in many ways—not the least of which was to help him confirm his decision to give up drinking. As he matured, he also commenced a religious quest that validated and strengthened his commitment to the Christian faith, which solidified his marriage and sobriety.

Bush lost a run for the U.S. House, and later returned to run for governor of Texas against the popular incumbent Ann Richards. Bush won. He was a popular governor who was generally conservative in his policies, occasionally offering surprisingly moderate positions, such as support for education, renewable energy, and the valuable place of voluntarism in public life.

GEORGE W. BUSH: ELECTION OF 2000

Soon after his 1998 re-election as governor, conjecture was abundant in the national media as to the possibilities of a Bush run for president in 2000. Portraying himself as a "compassionate conservative," he won the nomination and chose Richard Cheney as running mate.

The general election was hard-fought. Bush lost the popular vote by almost 600,000 votes, the first time since Benjamin Harrison that the winning president did not achieve at least a plurality of the people's votes. It was in the Electoral College that Bush attained his victory, and it was in Florida that the final decision was made. Before the resolution of the Florida vote, the electoral vote stood at 246 to 267.[1] Depending on the result in the Sunshine State, either candidate could win.

In Florida, the difference between the two candidates was less than six hundred votes statewide—with Bush ahead. The Democrats made a strategic error when they asked for recounts in only four counties, which were traditionally Democratic strongholds, instead of a statewide manual count. The hand count in Florida went on for a month before being brought to an end by the U.S. Supreme Court, which ruled five to four for Bush in *Bush v. Gore*. The Court stated the protracted recount was prejudicial because it violated the Fourteenth Amendment. It was one of the most controversial, and allegedly political, decisions in Court history.

Following Presidents John Quincy Adams, Rutherford B. Hayes, and Harrison, George W. Bush was only the fourth president in U.S. history to claim the White House without winning the popular vote. He would not be the last.

GEORGE W. BUSH: DOMESTIC POLICY AND BUSH TAX CUTS-I

President Bush had ambitious goals when he entered office and achieved many of them. He and Congress passed two major tax cuts, the first of which was one of the largest in U.S. history. The tax cuts were fiscally stimulative and helped deal with the recession early in his first term, but they were never offset by increased revenues as promised by supply-side economists. This—along with enormously increased military spending, which included the largely unfunded War on Terror and the wars in Afghanistan and Iraq—blew away the surplus his predecessor left him. During his two terms, the budget was never balanced. Bush more than doubled the national debt.

To address widespread concern about America's education system, President Bush partnered with Senator Edward Kennedy (D–Massachusetts) to advance No Child Left Behind, a restructuring of the country's school system. Using the paradigm of student testing in reading and math, significant progress was realized.

After his re-election, President Bush proposed an upgrade to the Medicare system, which added a prescription drug benefit to help seniors deal with the high cost of drugs. Medicare B was an important improvement in care for the elderly, but it increased annual expenditures without an off-setting funding mechanism.

GEORGE W. BUSH: DOMESTIC POLICY AND BUSH TAX CUTS-II

The Bush approach to the environment tended to reflect the intellectual bias of a Texas oil executive. He opposed U.S. participation in the Kyoto Protocol, an international agreement designed to curb greenhouse gases. Bush did not deny climate change and global warming, but he was ambiguous about whether the phenomenon is man-made or not. Instead, he advocated support for alternative energy technology (better batteries and hydrogen fuel cells) to deal with the climate crisis.

Perhaps one of Bush's greatest disappointments was the failure of the bipartisan Comprehensive Immigration Reform Act (2007), which, under the leadership of Senator John McCain, would have given protected status and work permits to millions of undocumented residents—along with an eventual path to citizenship. The proposal divided the Republican party and failed, largely from GOP opposition.

In early fall 2005, Hurricane Katrina devastated south Florida and then headed for New Orleans. Levee breaches resulting from the hurricane caused massive flooding in the city. The federal government's inept response to the crisis was attributed to Bush's incompetence in the formulation of policy and his choice of subordinates to manage the catastrophe. After Katrina, public opinion began to shift against President Bush. His bumbling response, combined with continual bad news from the Iraq War, permanently altered—for the worse—the president's relationship with the American public. The arc of his leadership never recovered.

GEORGE W. BUSH:
9/11 AND ASYMMETRIC WARFARE

On September 11, 2001, four airliners were high-jacked by dev-
otees of Osama Bin Laden, leader of Al-Qaida, the militant
Sunni Islam multinational organization. Two of the planes hit the
World Trade Center in New York City, one hit the Pentagon, and
the fourth crashed in the Pennsylvania countryside after an apparent passenger revolt against the high-jackers. The 9/11 attack was
an example of asymmetric or irregular warfare and is increasingly a
factor in modern life. Asymmetric conflict describes one in which
two or more weaker opponents attempt to exploit the weaknesses
of their stronger opponents in order to counterbalance their own
weaknesses.

The attacks on 9/11 were perpetrated on an international
power with a huge population—whose military resources and
economic supremacy was unequaled, perhaps in human history.
Yet, the group carrying out this attack had very few adherents by
comparison. One factor that led to the spectacular success of the
Trade Center attack was engineer Bin Laden's understanding of
the towers' structure. A plane hitting the towers at a quarter of
the distance from the top would cause the top floors to collapse
and then, through "pancaking" and sheer weight, take both towers
down.

To defend against such asymmetric attacks, a strong power must
be much more aware of its own weaknesses and prepare to defeat
attempts by disparate entities to exploit those weaknesses.

GEORGE W. BUSH:
WAR ON TERROR—AFGHANISTAN

From the moment the planes struck the World Trade Center in New York on September 11, 2001, President Bush had found his mission, "the central purpose of his administration." Within three days he was at ground zero and declaring. ". . . the people who knocked these buildings down will hear all of us soon."

Backed by an American public that demanded little more than revenge and protection from further attacks, he declared a War on Terror. Wielding virtually unchecked power and leadership that resembled Franklin D. Roosevelt in the weeks after Pearl Harbor, he proposed The Patriot Act, legislation designed to ferret out domestic and international terrorist threats. The act gave law enforcement broad new powers of investigation and incarceration, but also raised heightened concern among civil libertarians.

On September 20, President Bush demanded the Taliban leaders of Afghanistan surrender Osama bin Laden. When they refused, he attacked. British and American air attacks destroyed Taliban resistance and surrounded Al-Qaeda leaders in the mountain refuge of Tora Bora near the Pakistani border. The allies failed to capture bin Laden. Military leaders warned the Bush team that a continued allied presence was necessary to prevent a resurgence of Taliban power and Al-Qaeda influence. That allied presence remains today.

GEORGE W. BUSH:
WAR ON TERROR—IRAQ

President Bush, under strong pressure from Vice President Richard Cheney and other neo-conservatives, used the 9/11 attacks as a pretense to pursue what they considered unfinished business in Iraq.

The reason given to invade and overthrow Iraqi dictator Saddam Hussein was that Hussein was engaged in the manufacture and deployment of weapons of mass destruction, including nuclear arms. A major public relations campaign based on faulty information was employed to whip up congressional and public support for a war against a regime that had absolutely nothing to do with 9/11.

Essentially only Britain assisted the U.S. with the heavy lifting in this invasion, and at first it went well. Saddam's forces, weakened by the Iran–Iraq War and the first Gulf War, collapsed like a house of cards. Soon the dictator was captured and sent to the hangman's noose. Bush's problem was that he hollowed out the Iraqi leadership structure and imposed an alien allied occupation government that soon tossed up a civil war. In 2007, Bush sent an additional 21,500 troops to Iran to deal with the insurgency that had led to some of the most intensive fighting of the war.

The Iraq War changed the complexion of Middle Eastern politics. It ultimately redounded to the advantage of Iran, whose power and influence was enhanced when that nation moved into the power vacuum left with the departure of Hussein.

GEORGE W. BUSH:
ELECTION OF 2004

In the early months of 2001, President Bush's approval rating struggled to remain above 50 percent. That all changed with 9/11. The American people gave strong sanction to President Bush's single-minded focus on pursing those who had attacked the homeland and protecting the U.S. from future attacks. They rewarded the president and his party with a stumping victory in the mid-terms of 2002, reversing decades of electoral tradition in which the president's party was penalized in the first bi-election of his term.

His approval ratings were close to 90 percent and remained high until early 2004, when they began to decline.

Campaign strategist Karl Rove, whom James Moore and Wayne Slater identified in their book as "Bush's Brain," devised a slash-and-burn campaign. He built on strong Republican support and voter's approval of the president's war record. Since both parties expected another close election, Rove built in an insurance policy: constitutional amendments in key states against abortion and same-sex marriage.

Bush won a minute but absolute popular majority (50.7 percent to 48.3 percent), as did his father in 1988, but the election in the Electoral College was also close—286 to 251. It was the smallest winning margin for an incumbent president since President Woodrow Wilson in 1916.

GEORGE W. BUSH:
MID-TERM ELECTIONS 2006-I

In 2006, President Bush experienced the curse of the second-term presidency. Because of the Twenty-Second Amendment, all second-term presidents are immediately rendered with lame duck status.

Beginning almost from the moment of his re-election, George W. Bush faced growing skepticism about his presidential steward-ship. After 9/11, people valued the president's single-minded focus on revenge for the attacks and determination to prevent more. But voters change their minds.

In December 2004, President Bush's approval ratings dropped below 50 percent, began to decline, and never recovered. This was due primarily to the voter dissatisfaction and weariness about the Iraq War. There was a visible weakening of support among Republicans who were frustrated over the war, immigration, and out-of-control deficits due to expensive tax cuts that benefitted upper-income tax-payers, an unfunded Medicare expansion, and massive wartime expenditures. Other voters focused on the clear ineptitude of the Bush administration in the Katrina crisis, prisoner abuse in Iraq and Guantanamo Bay, and warrantless surveillance under the Patriot Act by the National Security Agency and other agencies. Voters were also concerned about torture and other "enhanced interrogation methods" such as water-boarding.

GEORGE W. BUSH:
MID-TERM ELECTIONS 2006-II

As the mid-term election of 2006 approached, Republicans were facing powerful challenges to their continued majority in Congress. In 2003 and 2004, a number of highly public scandals involving Republican politicians came to light. GOP lobbyists Jack Abramoff, Ralph Reed, and Grover Norquist were revealed to have charged excessive lobbying fees to Indian tribes seeking help in starting gambling casinos. In the course of the investigation, it was discovered that the lobbyists had also made illegal gifts and campaign contributions to Congressman Bob Ney (R–Ohio) and Tom Delay (R–Texas) for help with legislation. Bribery charges were levied against Congressman Duke Cunningham (R–California), who received financial favors for help in securing contracts for defense suppliers.

Given the negative headwinds facing Bush and the Republicans, the outcome of the 2006 mid-terms was almost predictable. The Democrats reclaimed control of both houses of Congress. In the House, the result was a 232–203 Democratic majority, and Nancy Pelosi became the first female speaker of the House. Races for governor went heavily for Democrats.

As a result of the elections, President Bush accepted the resignation of Defense Secretary Donald Rumsfeld, and as the congressional investigations mounted, in August 2007, he agreed with his resigning political strategist Karl Rove that it was "time to go."

GEORGE W. BUSH:
THE GREAT RECESSION

In late 2007, the United States entered what economists called the Great Recession, the longest economic contraction since World War II. In quick succession, the economy incurred a series of shocks: rapid stock market collapse, increased unemployment (7.2 percent) leading to the loss of over 2.6 million jobs, bank failures, and a severe housing market contraction.

The Bush administration advanced a $170 billion stimulus package, which included direct rebate checks to help give a boost to the shaky economy. In September 2008, the government took over the federal mortgage giants Freddie Mac and Fannie Mae and—after the collapse of the Wall Street powerhouse, Lehman Brothers—bailed out American International Group (AIG) for $85 billion.

At the beginning of the Bush years, the Dow Jones Industrial Average was at 10,587. It was at just over 14,000 right before the downturn. By the time President Bush relinquished the White House, it had gone below 8,000.

Voters blamed President Bush and the Republicans for this disaster. The party nominee Senator John McCain (R-AZO) had little chance and was overwhelmed by Barack Obama. He won a majority of the popular vote and a stunning victory in the Electoral College.

Joseph August / Shutterstock.com

GEORGE W. BUSH: LEGACY

In the history of the Gallop Presidential Approval Poll, President George Walker Bush has the distinction of having had the highest approval rating of any president (89 percent) in the wake of the World Trade Center attacks and the lowest rating (19 percent) seven years later in the midst of the Great Recession.

Bush introduced the largest tax cuts since those of President Ronald Reagan, but without a comparable reduction in the size and scope of federal program and responsibilities. At the same time, he led the nation into two very expensive wars and saddled Medicare with a new, largely unfunded, prescription drug program. These represented the largest expansion of the federal enterprise since the full term of Lyndon B. Johnson. This yielded an unbroken string of budget deficits and a massive increase—indeed doubling—of the national debt.

Whatever criticism might be leveled at President Bush for policies and actions, his clarion call for a unified national response to the attacks of 9/11 was inspiring. It stirred the nation to rise from its knees, shake off the blow, mourn its losses, and dedicate itself to eradicate the evil that had beset the republic. Leaving office with low approval ratings, however, is no disgrace as these may represent circumstances beyond a president's control. Indeed, President Bush has gradually reclaimed a measure of respect in a citizenry having to deal with a Republican successor whose approach to leadership is markedly different than his own.

44

BARACK OBAMA

BARACK OBAMA: LIFE PAGE

Born: August 4, 1961, Honolulu, Hawaii, as Barack Hussein Obama II

Education: Occidental College

                      Columbia University (BA)

                      Harvard Law School (JD)

Married: Michelle Robinson, 1992

Vocation: Attorney, Community Organizer, and Politician

Illinois State Senator: 1997–2004

United States Senator: 2005–2008

Forty-Fourth President of the United States: 2009–2017

Additional resources available for this president at www.amomentintime.com.

BARACK OBAMA: SENATOR

Barack Obama was the offspring of a racially mixed marriage. Having had little contact with his father as a child, the future president expressed concern in his writings over the social perception of his diverse heritage and divided home life. He lived for a time in Indonesia before returning to Honolulu for high school. By this time, Obama began demonstrating the intellectual horsepower that would take him through an excellent academic record at Columbia (1983) and Harvard Law School (1991). While in Cambridge, he worked as research assistant to famed constitutional scholar Lawrence Tribe and became the first African American elected as president of the *Harvard Law Review*. This distinction brought national notoriety and led to the publication of a memoir, *Dreams of My Father*.

After Columbia, he worked as a community organizer in Chicago and twice returned there as a summer intern in a legal firm while at Harvard. There he met and married Michelle Robinson. After graduation from Harvard, he returned to the Windy City and took up his community work again while he began teaching constitutional law at the University of Chicago. In 1993, Obama joined a small legal firm specializing in civil rights litigation and became partner in 1996.

He was elected to the Illinois Senate and served there until 2004 when he was elected to the U.S. Senate in a landslide.

BARACK OBAMA:
A TALE OF TWO SPEECHES

Obama faced the opportunity of a lifetime when he was chosen to make the keynote address at the Democratic National Convention in Boston, Massachusetts, on July 27, 2004. Obama wrote the speech himself, albeit with edits from the campaign leadership of presidential candidate John Kerry. Obama was disappointed with the time of the speech because it would not be carried by the major networks, but that mattered little; the coverage was near-universal and almost completely positive.

His speech climaxed with the stirring peroration: "There is not a black America and a white America and Latino America and Asian America—there's the United States of America. . . . Hope! Hope in the face of difficulty! . . . The audacity of hope! . . . A belief that there are better days ahead." With the election of Kerry and John Edwards, "this country will reclaim its promise, and out of this long political darkness, a brighter day will come."

This speech was the beginning of Obama's campaign for president, but another speech help set his candidacy in perspective. On March 18, 2004, Obama, in his speech "A More Perfect Union," moved to distance himself from incendiary remarks of his longtime pastor, Reverend Jeremiah Wright. The speech received widespread affirmation across the political spectrum and helped Obama deflect criticism that might have derailed his candidacy. It also reflected his sincerely held conviction that America could rise above its obsession with race.

BARACK OBAMA: ELECTION 2008

Having caught the attention of the political world with his stunning keynote address at the Democratic National Convention in 2004 and fearlessly dealing with America's struggle with race, Senator Barack Obama moved to advance his candidacy for the Democratic nomination in 2008.

Using the theme of hope and change, Obama announced his run at the Old State Capitol Building—the site of Abraham Lincoln's 1858 "House Divided" speech. He re-affirmed his opposition to the Iraq War and his goal of transforming the nation's healthcare system. While the nomination struggle attracted many candidates, the real battle evolved into a skirmish between Obama and Senator Hillary Clinton (D–New York). It was a closely fought duel, but Obama pulled ahead due to superior organization and well-considered campaign tactics. Clinton ended her effort in early June and, at the Denver Convention, spoke in Obama's favor, urging her supporters to back the nominee.

Obama chose Senator Joseph R. Biden (D–Delaware) as his running mate, and they faced Senator John McCain (R–Arizona) and Governor Sarah Palin (R–Alaska) in the general election. The campaign was marked by serious questions about Palin's qualification and the onset of the economic collapse that led to a severe economic contraction, a collapse in the housing market, and the Great Recession. Obama won a convincing popular majority (52.9 percent to 45.7 percent) and a large margin in the Electoral College (365 to 173).

BARACK OBAMA:
GREAT RECESSION

As soon as he was inaugurated, President Obama was faced with a national economy in turmoil. In his first month, he signed a large stimulus package—the American Recovery and Reinvestment Act (2009)—pumping close to $800 billion into the ailing economy. A month after that, he intervened to boost the real estate market and the sickly automobile industry. These measures tended to increase the federal deficit, and over the next two years, Obama worked with Congress to set up a process for steady budget reduction.

The economy began to grow in the third quarter of 2009 and continues to produce moderate growth into the Trump years.

After the mid-term elections of 2010, President Obama and Democratic leadership produced another huge stimulus package that further boosted economic growth into 2011 and 2012. As a result, economists noted that in late 2010, the Great Recession—the longest continuous economic contraction since World War II—was finally over. The multiple jolts of government investment in the economy succeeded in moving the U.S. economy out of the recession, and in a much quicker fashion than the austerity measures applied by the European Union. This in turn helped Europe eventually recover, as international trade began to pick up.

BARACK OBAMA: OBAMACARE

Perhaps the singular achievement of President Obama's time in office was the Affordable Health Care Act (2010) or, as it was at first derisively called, "Obamacare." One of Obama's campaign promises, the proposal involved a $900 billion investment over ten years. His intent was to cover those not covered by health insurance, to reign in the growth of health insurance premiums, to permit people to retain their insurance when they quit work or moved jobs, and to block companies from denying coverage to people who were ill or had pre-existing conditions.

Congressional leaders presented the plan in July 2009, Obama pushed the plan in a speech before Congress in September, and by December, both the House and Senate had passed the core of the measure. The bill Obama signed in March 2010 expanded eligibility for Medicaid and subsidized insurance for those who made up to 400 percent of the federal poverty level. The measure also encouraged businesses to offer health insurance and prohibited the denial of coverage and claims based on pre-existing conditions.

There were legal challenges at the Supreme Court to Obamacare, but the Court left the program largely intact. After all the features of the program went active in 2014, participation began to grow and the number of uninsured in America began to decline.

BARACK OBAMA: DOMESTIC POLICY

The president addressed a number of other domestic issues during his two terms. On environmental policy, Obama demonstrated a heightened intensity given the threat of global climate change. New regulations were forthcoming on petroleum refinement facilities, electrical generating installations, and industrial plants.

Beginning in 2005, the TransCanada Corporation began laying plans for a pipeline network to carry crude oil from the oil sand fields around Hardesty, Alberta, to various destinations in the U.S. This Keystone Pipeline became a cause celèbré among environmentalists who were concerned about oil leaks from the pipeline itself and its long-term impact on global climate change in general. President Obama had already halted oil exploration in the Artic and vetoed legislation authorizing Keystone XL, the fourth phase of the pipeline. Early in his administration, President Donald Trump reversed Obama's decision.

In the wake of repeated mass shootings, often in public schools, President Obama struggled to assemble a consensus around what he called "common-sense gun reform." He signed a number of Executive Orders but was not able to get Congress to renew the Bush-era ban on military-style assault weapons.

BARACK OBAMA: FOREIGN POLICY-I

Having expressed opposition to the second Gulf War in 2003, one of President Obama's foreign policy goals was to end U.S. military involvement in Iraq. This proved to be more difficult to achieve than to promise given the volatility of the region.

One of the outcomes of the Iraq War was the emergence of the Islamic State in the Levant (ISIL). The organization, also known as ISIS, captured the ancient city of Mosul in northwestern Iraq, the largest city of the so-called Islamic State. Because of ISIS massacres and ethnic cleansing in the region, in 2014, President Obama sent U.S. troops back into Iraq and began to reassemble the international coalition in the support of the Iraqi Army. Coalition air forces directed thousands of aircraft sorties against ISIS targets. With the re-capture of the city following the Battle of Mosul in 2017, ISIS received a severe setback, but it continues to be a profound threat to peace and stability in northwestern Iraq and eastern Syria.

In early 2009, and again in December of that year, the president strengthened U.S. forces in Afghanistan, at the same time announcing a phased withdrawal. Continuing instability in that country has prevented a complete drawdown of U.S. forces or its coalition allies.

BARACK OBAMA: FOREIGN POLICY-II

Determined to end the development of nuclear weapons by Iran, the Obama administration and several international powers engaged the Iranian Revolutionary Regime in a sequence of negotiations. In 2015, these talks led to the "Joint Comprehensive Plan of Action," which paired the removal of financial sanctions with measures designed to prevent Iran from obtaining nuclear arms.

Influenced by Pope Francis, in July 2015, Cuba and the U.S. normalized diplomatic relations, upgraded their "interests sections," and opened embassies in Washington and Havana.

President Obama was a strong supporter of the State of Israel, but not an unquestioning supporter. On one side, he increased military aid to Israel and permitted enlarged consultations between Israeli and U.S. defense specialists. During the 2014 Israel–Gaza conflict, he supported Israel's right to defend itself and continued to identify with traditional pro-Israel, pro-Jewish positions. In the early years of the administration, the U.S. stood alone in resistance to international condemnation of Israeli west bank settlements. By 2013, however, the president was growing concerned that Israel's continued pursuit of these settlements was increasing Israel's international isolation. In 2016, President Obama abstained and therefore allowed the passage of U.N. condemnation of expanded Jewish settlements.

BARACK OBAMA:
DEATH OF OSAMA BIN LADEN

Since it became clear following the 2001 World Trade Center and Pentagon attacks that the militant Islamist terrorist group Al-Qaeda was responsible, the U.S. had been pursuing the group's leader, Saudi-born Osama bin Laden.

After his escape into the borderlands between Afghanistan and Pakistan near Tora Bora in 2001, allied intelligence services had been on the lookout for any signs of bin Laden's location.

In the middle of 2010, the Central Intelligence Agency (CIA) began to zero in on information that indicated bin Laden was hiding in a compound near Abbottabad, not far from Islamabad, Pakistan. Over the next several weeks, the CIA sought further affirmation of the location of the suspect. Obama rejected a bombing raid because that would indiscriminately risk civilian deaths and ultimately fail to confirm bin Laden's death. Instead, the president ordered members of Seal Team Six to prep for a precise human raid. On May 1, 2011, the operation killed Osama bin Laden and captured a priceless trove of records and computer information. No members of the raiding party were killed.

That evening, President Obama announced the death of bin Laden in a nationally televised address. This news was greeted by riotous impromptu street celebrations in front of the White House, at Ground Zero, and at Times Square in New York City.

BARACK OBAMA: ELECTION 2012

President Obama and Vice President Biden were nominated for re-election at the Democratic National Convention on September 4-6, 2012. They faced former Massachusetts Governor Mitt Romney and Congressman Paul Ryan in the general election. In the course of the campaign, Obama's reminder that the U.S. had a mixed economy in which entrepreneurs benefitted from the infrastructure provided by government was the subject of severe Republican criticism.

Romney then complained in the third presidential debate that the U.S. Navy was smaller than at any time since 1917. Obama agreed that the U.S. Navy had fewer ships than in 1916. "Well, governor, we also have fewer horses and bayonets, because the nature of our military's changed."

However, it was Romney's seeming denigration of 47 percent of voters at a private fundraiser that was most decisive. In the speech, secretly taped and released, he said that none of them would ever vote for him because they are "dependent upon the government … I will never convince them they should take personal responsibility and care for their lives."

In the election, Obama/Biden won with a popular majority of 51 percent to 47.2 percent and an Electoral College vote of 332 to 206. It was the first time since Franklin D. Roosevelt that a Democrat had won the popular majority twice in a row.

BARACK OBAMA:
GENDER-NEUTRAL MARRIAGE[1]

Perhaps no social and legal transformation in U.S. history has been as swift as that concerning homosexuals. While there remains a bitterly resistant minority, strong majorities in American society now support unimpeded participation of homosexuals in all social, legal, economic, and even religious parts of life. The Obama administration intervened when possible to buttress legal arguments on behalf of lesbian, gay, bisexual, transgender, and questioning (LBGTQ) litigants.

In *Loving v. Virginia* (1967), the Supreme Court decision struck down laws banning interracial marriage. This ruling became the basis for eliminating legal discrimination against LBGTQ citizens. Having upheld Georgia's anti-sodomy law in *Bowers v. Hardwick* (1986), the Court reversed course. It dismantled discrimination in four key decisions. In *Lawrence v. Texas* (2003), the court reversed the Bowers decision, striking down anti-sodomy laws nationwide. The Court, in *Hollingsworth v. Perry* (2013), accepted lower court rulings that declared anti-same sex marriage California statutes to be unconstitutional.

In *United States v. Windsor* (2013), the Supreme Court struck down DOMA (Defense of Marriage Act). The Supremes said DOMA violated the Fifth Amendment's prohibition against depriving a citizen of life and liberty. The case expanded individual state recognition of same-sex relationships to the entire nation and extended federal marriage benefits to same-gender couples. In *Obergefell v. Hodges* (2015), the court ruled that same-gender couples could marry on the same terms as opposite-gender couples—a privilege guaranteed in the Due Process and Equal Protection Clauses of the Fourteenth Amendment.

Dr. Martin Luther King Jr. often quoted nineteenth-century clergyman Theodore Parker: "The arc of the moral universe is long, but it bends toward justice." The arc for African Americans has been long and still requires heavy effort for bending. The experience of homosexuals shows that legal transformation can be breathtakingly swift. In both cases, transforming the inclinations of a resistant minority takes much, much longer.

BARACK OBAMA: LEGACY

As the first African American to be elected President of the United States, Barak Obama already had a well-establish legacy, but in his two terms, he accomplished many goals. Perhaps the most significant triumph was the passage of the Patient Protection and Affordable Care Act (2010). Despite multiple attempts of Republicans to undo this transformation of the nation's healthcare system, Obamacare remains largely intact and has brought health care to millions of uninsured Americans.

Obama helped lift the nation from its worst economic contraction since the Great Depression. In his two terms, 11.3 million jobs were created, a pattern of growth that continued far into the early years of President Donald Trump's first term. Additionally, the expansion of hate crimes legislation to include crimes committed against the lesbian, gay, bisexual, transgender, and questioning (LBGTQ) community helped protect gay persons as they seek to fully participate in the rites of citizenship. Obama's repeal of "Don't Ask, Don't Tell" removed the obstruction preventing gay men and women from openly serving their country in the military.

The president reduced, but was not able to permanently eliminate, U.S. combat participation in Iraq, Afghanistan, or other centers of international conflict. In 2012, the president established Deferred Action for Childhood (DACA), an immigration program that provided protection from deportation for "Dreamers," children and young adults brought to the United States by their immigrant parents. President Trump has tried to end the program, but various legal challenges have stayed his hand. Barak Obama left office with a strong popular approval rating (60 percent) and has continued to experience an increased level of assessment in surveys of historians and political scientists.

45

DONALD TRUMP

DONALD TRUMP: LIFE PAGE

Born: June 14, 1946

Education: Fordham University

The Wharton School of the University of Pennsylvania (BS in Economics)

Married: Ivana Zelníčková, 1977; divorced, 1992

Marla Maples, 1993; divorced, 1999

Malania Knauss, 2005

Vocation: Real Estate Investment and Management

Reality Television Actor: 1971–2015

Forty-Fifth President of the United States: 2017–Present

Additional resources available for this president at www.amomentintime.com.

DONALD TRUMP:
REAL ESTATE AND REALITY ACTOR

Trump was not known as a particularly gifted or inquiring student, and after college graduation, he joined the family real estate business.

This pattern of using other people's money, the creative use of debt, tax incentives growing out of political connections, and the re-structuring of debt through bankruptcy laws served Trump well throughout his career. After bankruptcies involving six of his major hotel or casino properties between 1991 and 2009, banks declined to do business with the Trump Organization (with one exception, Deutsche Bank). Faced with declining opportunities, Trump very cleverly used the ongoing visibility of his name to begin a lucrative licensing of the Trump name. This generates approximately $59 million a year to his company, though affixing his name to various consumer ventures has declined in its appeal.

None of his side ventures were particularly successful. Never-theless, in 2019 *Forbes* estimated his net worth to be $3.1 billion. Perhaps his most successful pre-presidential venture, something that laid the foundation for his political career, was *The Apprentice* on NBC. From 2003 to 2014, he was host and executive producer of this extraordinarily popular fake recruitment television reality series. It was fascinating and powerful political theater. With contestants fearing to hear his words, "you're fired," Trump was able to convey the impression that he was a successful, hard-driving businessman.

DONALD TRUMP:
ELECTION OF 2016-I

The election of 2016 did not begin in 2015 when Donald and Melania Trump rode down the escalator in Trump Tower to announce his candidacy to a cheering crowd. It began in 2003 on the *Apprentice*, where he established a connection to potential voters.

Flirting with running in 2000, 2004, and 2012, he shifted to the Republican Party. According to *The New York Times*, his determination to succeed in this realm was intensified when he was ridiculed by President Barak Obama at the White House Correspondents Dinner in April 2011.

There is an extraordinary connection between Trump and his base voter, and he demonstrates a high level of political shrewdness in cultivating that demographic—white, rural, working class voters. He understands that many white voters are nervous about the growing diversity of America and the threat of immigration. Trump instinctively grasps that for all their protestations to the contrary, the vast majority of voters are proto-socialists and have embraced a mixed economy with a strong safety net embodied in Social Security, Medicare, Medicaid, and support for government involvement in infrastructure projects. This remarkable mixture of populist positions from all parts of the political spectrum, effectively presented, overcame a powerful counter narrative about his personal shortcomings and his questionable association with the truth.

DONALD TRUMP:
ELECTION OF 2016-II

During the election season of 2016, Donald Trump had three distinct advantages. First of all, presidents in America are not decided by popular vote. Elections are won in the Electoral College. Trump's second advantage was that in certain places his opponent was marginally as unpopular as was he. When faced with two unpopular presidential choices, most Americans retreat into their tribal corners—Republicans to theirs, Democrats to theirs. Others, sometimes a decisive number, choose a third-party candidate. Still others are willing to take a chance on a traditional party candidate about which they know little, hoping that any fears they have about his or her candidacy are unfounded or that, once elected, that candidate will revert back to those norms of behavior expected of a U.S. president.

Finally, Americans, absent a national crisis such as war, are rarely willing to give a single party multiple consecutive terms in the White House. Trump found himself in the right place in the right time. His opponent in 2016 was considered by many to be one of the most intelligent, accomplished, and popular women in America—former first lady, senator, and secretary of state, Hillary Rodham Clinton. She also was quite unpopular in some segments of the electorate. That unpopularity was often inchoate, visceral, emotional, and, at times, unexplainable.

DONALD TRUMP:
ELECTION OF 2016-III

Hillary Clinton was assumed to have an easy route to the nomination, but she faced a formidable opponent in Senator Bernie Sanders (I–Vermont). The intraparty struggle was lively, but, in the end, Clinton prevailed. Sanders endorsed Clinton, but there was lingering resentment among Sanders's voters.

Seventeen Republicans entered the nomination race in 2016, the largest number of candidates in a party nomination race in U.S. history. Gradually, Trump overcame all resistance. After becoming the presumptive nominee, Trump named Governor Mike Pence (R–Indiana) as his running mate.

Trump's campaign demonstrated poor organization, but his choice of Steve Bannon, former Chairman of Breitbart News, reflected Trump's willingness to fish in far-right waters—particularly among white, working-class voters in the Midwest. His personal morality became a theme for his opponents, particularly after the release of a 2005 Access Hollywood interview in which Trump made sexually explicit remarks. Later in a campaign broadcast, he admitted to having made those comments, but he dismissed them as mere "locker room banter." At first, even Republicans blanched at having to defend Trump's language, but soon, in the heat of the campaign, they returned to their support for Trump.

DONALD TRUMP:
ELECTION OF 2016-IV

Clinton was plagued with questions about her personal integrity and, in particular, her use of a personal email server while secretary of state. When the FBI reopened and then—just days before the election—reclosed its investigation, post-election pundit analysis speculated that this tipped the election to Donald Trump.

Clinton decisively won the national popular vote (48.18 percent to 46.09 percent). Trump triumphed in the Electoral College (304 to 227). They managed to carry three states—Michigan, Pennsylvania, and Wisconsin—that had voted for President Barak Obama in 2008 and 2012 and had been a part of the so-called Blue Wall since the 1990s. In fact, the margin of victory in each of these states was less than 1 percent, or a total of 74,744 in all three.

One interesting factor in Clinton's loss in these three states (Michigan, Wisconsin, and Pennsylvania) was the total number of votes in these three states for Green Party Candidate Jill Stein, whose appeal was clearly to a liberal constituency. In each state, Stein's total vote exceeded the margin of Trump's victory total in that state.

Another interesting factor leading to Trump's victory in those states was the substantial reduction in the number of African Americans who voted in 2016 over 2012.

Though it would not be recognized until after the election, another theretofore unrecognized influence was at play—not just in those crucial states, but in the vote nationwide.

DONALD TRUMP:
RUSSIAN INTERFERENCE-I

During the campaign of 2016, Federal Bureau of Investigation (FBI) investigations into circumstances surrounding the elections were underway. The first, a criminal investigation, was highly public and was focused on the use of a private email server by the former secretary of state and Democratic presidential candidate, Hillary Clinton. The FBI announced in July that it was ending this investigation and had found there was no evidence of criminal activity by the secretary, but FBI Director James Comey took Clinton to task for her "reckless" use of the server.

This public criticism was highly unusual. In most cases, when the FBI concludes there will be no charges, it just closes out the investigation with no fanfare. Republican candidate Donald Trump was able to use this public dressing down of Clinton to advance his "Crooked Hillary" epithet in his campaign. Then, eleven days before the election, Comey informed Congress that thousands of emails had been discovered on the laptop of disgraced former Congressman Anthony Weiner—the husband of long-time Clinton aide Huma Abedin. The FBI publicly re-opened its investigation. Then two days before the election, they concluded there was nothing there. The emails were simply duplicates of emails already in the possession of the FBI. Clinton remains convinced that Comey's announcement late in the campaign—which was clearly in violation of the Department of Justice protocols concerning investigations so close to the election—tipped the contest to Donald Trump.

DONALD TRUMP:
RUSSIAN INTERFERENCE-II

Yet, there was another investigation taking place, a secret counter-intelligence investigation. Acting on information from the Australian government, the Federal Bureau of Investigation (FBI) began delving into evidence that members of the Trump campaign—not the candidate himself—were working with the Russian government to influence the campaign against Secretary Hillary Clinton.

After the election and shortly before President-elect Trump was to be inaugurated, the American Intelligence Community concluded "with high confidence" that the Russian government interfered in the 2016 presidential election to benefit the candidacy of Donald Trump.

It has been confirmed that Trump's first National Security Advisor Michael T. Flynn, Trump's Campaign Chair Paul Manafort, and the president's close friend Roger Stone had connections to the Russian government. All three have now been convicted as felons on information growing out of this investigation.

In the three years since the campaign, President Trump has promoted an alternative theory suggesting that election interference came from Ukraine and not Russia. This theory says Fiona Hill, Senior Director for Europe and Russia on President Trump's National Security Council (2017–2019), is in fact an agent of Russian Military Intelligence. It has been advanced at the behest of Russian President Vladimir Putin.

On February 13, 2017, President Donald Trump fired National Security Advisor Michael T. Flynn ostensibly for lying about his contacts with Russians during and after the 2016 election. The next day, Trump met with FBI Director James Comey for a terrorist briefing. After the meeting, Trump told Comey, "I hope you can see your way clear to letting this go, to letting Flynn go."

Comey memorialized the event in written notes. On May 9, 2017, President Trump fired Comey. The original story from the White House was that he had done so on the recommendation of Attorney General Jeff Sessions and Deputy Attorney General Rod Rosenstein, but days later he admitted in an interview with *NBC News* Anchor Lester Holt that he fired Comey because of the Russia investigation.

Due to his Trump campaign involvement, the attorney general had recused himself from the Russia probe; on May 17, 2017, the deputy attorney general appointed the highly respected former Director of the FBI Robert Mueller as special counsel to investigate Russian interference with the 2016 presidential election. According to sources close to the president, he was incensed, seeing this as a guarantee of an investigation that would do him harm politically and personally. According to testimony assembled for Volume Two of Mueller's report, President Trump expressed a desire to fire Robert Mueller and close the investigation, but his staff succeeded in persuading him otherwise.

DONALD TRUMP: MUELLER PROBE-II

Robert Mueller's investigation was exhaustive and resulted in multiple indictments of Trump associates and Russian military intelligence operatives. He presented his findings to Attorney General William Barr on March 22, 2019. Barr issued a short preliminary summary that absolved the president of any criminal conspiracy—though it did not exculpate him from obstruction of justice.

A heavily redacted version of the Mueller Report was released a month later. Volume One concluded that Russia engaged in pervasive interference with the election to benefit Trump and impede Hillary Clinton's candidacy. What his report did make clear was that the foreign interference was illegal and systematic. Mueller described in detail how various members of the Trump campaign directly and indirectly welcomed and encouraged the Russian activity in hopes that it would benefit their campaign.

Volume Two detailed repeated alleged instances of obstruction of justice by the president. Mueller could not be assured of Trump's innocence, but he was unable to pursue an indictment of the president because of a Justice Department memorandum by the Office of Legal Counsel (OLC). The bottom line on obstruction: No indictment, but no affirmation that the president was blameless. President Trump saw it differently. He saw Mueller's report as a complete exoneration.

DONALD TRUMP: RACISM, NATIONALISM, AND WHITE SUPREMACY

President Trump has asserted, "I am the least racist person there is anywhere in the world." Many of his supporters believe him, yet others are not as sanguine. They look at a record that is problematic.

He and his father settled a 1973 Justice Department lawsuit alleging housing discrimination against black renters. He publicly supported prosecution of black and Latino teenagers who were accused of rape in the famed 1989 Central Park jogger case. Trump held to his accusations even after the youths were acquitted in 2002 by DNA evidence. President Trump activated his run for the White House in 2011 through the "birther" controversy, asserting the false narrative that President Barak Obama was born not in Hawaii, but in Kenya. After the violent August 2017 Charlottesville "Unite the Right" rally, he implied an equivalent morality between marchers asserting white supremacy and those who opposed them.

Many of the president's supporters defend his actions and comments as part of a campaign against "politically correct" language. Others see them as part of a sinister pattern of behavior that if not racist, at least gives permission to those who hold racist opinions to act and speak with racial animus.

DONALD TRUMP: DOMESTIC POLICY AND JUDICIAL APPOINTMENTS

The economic expansion that began in the second year of President Barak Obama's administration has continued into President Trump's term. One of the drivers of this growth was the Tax Cuts and Jobs Act of 2017. It temporarily reduced personal tax brackets, permanently reduced business tax rates, increased the child tax credit, increased the estate tax exemption, and limited the state and local tax deduction to $10,000. This tax bill was a powerful stimulus to an already highly stimulated economy. President Trump has also worked to cut back on government regulations.

Soon after taking office, Trump took the U.S. out of the Trans-pacific Trade Partnership and threatened a prospective trade war with China. He has repeatedly asserted, incorrectly, that import tariffs are paid into the U.S. Treasury. In reality, import tariffs are indirectly passed onto American consumers, who pay higher prices for imported goods.

One of his campaign promises was to nominate a large number of conservative judges to seats left open because of the political strategy of Senate Majority Leader Mitch McConnell (R-Kentucky). Since the beginning of Trump's term, the Senate has confirmed over 180 conservative Republican district appeal court judges and two new conservatives, Justices Neil Gorsuch and Brett Kavanaugh, to the Supreme Court.

On July 25, 2019, the day after Special Counsel Robert Mueller presented his report to Congress on Russian election interference, President Trump spoke by phone with newly elected Ukranian President Volodymyr Zelensky. According to the White House summary (not a verbatim transcript) of the call, President Trump asked Zelensky to announce an investigation into the son of one of Trump's principal adversaries in the 2020 election, former Vice President Joseph R. Biden. He also requested the Ukrainians advance the debunked Russian narrative that the Ukrainian government had worked to help Hillary Clinton along with Democrats, the digital forensics company CrowdStrike, and the FBI.

Trump requested that Zelensky get in touch with Attorney General William Barr and Trump's personal attorney, Rudolf Giuliani, to facilitate these investigations. President Trump then refused to extend to the Ukrainian a coveted Oval Office visit and held up nearly $400 million in military aid that Ukraine needed to protect itself from Russia until Ukraine began the requested investigations.

DONALD TRUMP: IMPEACHMENT-II

In August, a government whistle-blower, whose name has remained an official secret to this point, called the phone call to the attention of Congress. In response—seen as a possible breach of national security—on September 24, 2019, House Speaker Nancy Pelosi commenced a formal impeachment inquiry into President Trump's actions vis-à-vis Ukraine. The president then rejected all subpoenas for documents and tried to block the testimony of witnesses to House committees. After an extensive investigation of the call by the House Intelligence Committee, testimony from officials familiar with the call, and attending actions of the president, the House Judiciary referred two articles of impeachment to the full house. On December 18, 2019, the United States House of Representatives voted to impeach President Donald John Trump for abuse of power and obstruction of Congress.

President Trump was tried by the United States Senate. In the course of the trial the case for impeachment was made by House Managers (essentially prosecutors) and the President's defense team. In the most consequential vote of the proceedings, all but two Republicans voted to block any further witnesses and documents.

President Donald John Trump was acquitted of both articles of impeachment on a party-line vote, with the exception of one Republican senator (Mitt Romney of Utah), on February 5, 2020.

Evan El-Amin / Shutterstock.com

DONALD TRUMP:
LEGACY IN THE MAKING

These chapters are being finalized in the early weeks of 2020. President Donald John Trump has been impeached, was tried, and was acquitted by the U.S. Senate on February 5, 2020.

Though impeachment has cast a cloud over the Trump presidency, he is establishing a legacy for which he will be remembered. Trump followed through with a huge tax cut. He delivered a significant increase in the number of conservative judges in the federal judiciary and two new justices on the Supreme Court.

President Trump failed in his attempt to repeal and replace the Affordable Care Act, but on social issues, he stood firm in the center of Republican orthodoxy. He currently stands firmly against gun control legislation, though his position over the years has shifted. His administration has negatively altered some Obama-era workplace protections for LBGTQ citizens.

As an impeached president, he faces substantial challenges to his re-election. His supporters regularly defend him against accusations that he has a questionable relationship with the truth and suffers from a deficient personal morality. Whether he can rise above the challenges and buck electoral headwinds to win a second term will continue to fascinate those seeking to master presidential history in the modern era.

ENDNOTES

INTRODUCTION

1. Washington, Jefferson, Madison, Monroe, Jackson, Tyler, Polk, and Taylor owned slaves while serving as president. Andrew Johnson and Ulysses S. Grant were slaveholders but either manumitted their slaves before the war or freed them at the time of the Emancipation Proclamation. Van Buren's only slave escaped in 1814 and never returned to enslavement. Harrison inherited a number of slaves and worked to bring slavery into the Indiana Territory when he was governor, but he held no slaves when he was in the White House. Van Buren, Harrison, Fillmore, Pierce, and Buchanan were either sympathetic to or acquiesced in the desires of the slave interest for political reasons. Van Buren later shifted his political position and opposed the spread of slavery to the territories as a member of the Free Soil Party.

2. Political scientists identify as many as six party systems:
   1. First Party System: Federalist Party v. Democratic-Republican Party (1800)
   2. Second Party System: Democratic Party v. Whig Party (1836)
   3. Third Party System: Republican Party v. Democratic Party (1860)
   4. Fourth Party System: Republican/Progressive Party v. Democratic/Progressive Party (1896)
   5. Fifth Party System: Democratic Party (New Deal) Party v. Republican Party (1932)
      And possibly:
   6. Sixth Party System: Republican (Southern) Party v. Democratic Party (1968)

3. During the Antebellum Era, Jim Crow was a legendary character among African American slaves, a charlatan who cleverly outwitted un-suspecting gullible whites in his ratty attire and by fake foolishness. In the 1830s, white actor Thomas D. Rice created and performed on stage a demeaning, racist character not surprisingly named Jim Crow. Dressed in rags and with his face turned black using burnt cork, Thomas imitated the dialect of poor African Americans, speaking and singing in that vernacular. As part of his act, he revised and promoted the song, "Jump Jim Crow" an irreverent depiction of what a white person thought

an ignorant black field hand looked and acted like. His work helped to disseminate the genre of minstrel singing with all its belittling inferences, but also reinforced for his audiences all the ethnically stereotypical views Americans held about black people. Most whites considered African Americans to be inferior in character, lacking a work ethic comparable to whites, and that they were "lazy, stupid, inherently less human, and unworthy of integration."

By 1840, "Jim Crow" was used by American whites to refer to Negroes. This negative racist epithet continued to the end of the century when so-called "Jim Crow Laws" were enacted in the South to reverse the intent and effect of the Fourteenth and Fifteen Amendments to the Constitution, ratified after the Civil War to protect the rights of freedmen. These laws were designed to enforce racial segregation and keep blacks "in line" through the use of humiliating laws passed by southern Democratic-dominated legislatures. They mandated segregation in all public facilities—restrooms, restaurants, drinking fountains—continued the segregation of public schools, and extended this separation to interstate transportation. After the Supreme Court enshrined the principle of "separate, but equal" facilities in Plessy vs. Ferguson (1896), white legislatures had free reign to assign blacks to second-class citizenship.

In addition to restricting access by African Americans to public accommodations, their civil rights were legally proscribed. Beginning in 1890, nearly all of the states that had formed the Confederacy adopted new constitutions or amendments that marginalized the civil rights of most blacks and thousands of poor whites. Using such clever devices as poll taxes, literacy and comprehension tests, residency and record-keeping requirements, and grandfather clauses, white governments virtually locked blacks out of the rites of citizenship. It also effectively prevented any political alliance between blacks and lower-class whites that might have been formed to improve the circumstances of both.

4. Whig Party doctrine tended to defer to Congress on legislative initiatives. Without hesitation, Abraham Lincoln, formerly a Whig Party congressman, seized the reigns of control of the armed forces and went after domestic threats to the nation during the Civil War. Nevertheless, he generally deferred to Congress on advancing domestic legislation, such as the Transcontinental Railroad and the Homestead Act. He signed the laws and enforced them, but in standard Whigish fashion (with some

major exceptions, such as the effort to end slavery in the Thirteenth Amendment) focused his attention on national security.

JOHN ADAMS

1. As a word, "obsequy" is a bit arcane, but it is a delicious alternative to the more ponderous "obsequiousness". In the vernacular, it simply means "ass-kissing."

2. Elbridge Gerry (pronounced "Gary" not "Jerry") was a Massachusetts politician and American statesman and diplomat. After his election as governor in 1810, the Republican dominated legislature created new state senate boundaries, some with highly creative shapes. Gerry signed the legislation. One of those districts in Essex County attracted the ire of a Federalist newspaper, which described it as resembling a salamander, which was dubbed a "gerry-mander." Few people remember the contributions of Elbridge Gerry as a statesman or diplomat, but few observers of the political scene are ignorant of "gerrymandering." Election districts artfully designed for partisan benefit remain a regular and pernicious part of American political life.

3. Private persons or ships under contract or commission to the French government.

THOMAS JEFFERSON

1. Disestablishment was removing the Anglican (Episcopal) Church from established or privileged status in the Commonwealth. An established church received financing from the state either through direct governmental subsidy or legal requirements for members and non-members alike to provide funding for the conduct of ministry. In Virginia's case, Anglican pastors were paid either in cash or pounds of tobacco. Being the established church also insured that no other church could compete for converts in Virginia or, in some cases, even conduct worship services in church-style buildings.

JAMES MADISON

1. Impressment was particularly galling to Americans. British behavior in this regard was particularly egregious. The Brits would stop an American ship suspected of trading with France, confiscate the goods, and "im-

press," or press into British service, American sailors either native-born or British deserters in U.S. service. This was a humiliating practice and one of the important factors leading to the War of 1812.

2. During the Battle of Baltimore, on September 13–14, 1814, slave-holding Maryland lawyer, author, and poet Francis Scott Key observed the bombardment of Fort McHenry from the deck of HMS *Tonnant*. He was on board negotiating for the release of prisoners. Because he knew of British plans, he was held and was on deck at dawn and saw the American flag still flying over the ramparts of the fort. Within a week he had penned "The Defense of Fort McHenry" and later had it put to music. By the time of the American Civil War, it was popularly considered the unofficial national anthem, *The Star-Spangled Banner*. Despite its popularity, it was and continues to be difficult to sing. A century after Key penned the epic verses, President Woodrow Wilson declared it the national anthem by executive order. Congress later adopted it as such, and President Herbert Hoover signed the legislation in 1931.

JAMES MONROE

1. Only a single elector voted against Monroe. He explained his vote against Monroe: because he felt the president to be incompetent.

2. The debate was between "restrictionists," those who wished to prevent states in the Louisiana Purchase from becoming slave states. On the other side were "anti-restrictionists" southern pro-slavery representatives and their Northern allies who believed Congress had no right to restrict the spread of slavery into the territories.

JOHN QUINCEY ADAMS

1. Contingent elections are extremely rare in U.S. history. They occurred in 1800, in which Thomas Jefferson was elected by the House; 1824, in which John Quincy Adams was elected by the House; and 1836, in which Richard Mentor Johnson was elected vice president by the Senate. This is an emergency process proscribed by the Constitution and modified by the Twelfth Amendment in 1804.

ANDREW JACKSON

1. Peggy Eaton's first husband, John B. Timberlake, was a U.S. Navy purser.

The couple befriended the newly widowed John Eaton when he came to Washington to join Jackson's Cabinet. Timberlake died of pneumonia while at sea, but rumors flew that he committed suicide because he suspected an affair between Eaton and his wife. While he was at sea, Peggy was rumored to have had a miscarriage from a pregnancy—the timing of which could only have come from relations with another man. When word came of Timberlake's death, Peggy and John immediately married, avoiding the socially required period of mourning.

MARTIN VAN BUREN

1. The Bucktails, also known as the Albany Regency, was a political clique led by Van Buren and opposed to aristocratic politicians such as Governor DeWitt Clinton. They were allied with the New York City–based working-class machine of Tammany Hall. The group derived its name from the Tammany insignia, a deer's tail worn in the hat. While in office, Clinton supported government expenditure for internal improvements such as the Erie Canal. Though Van Buren supported the Erie Canal because it benefited his home state, he generally opposed other such projects as too expensive and constitutionally suspect.

WILLIAM HENRY HARRISON

1. Barnburners were an anti-slavery faction in New York state politics led by Van Buren. They also opposed federal support of corporations and advocated local control of state politics in opposition to agents of President James K. Polk, who were attempting to organize an anti-Van Buren faction in the state.

JOHN TYLER

1. The Independent Treasury (1840–1841, 1846–1913) was a program designed to keep all government funds out of banks and in gold and silver (specie) in government hands either in the Treasury building or in scattered sub-treasuries around the country.

   The intention of this policy was to keep federal funds out of poorly managed state-chartered banks. These banks often used federal deposits as collateral to back loans—often unwise or risky loans—to small and large corporations and needy individuals. Depositing federal funds in these state banks had a tendency to increase the money supply and, if not restrained, could create a burst of inflation. On the other hand, keeping funds in the Independent Treasury had a restraining (deflationary) effect on economic activity. Because of this, in times of economic contraction, recession, or panic, the government had few tools to stimulate the economy other than simply printing more money, which was something policy makers were loath to do.

The Independent Treasury was instituted in 1840, repealed in 1841, re-established in 1846, modified with little success over the decades, and brought to an end with the passage of the Federal Reserve Act (1913).

2. Virginia broke ranks with the Democrats and voted for the Whig candidate in 1840 and 1848. Tyler, a slaveholder, was put on the 1840 Whig ticket as an attempt to achieve geographical and ideological balance. This theory proved correct in 1840 when Virginia voted for William Henry Harrison and the state's native son, John Tyler. When conflict over the Bank brought about President Tyler's banishment from the Whig Party, he had successfully burned bridges connecting him to both major political parties.

JAMES POLK

1. The term "dark horse" candidate originated in the world of horse racing. A dark horse was a contender about which little is known, thus complicating the betting odds. The obscure runner then comes out of nowhere to win the race.

2. Manifest Destiny was an aspirational concept that hoped to harness the vision and energies of America to spread the boundaries of the United States ever westward until lapping on the shores of the Pacific. It also advocated that the evangelical belief system articulated in the Declaration of Independence would proliferate world-wide to brighten the corners of mankind held in darkness and enlighten minds hungry for life, liberty, freedom, and the pursuit of happiness. Four themes distinguished such thinking:
   1. Continent-wide expansion of the borders of the United States: Canada to Mexico—Atlantic to Pacific.
   2. The virtue of Americans and their traditions.
   3. The mission of transforming and reshaping the world in the likeness of the United States.
   4. The understanding that this was a mission with deific imperative and divine assistance. This was God's work.

3. With U.S. forces under Zachary Taylor camped on the Rio Grande in disputed territory, Mexican President Mariano Paredes sent General Mariano Arista to repel the Yanks. He arrived on April 24, 1846, and almost immediately sent General Anastasio Torrejón with a force of one-thousand six-hundred troops across the Rio Grande upriver from Taylor's camp. Old Rough and Ready sent Captain Seth B. Thornton with eighty men to reconnoiter the crossing, and they were quickly overcome by Arista's much-larger force. Except for a few wounded men sent back to Taylor, the majority of Thornton's unit was either killed or captured. The prisoners were eventually released in an exchange after the Mexican defeat at the Battles of Palo Alto and Resaca de la Palma.

MILLARD FILLMORE

1. The legislative process—with all the compromises, swapping, and horse-trading necessary to craft laws—has long been compared to the making of sausage. The observer needs to have a genuine love of the process or strong tolerance of disagreeable behavior to see it as salutary enterprise. In 1869, the following was attributed to John Godfrey Saxe: "Laws, like sausages, cease to inspire respect in proportion as we know how they are made." In the 1930s, the same sentiments began to be attributed to German Chancellor Otto von Bismarck, who is alleged to have opined, "Those who love sausage or legislation should *never* watch either being made." Whoever originated the witticism would surely have recognized the process in the crafting of the Compromise of 1850.

FRANKLIN PIERCE

1. Styled after similar reform movements in Europe, Young America was a political and cultural program that advocated expansion, free trade, internal improvements, the use of technology, and aggressive commercial development. Young Americans were committed to "Manifest Destiny," the idea that American freedom and liberty were destined to spread not just to the confines of the continent, but also into the Caribbean and beyond. Allied with the movement was an artistic component. Authors such as Herman Melville, Nathaniel Hawthorne, and William Cullen Bryant identified with the Young Americans, as did the painters of the Hudson River School.

ABRAHAM LINCOLN

1. From the Latin, literally "show me the body." This was the ancient common law prohibition against arbitrary arrest and incarceration. Served with a writ of *habeas corpus*, law enforcement must produce a prisoner and subject him or her to a trial before an independent judicial officer. In the Constitution, only Congress is empowered to suspend this writ. Congress would not be in session until July 1861, and Lincoln felt the rebellion required the immediate response only a Commander in Chief could implement. Lincoln later requested and received congressional affirmation of his actions—albeit retroactively.

2. Chapter 159 from *Master American History in One Minute a Day*, Dan Roberts. Sanger, California: Familius. 2019.

3. Copperheads, or extreme Peace Democrats, were strongest in the southern parts of mid-western states, where many Southerners had settled before the war. They were traditionalists, highly suspicious of the transformation of national life by the Republicans. They harbored intense racial hatred of blacks and were opposed to tariffs, national banks, and federal support for internal improvements (roads, canals, bridges). Copperheads were markedly naïve when considering Southern interest in restoring the Union and often acted to undermine the Union war effort. Some encouraged Northern soldiers to desert. The movement was most influential when Northern military fortunes were on the wane, but when the Union armies began to triumph, "Copperheadism" collapsed.

4. Chapter 167 from *Master American History in One Minute a Day*, Dan Roberts. Sanger, California: Familius. 2019.

5. Chapter 168 from *Master American History in One Minute a Day*, Dan Roberts. Sanger, California: Familius. 2019.

ANDREW JOHNSON

1. Impeachment is investigated and confirmed as an indictment in the U.S. House of Representatives and then sent to the Senate, where House representatives act as prosecutors in a trial before the Senate and presided over by the Chief Justice of the Supreme Court.

2. The constitution required senators be elected by the legislatures of the several states. The Founders hoped this would tie the states to the federal government in early years and would allow senators to conduct national

business free from popular pressure. The Seventeenth Amendment (1913) mandated the popular election of senators.

ULYSSES S. GRANT

1. See discussion of Jim Crow in Note 3 of Introduction.
2. Excerpts from Amendments:

THIRTEENTH AMENDMENT

Section 1. Neither slavery nor involuntary servitude, except as a punishment for crime whereof the party shall have been duly convicted, shall exist within the United States, or any place subject to their jurisdiction.

Section 2. Congress shall have power to enforce this article by appropriate legislation.

FOURTEENTH AMENDMENT

Section 1. All persons born or naturalized in the United States, and subject to the jurisdiction thereof, are citizens of the United States and of the State wherein they reside. No State shall make or enforce any law which shall abridge the privileges or immunities of citizens of the United States; nor shall any State deprive any person of life, liberty, or property, without due process of law; nor deny to any person within its jurisdiction the equal protection of the laws.

Section 2. Representatives shall be apportioned among the several States according to their respective numbers, counting the whole number of persons in each State, excluding Indians not taxed. But when the right to vote at any election for the choice of electors for President and Vice President of the United States, Representatives in Congress, the Executive and Judicial officers of a State, or the members of the Legislature thereof, is denied to any of the male inhabitants of such State, being twenty-one years of age, and citizens of the United States, or in any way abridged, except for participation in rebellion, or other crime, the basis of representation therein shall be reduced in the proportion which the number of such male citizens shall bear to the whole number of male citizens twenty-one years of age in such State.

Section 3. No person shall be a Senator or Representative in Congress, or elector of President and Vice President, or hold any office, civil or military, under the United States, or under any State, who, having previously taken an oath, as a member of Congress, or as an officer of the United States, or as a member of any State legislature, or as an executive or judicial officer of any State, to support the Constitution of the United States, shall have engaged in insurrection or rebellion against the same, or given aid or comfort to the enemies thereof. But Congress may, by a vote of two-thirds of each House, remove such disability.

Section 4. The validity of the public debt of the United States, authorized by law, including debts incurred for payment of pensions and bounties for services in suppressing insurrection or rebellion, shall not be questioned. But neither the United States nor any State shall assume or pay any debt or obligation incurred in aid of insurrection or rebellion against the United States, or any claim for the loss or emancipation of any slave; but all such debts, obligations and claims shall be held illegal and void.

Section 5. The Congress shall have power to enforce, by appropriate legislation, the provisions of this article.

FIFTEENTH AMENDMENT

Section 1. The right of citizens of the United States to vote shall not be denied or abridged by the United States or by any State on account of race, color, or previous condition of servitude.

Section 2. The Congress shall have power to enforce this article by appropriate legislation.

3. Presidents with military service: George Washington, Andrew Jackson, William Henry Harrison, Zachary Taylor, Franklin Pierce, Abraham Lincoln, Ulysses S. Grant, Rutherford B. Hayes, James A. Garfield, Benjamin Harrison, Theodore Roosevelt, Harry S. Truman, Dwight D. Eisenhower, John F. Kennedy, Lyndon B. Johnson, Richard M. Nixon, Gerald R. Ford, Jimmy Carter, Ronald Reagan, George Bush, and George W. Bush. Voters were often drawn to them because of their service during periods of national crisis or advance.

RUTHERFORD B. HAYES

1. See discussion of Jim Crow in Note 3 of Introduction.

2. Not speaking of it publicly, where it might have done some good or swayed public opinion, but writing in his diary, he noted his conversion

to transformational change, "Money isower . In Congress, state legislatures....in the courts...in the press, in the pulpit...its influence is growing greater and greater. Excessive wealth in the hands of the few means extreme poverty, ignorance, vice, and wretchedness as the lot of the many...Let the people be fully informed and convinced as to the evil. Let them earnestly seek the remedy and it will be found."

THEODORE ROOSEVELT

1. See discussion of Jim Crow in Note 3 of Introduction.
2. The Peter Principle is an organizational theory developed by Laurence J. Peter that articulates people in a hierarchy tend to rise to their "level of incompetence." This idea describes the progression of a successful employee who is promoted based on their achievements in previous jobs, until they reach a position in which they are no long competent. Skills in one job do not necessarily translate to another. The concept was explored in *The Peter Principle* by Laurence J. Peter and Raymond Hull (New York: William Murrow and Company, 1969).

   Taft was a brilliant achiever in every job he ever tackled, but he had never run for or served in an elective political office. He did not like electoral politics. Having no elective political experience, in his election as President, he rose to his level of incompetence.

WOODROW WILSON

1. Tying and exclusive dealing are ways in which corporations engage in restraint of trade. Tying requires customers to buy additional products if they wish to buy the product they desire. The additional products are "tied" to the desired product.

1. See discussion of Jim Crow in Note 3 of Introduction.

2. See discussion of Wilson's 1916 second spurt of progressive legislation in 28-D3: New Freedom Agenda-III.

3. See discussion of Jim Crow in Footnote 2 in Introduction Elections.

WARREN G. HARDING

1. Harding's front-porch campaign was in marked contrast to his opponents, Governor James M. Cox and Franklin D. Roosevelt, who barnstormed the nation, giving dozens of speeches to large crowds. The

future president's unique call for a "return to 'normalcy'" resonated with an electorate weary after a decade of policy innovation and war, but many observers were less than enthusiastic with Harding's bland rhetoric. Former Treasury Secretary William McAdoo remarked that a Harding speech was like "an army of pompous phrases moving over the landscape in search of an idea." Even more scathing was H.L. Mencken, who wrote of Harding's efforts, "it reminds me of a string of wet sponges....tattered washing on the line...stale bean soup, of college yells, of dogs barking...It is so bad that a kind of grandeur creeps into it." Ironically, such criticism of his grandiloquence presaged the general criticism of Harding's presidency in the decades following his death.

FRANKLIN D. ROOSEVELT

1. At that time, New York gubernatorial terms were two years.

2. See discussion on realignment elections in the Introduction.

3. As articulated, refined, and built-upon by Cambridge macroeconomist John Maynard Keynes, the idea is that during times of economic contraction, governments could spend the national economy out of recession by stimulating demand with deficit spending. Keynes was perfectly willing to advocate balanced budgets, but only when the economy was strong during times of growth. By the time of Keynes's death in 1946, most governments were moving toward this understanding of monetary and fiscal policy. Franklin Roosevelt was hardly a philosophical Keynesian, but he did understand that spending by government and business during times of recession helped lift the economy.

4. From the world of tailoring came the idea that sewing a small rip prevents having to repair a much larger hole later on—"a stitch in time saves nine." It was an Anglo-Saxon phrase discouraging laziness—"never put off till tomorrow a task that should be done today." When the Supreme Court began to eschew its conservative bias and stop blocking Roosevelt's program, political wags said it was a "switch in time that saved nine."

5. U.S. forces would capture one island under Japanese control, cut it off, and skip the next one, leaving Japanese forces on the skipped island to starve for lack of supply.

6. Irascible as ever, Truman told his biographer, Merle Miler in 1972, "I fired [MacArthur] because he wouldn't respect the authority of the

president. I didn't fire him because he was a dumb son of bitch, although he was, but that's not against the law for generals. If it was, half to three-quarters of them would be in jail."

JOHN F. KENNEDY

1. For an exploration of the wit of John Fitzgerald Kennedy, consider chapter 276 in Dan Roberts's *Master American History in One Minute a Day*. Sanger, CA: Familius, 2019.

2. Theodore Roosevelt was the youngest man to serve as president, as he came to the office as a result of President William McKinley's assassination.

LYNDON B. JOHNSON

1. Lyndon Johnson sent forward and brilliantly maneuvered a large number of bills through a receptive Congress:
   1. a voting rights law (1965),
   2. a fair housing law (1968),
   3. the Office of Economic Opportunity (1964),
   4. food stamps (1964),
   5. the Head Start program (1964),
   6. a standard for job training (1964),
   7. environmental laws (1965),
   8. conservation (1965–1968),
   9. consumer protections (1965–1968),
   10. natural gas safety laws (1965–1968),
   11. truth in lending laws (1965–1968),
   12. the Department of Housing and Urban Development (1965),
   13. the Model Cities program (1966),
   14. the Department of Transportation (1966),
   15. Medicare (1965),
   16. Medicaid (1965),
   17. federal aid to elementary, secondary, and higher education (1965),
   18. a family- and skill-based immigration law (1965),
   19. the Public Broadcasting System (1967),
   20. the National Endowment for the Arts (1965),
   21. the National Endowment for the Humanities (1965),

22. the Freedom of Information Act 1966), and

23. the Kennedy Center for the Performing Arts (1967).

RICHARD NIXON

2. The end of the Vietnam War also brought significant changes in the way the armed forces were organized and the way America's warrior class relates to the society for which they fight. The draft was gradually ended, and by 1973, the U.S. military establishment had become an all-volunteer enterprise.

RONALD REAGAN

1. The choice of the Neshoba County Fair for the campaign kick-off has been a subject of controversy between Reagan partisans and critics over the years. To pick a venue just a short distance from the dam under which the three murdered civil rights martyrs (Cheney, Goodman, and Schwerner) were buried in the Freedom Summer (1964) was either a bountiful exercise in historical and geographical ignorance or a brilliant vote-getting strategy. That Reagan knew just what he was doing is clear from the way he hammered away at the old racist theme of states' rights and the fact that he immediately left for New York City and an appearance before the Urban League. It is notable that his reception at the civil rights meeting following his foray into Mississippi was "cautious," if not chilly. Some observers asserted that Reagan's joint appearances were a simple coincidence or that it revealed a genuinely benign approach to racial issues. Others attribute darker motives to the choice of Mississippi for the campaign inaugural speech. They emphasize that the Urban League appearance was a too-clever-by-half attempt to deflect attention away from a naked appeal to those for whom the assertion of states' rights was a buttress against advancing black civil rights. In November, Reagan carried both Mississippi by an 11,808 plurality and Neshoba County by a 1,293 vote majority. In 1976, Jimmy Carter carried both.

2. Andrew Jackson was not wounded in two attempts. Abraham Lincoln and John F. Kennedy endured head wounds from which they could not survive. Had James A. Garfield and William McKinley had the kind of modern medical treatment Reagan enjoyed, their assassin's bullets would have been easily found and extracted in a sterilized environment. This

would have prevented the onset of sepsis, infections, and death.

3. The most serious threat to U.S. dominance in the Olympics were the Soviets, but they were not present. They had declined to participate, in retaliation for President Jimmy Carter's boycott of the 1980 Moscow Olympics after the Soviet invasion of Afghanistan.

GEORGE H. W. BUSH

1. Harvey LeRoy "Lee" Atwater was one of the most successful political operatives of the late twentieth century. His hard-fisted tactics were honed in the rough and tumble of South Carolina politics, notably the vicious 1980 congressional campaign in which Floyd Spence prevailed over Tom Turnipseed. During the 1988 campaign, Atwater attempted to affix Michael Dukakis with blame for the release of rapist and murderer Willie Horton. In order to give Bush the ability to deny such a direct and unfair attack on Dukakis, Atwater arranged to have an independent group run ads which furthered Atwater's determination to "make Willie Horton his [Dukakis's] running mate.

     One of the most poignant parts of the Atwater saga was his repentance prior to his death. Diagnosed with terminal brain cancer in 1990, Atwater penned a number of letters to those he recognized he had abused over the years, repenting of his cruelty and seeking forgiveness. Atwater died in 1991, thus ending the mixed career of one of the key architects of the bitter fragmentation of modern American politics.

2. The combined popular total of Bush and Ross Perot was a whopping 57 percent compared to Bill Clinton's modest plurality of 42 percent. In the Electoral College, Clinton's strength was more apparent at 370 to 168.

GEORGE W. BUSH

1. Al Gore's total electoral votes after the voting were 267, but a faithless Gore-pledged elector abstained in the Electoral College vote so that the final vote was 266.

BARACK OBAMA

1. This chapter expands the discussion in Chapter 300 in Dan Roberts's *Master American History in One Minute a Day*. Sanger, CA: Familius, 2019.

GENERAL BIBLIOGRAPHY*

Amar, Akhil Reed. *America's Constitution: A Biography.* New York: Random House, 2005.

——. *The Law of the Land: A Grand Tour of Our Constitutional Republic.* New York: Basic Books, 2015.

Barilleaux, Ryan J. and Christopher S. Kelley, eds. *The Unitary Executive and the Modern Presidency.* College Station: Texas A&M University Press, 2010.

Bausum, Ann. *Our Country's Presidents.* Washington, D.C: National Geographic Partners, LLC, 2017.

Best, Judith. *The Case Against Direct Election of the President.* Ithaca: Cornell University Press, 1975.

Beschloss, Michael. *Presidential Courage: Brave Leaders and How They Changed America 1789–1989.* New York: Simon & Schuster, 2007.

Brinkley, Alan and Davis Dyer. *The American Presidency.* Boston: Houghton Mifflin Company, 2004.

Calabresi, Steven G. and Christopher S. Yoo. *The Unitary Executive: Presidential Power from Washington to Bush.* New Haven: Yale University Press, 2008.

Dean, John. *Broken Government.* New York: Viking, 2007.

Diamond, Martin. *The Electoral College and the American Idea of Democracy.* Washington: American Enterprise Institute of Public Policy Research, 1977.

Edwards, George C. III. *Why the Electoral College is Bad for America.* New Haven: Yale University Press, 2011.

Ellis, Joseph J. *Founding Brothers.* New York: Vintage Books (Random House), 2002.

Fisher, Louis and Leonard W. Levy. *Encyclopedia of the American Presidency.* New York: Simon & Schuster, 1994.

Freidel, Frank and Hugh Sidey. *The Presidents of the United States.* Washington, D.C.: The White House Historical Association, 2009.

French, Allen. *The First Year of the American Revolution.* Boston: Houghton Mifflin Company, 1934.

Goodwin, Doris Kearns. *Leadership in Turbulent Times.* New York: Simon & Schuster, 2018.

Goethals, George R. *Realignment, Region, and Race: Presidential Leadership and Social Identity.* Bingley, U.K., 2018.

Gould, Lewis L. *The Modern American Presidency*. Lawrence, Kansas: University Press of Kansas, 2003.

Higgenbotham, Don. *The War of American Independence*. Bloomington, Indiana: Indiana University Press, 1971.

Jensen, Merrill, ed. *English Historical Documents*, Vol. IX: *American Colonial Documents to 1776*. London: Eyre and Spottiswoode, 1964.

Jensen, Merrill. *Founding of the American Nation: A History of the American Revolution, 1763–1776*. New York: Oxford University Press, 1968.

Jones, Charles O. *The American Presidency: A Very Short Introduction*. New York: Oxford University Press, 2016.

Knollenberg, Bernhard. *Origin of the American Revolution*. New York: Macmillan, 1960.

Lessig, Lawrence and Cass Sunstein. "The President and the Administration," *Columbia Law Review*. 94 (1994).

Meacham, John. *The Soul of America: The Battle for our Better Angels*. New York: Random House Books, 2018.

Middlekauff, Robert. *The Glorious Cause: The American Revolution, 1763–1789*. New York: Oxford University Press, 2005.

Miller, James and John Thompson. *Almanac of American History*. Washington, D.C.: National Geographic Society, 2006.

Morison, Samuel Eliot. *By Land and By Sea: Essays and Addresses*. New York: Alfred A. Knopf, 1954.

Sabato, Larry J. and Howard R. Ernst. *Encyclopedia of American Political Parties and Elections*. New York: Facts on File, Inc., 2006.

Scheer George F. and Hugh F. Rankin. *Rebels and Redcoats*. Cleveland: World Publishing Company, 1957.

Schlesinger, Arthur M. *Imperial Presidency*. Boston: Houghton, Mifflin, 1973.

Watson, J. Steven. *The Reign of George III, 1760–1815*. New York: Oxford University Press, 1960.

Ward, Christopher. *The War of the Revolution*. ed. John Richard Alden. New York: Macmillan, 1952.

*Additional resources available for each president at www.amomentintime.com.

ABOUT THE AUTHOR

Dan Roberts is Executive Producer and Host of the award-winning radio series *A Moment in Time*. Created to excite and enlighten the public about the past and its relevance to the present and impact on the future, *A Moment in Time* is a captivating historical narrative that is currently broadcast worldwide.

After receiving a BA in history from Presbyterian College in 1969, Roberts served as an officer in the US Army, including a tour in Vietnam where he was awarded the Bronze Star in 1971. Roberts began training as a Presbyterian minister and completed his professional education at Princeton Theological Seminary in 1974. In August, 1986, he served as guest chaplain of the United States Senate.

In 1990, Roberts obtained a master's degree from the University of Richmond and, in 1997, a PhD in early modern British history and American colonial history from the University of Virginia. He is currently a Professor of Liberal Arts and History at the University of Richmond and serves as Chair of the Department of Liberal Arts at the School of Professional and Continuing Studies. He has been a guest contributor and columnist for *Education Week*, *USA Today*, *Scripps-Howard* papers, and *Richmond Times-Dispatch*. He is often heard as a history commentator on CNN, CNN Headline News, and Fox News.

Dan is a popular jazz pianist and an avid reader. He travels each year to a part of the world for research in his continuous quest to bring history to life. Roberts is married to Mario Mejia Roberts.

Roberts has three children: Heather Elizabeth Roberts Gill, Kathleen Roberts, and Daniel McDonald Roberts, III. He also has two lovely granddaughters: Ava McKenzie Hunt and Gerika Gill.

ABOUT FAMILIUS

VISIT OUR WEBSITE: WWW.FAMILIUS.COM

Familius is a global trade publishing company that publishes books and other content to help families be happy. We believe that the family is the fundamental unit of society and that happy families are the foundation of a happy life. We recognize that every family looks different, and we passionately believe in helping all families find greater joy. To that end, we publish books for children and adults that invite families to live the Familius Nine Habits of Happy Family Life: *love together, play together, learn together, work together, talk together, heal together, read together, eat together,* and *laugh together.* Founded in 2012, Familius is located in Sanger, California.

JOIN OUR FAMILY

There are lots of ways to connect with us! Subscribe to our newsletters at www.familius.com to receive uplifting daily inspiration, essays from our Pater Familius, a free ebook every month, and the first word on special discounts and Familius news.

GET BULK DISCOUNTS

If you feel a few friends and family might benefit from what you've read, let us know and we'll be happy to provide you with quantity discounts. Simply email us at orders@familius.com.

CONNECT

Facebook: www.facebook.com/paterfamilius

Twitter: @familiustalk, @paterfamilius1

Pinterest: www.pinterest.com/familius

Instagram: @familiustalk

FAMILIUS

*The most important work you ever do will
be within the walls of your own home.*